Literati Storytelling
in Late Medieval China

Literati Storytelling
in Late Medieval China

Manling Luo

UNIVERSITY OF WASHINGTON PRESS   *Seattle and London*

THIS BOOK IS MADE POSSIBLE BY A COLLABORATIVE GRANT
FROM THE ANDREW W. MELLON FOUNDATION.

*Publication of this book was also supported by a
grant from the Association for Asian Studies First
Book Subvention Program.*

© 2015 by the University of Washington Press
19 18 17 16 15   5 4 3 2 1

University of Washington Press
www.washington.edu/uwpress

Publication of this Book was also supported by a
grant from the Association for Asian Studies First
Book Subvention Program.

Library of Congress Cataloging-in-Publication Data

Luo, Manling.
Literati storytelling in late medieval China /
Manling Luo.
pages cm. — (Modern language initiative)
Includes bibliographical references and index.
ISBN 978-0-295-99414-7 (hardcover : acid-free paper)
ISBN 978-0-295-99415-4 (pbk. : acid-free paper)
1. Chinese literature—Tang dynasty, 618–907—
History and criticism. 2. Chinese literature—Five
dynasties and the Ten kingdoms, 907–979—History
and criticism. 3. Storytelling in literature.
4. Storytelling—China. 5. Literature and society—
China—History—To 1500. 6. China—Intellectual
life—Tang dynasty, 618–907. 7. China—Intellectual
life—Five dynasties and the Ten kingdoms, 907–979.
I. Title.
PL2283.L86 2014
895.109′003—dc23   2014023341

For Jiping

CONTENTS

ACKNOWLEDGMENTS

The completion of this book has finally given me the opportunity to tell my own story of indebtedness to the many people who have made the book possible. Robert E. Hegel has been a constant source of support and encouragement. From the earliest drafts to this present form, he has offered numerous suggestions, always insightful and enlightening. His critical acumen and fine scholarship have never ceased to inspire me.

Beata Grant, Lingchei Letty Chen, Steven Miles, Elizabeth A. Oyler, and Linda Nicholson deserve special credit for their thought-provoking comments and questions. They prompted me to reconsider the focus and framework of my project and to venture beyond my comfort zone into the little-explored territories of Tang anecdotal literature. Like the Bodhisattvas that she teaches about, Grant generously gave me much of her time and other invaluable assistance. Oyler has always reached out to me whenever I have needed help and went well beyond her call of duty.

I was fortunate to come to Indiana University, where I found an amazing intellectual community. Lynn Struve has read pretty much everything I have written, sometimes more than once. I have benefited tremendously from her always timely and insightful critiques and corrections. My comrades in a writing group, Heather Blair, Kevin Tsai, and Kevin Martin, sustained me through the long journey of writing and rewriting with their knowledge, insights, patience, and humor. Dubbed "the queen" of the writing group, Heather's "relentless" enforcement of deadlines was crucial in keeping me on track. She even read my drafts outside our group schedule, and her incisive questions and suggestions have been invaluable in my struggle to gain conceptual clarity in this project. Scott O'Bryan and Ellen Wu kindly read parts of the final manuscript and offered very useful comments. A great mentor, Edie Sarra has given me all sorts of much-needed help, from feedback on my writing to tips for teaching. Michiko Suzuki has generously shared with me her successful proposals and given much of her time to comment on my drafts and advise me on how to present my project to a broad audience. In addition to her, I also learned a great deal about grant writing from Sara Friedman, Scott Kennedy, Michael Foster, Ellen Wu, and Jason McGraw, all superb in grantsmanship. Successive chairs of the Department of East Asian Languages and Cultures, Bob Eno, Michael Robinson, and Natsuko Tsujimura, and the director of the East Asian Studies Center, Heidi Ross, have been very generous in supporting my research endeavors through the years.

I have also been blessed with the kindness of many people beyond my university. I particularly appreciate Paul W. Kroll's encouragement in the early stages of the project, and his continuing support has been indispensable for its completion. Ronald Egan offered me thoughtful comments and suggestions on more than one occasion. Despite his busy schedule, James Hargett is always willing to give me a hand; he read most of the final manuscript and gave me very useful feedback. Zhang Jie's comments on my introductory chapter and Brian Walter's on various parts of the manuscript enabled me to fix issues of which I was unaware. Zong-qi Cai has been very generous with his time and advice. Rebecca Copeland enabled me to do research in Japan; my work and life there was made much easier through the help of Liu Xunning, Onozawa Masaki, Oki Yasushi, and Mizobe Yoshie, as well as Nemoto Tatsushi and his friends. While doing research in China, I was very fortunate to receive assistance from Wang Lijia, Cheng Yizhong, and Li Pengfei. Without any complaint, my friend Xu Shengli bought and mailed books to me on short notice when I was in need of certain materials.

I am also grateful to Indiana University's East Asian librarian Wen-Ling Liu, who often does magic in solving my problems with databases and book searches, as well as the Interlibrary Loan staff, who have been very efficient and accommodating. I also wish to thank the library staff at the East Asian Library of Washington University in Saint Louis, the National Library of China, the Peking University Library, the Shanghai Library, the University of Tsukuba Library, the University of Tokyo Library, and the Institute for Advanced Studies on Asia at the University of Tokyo.

Daniel Hsieh and Elizabeth Oyler kindly invited me to present my work in progress at Purdue University and the University of Illinois at Urbana-Champaign, respectively, and I benefited greatly from invigorating discussions with them and with my audiences. I also had opportunities to present papers and receive very helpful feedback from fellow presenters, discussants, and audiences at the Association for Asian Studies Annual Conference, the Annual Meeting of the American Oriental Society, the American Oriental Society Western Branch Annual Meeting, and the T'ang Studies Twenty-Fifth Anniversary Conference.

The generous support I have received from various institutions has also been indispensable for the initiation, expansion, and completion of my project. A scholarship from the Association of International Education Japan funded my first research in Japan. I was able to further expand my research in China and Japan with the support of a New Frontiers in Arts and Humanities Grant from the Office of the Vice Provost for Research and a Travel and Research Grant from the College Arts and Humanities Institute at Indiana University. Supplementary research funding from the Department of East Asian Languages and Cultures was also crucial for this scholarly undertaking in its various stages. Subsequently, an ACLS Fellowship from the American Council of Learned Societies, an American Fellowship from the American Association of University Women, and a Research Leave Supplement Grant from Indiana University's Office of the Vice Provost for Research provided me the much-needed leave time to complete the manuscript.

Although some of the passages quoted in this book have previously been translated by James R. Hightower, Paul W. Kroll, Stephen Owen, William H. Nienhauser Jr., and others, for stylistic consistency I have undertaken to do all of the translations myself, while admiring and aspiring to the translation skill of masters who have gone before me. Because of space limitations, I refer specifically in my notes only to studies directly related to my discussions. Throughout my study, however, I have benefited from the work of many other scholars, to whom I extend my gratitude. The second part of chapter 1, "Political Intimacy: The Illustrious Emperor as Ruler of His Court," and the fourth part of chapter 3, "A Daughter's Romantic Deviation: The Paradox of Subversion and Submission," appeared earlier in *T'oung Pao: International Journal of Chinese Studies* and *Nannü: Men, Women and Gender in China*, respectively. I thank the editors for permission to incorporate and adapt parts of those articles.

For the publication of the book, my special thanks go to editor Lorri Hagman, who was responsive to all of my questions and who was impressively efficient in managing my manuscript. Tim Roberts was an effective managing editor, and I appreciate Kerrie Maynes's help with the copyediting. I would also like to take this opportunity to thank Lanya Lamouria, Angelica Zeller-Michaelson, Burton Pu, Ruth Berson, Rosa Brefeld, Brian Walter, and Julia Whyde for their excellent editorial assistance in one way or another over the years. I was very lucky to have Ben Garceau read through my final draft. My debt to the two perspicacious readers for the manuscript is particularly great because they offered important suggestions and corrections that saved me from embarrassing pitfalls. The remaining errors and deficiencies are solely my responsibility.

To Liu Jun I owe the deepest debt of gratitude, for he has done so much for me and for our family, and without him we would not have made it this far. I am extremely thankful that my father-in-law Huang Zhengquan has helped us through challenging times and that my father Luo Yuru has always been a source of comfort for me. Although my mother Luo Ruiying and my mother-in-law Liu Yongling did not get to see the publication of this book, they are always in my thoughts. My son Jiping grew up with this book and, from early on, has enthusiastically volunteered to help, trekking to the libraries with me and hitting the keyboard randomly to show me how productive I should be. This book is for him, since he loves to hear and read stories and to ask why.

The Chinese family name precedes the given name. Although a person could also be referred to by his style name, sobriquet, or honorific title, given the large number of storytellers and characters discussed in the book, I have adopted only the family name and the given name in my discussion, for the sake of consistency and clarity.

No biographical dates are given for many figures because they were obscure or fictive. Although better-known historical figures, whose biographical information can be extracted from other sources, are often featured in late medieval stories, this does not necessarily mean that the events described actually happened. In fact, when historical sources are available for cross-examination, many stories turn out to be apocryphal. My analysis, however, is concerned not with the historical accuracy of stories but with their narrative representations.

Many figures discussed in the book are said to have held positions in the officialdom, which consisted of nine ranks, each further divided into different grades. The official titles are translated according to Charles O. Hucker's *A Dictionary of Official Titles in Imperial China*.

CHRONOLOGY

THE TANG DYNASTY

Gaozu (r. 618–626)
Taizong (r. 626–649)
Gaozong (r. 649–684)
Empress Wu Zetian of the Zhou dynasty (r. 690–705)
Zhongzong (r. 684; 705–710)
Ruizong (r. 684–690; 710–712)
The Illustrious Emperor (Minghuang) or Xuánzong (r. 712–756)
Suzong (r. 756–762)
Daizong (r. 762–779)
Dezong (r. 779–805)
Shunzong (r. 805)
Xianzong (r. 805–820)
Muzong (r. 820–824)
Jingzong (r. 824–827)
Wenzong (r. 827–840)
Wuzong (r. 840–846)
Xuānzong (r. 846–859)
Yizong (r. 859–873)
Xizong (r. 873–888)
Zhaozong (r. 888–904)
Aidi (r. 904–907)

THE FIVE DYNASTIES

Later Liang (907–923)
Later Tang (923–936)
Later Jin (936–947)

Later Han (947–950)
Later Zhou (951–960)

THE TEN KINGDOMS

Wu (902–937)
Former Shu (907–925)
Wu-Yue (907–978)
Min (909–945)
Southern Han (917–971)
Jingnan (or Nanping) (924–963)
Chu (927–963)
Later Shu (934–965)
Southern Tang (937–975)
Northern Han (951–979)

Literati Storytelling
in Late Medieval China

Introduction

For we dream in narrative, day-dream in narrative, remember,
anticipate, hope, despair, believe, doubt, plan, revise, criticize,
construct, gossip, learn, hate, and love by narrative. In order
really to live, we make up stories about ourselves and others,
about the personal as well as the social past and future.

—BARBARA HARDY[1]

Stories make us human, but in what specific ways? The basic idea
that life is narrative, or that "a life as led is inseparable from a life
as told," conveys a now widespread recognition that telling stories is
instrumental to and constitutive of individuals' sense of reality.[2] The
importance of stories for the unity and continuity of communities is
also beyond question, for stories "combine over time . . . into a kind
of epic of his community, her tribe, their family, and the relationship among them all."[3] Their universal, omnipresent power notwithstanding, stories are also intrinsically specific, for they are products of
specific historical and cultural conditions, while they simultaneously
help constitute those very conditions. The relationship between narrative and history leads us to ask: What concrete forms and subjects
do stories take, what particular meanings do they hold in a certain
historical moment, and what distinctive roles do they play for the very
community that tells them?

This book explores these issues by examining the instrumental
function of storytelling for Chinese literati (or scholar-officials), more
specifically, how storytelling constructed their collective identity during the late medieval period, a turning point in Chinese history. Generally referred to as *shi*, the literati or scholar-officials were the social
group that monopolized literacy, social prestige, and political participation in traditional China.[4] The origins of this elite group have
been dated back to the Spring and Autumn period (770–476 BCE),
when people with military, political, and cultural expertise were distinguished from farmers, merchants, and artisans.[5] For more than

two millennia, until the founding of the republic in 1911, the literati communities adapted remarkably well to historical changes and
maintained their dominant status in traditional Chinese society.

The late medieval period, from the mid-eighth to the mid-tenth
century, was a critical interval during the so-called Tang-Song Transition in Chinese history.[6] From the Tang dynasty (618–907) to the
Song dynasty (960–1279), hereditary aristocracy gave way to a meritocracy based on civil service examinations ostensibly open to all.
Specifically, the great aristocratic clans that had dominated the upper
echelons of the bureaucracy disappeared with the fall of the Tang; by
the beginning of the Song, a new elite with a much broader social base
had emerged. Committed less to pedigree than to a merit-based ideal
of individual advancement, the Song elite pursued social eminence
through many means, including examinations, landholding, marriage, migration, patronage, military careers, and commercial activi-
ties.[7] This reconfiguration of the Chinese elite occurred along with
social, economic, and religious changes that laid the foundation for
the next millennium.[8]

In this long process of the Tang-Song Transition, the late medieval
era, between the outbreak of the An Lushan Rebellion in 755 and
the founding of the Song dynasty in 960, was particularly volatile
and formative. The rise of autonomous or semiautonomous military
governors in the aftermath of the rebellion created political instabilities, exacerbating existing tensions and spurring institutional, social,
and cultural changes that had far-reaching implications for the Song
and later dynasties.[9] Although great clans continued to dominate the
upper echelons of the court, provincial hierarchies opened up new
means for men of lesser backgrounds to advance their careers, inten-
sifying the competition for official positions in general. Moreover,
despite their small scale, Tang civil service examinations, especially
the literary examination for the Presented Scholar (*jinshi*) degree,[10]
became more prominent because of their meritocratic promises and
because the court tried to promote civil values in the face of post-
rebellion upheaval. These institutions later served as the blueprint for
the Song system of civil service examinations, which became the primary means for bureaucratic recruitment until the system was abol-
ished in 1905.[11]

The late medieval period also witnessed the emergence of an
unprecedentedly large number of recorded stories, both singly and in
collections, creating a range of new thematic and narrative prototypes

that would have enduring influences on later Chinese writers. The Tang dynasty has been hailed as the golden age of Chinese poetry because it produced so many poems as well as new and influential poetic forms. Literary historians have long been puzzled, however, by the disparity between the developmental trajectories of Tang poetry and Tang tales. Whereas poetry began to flourish after the establishment of a unified Tang empire and continued through the second half of the dynasty, the writing and compilation of stories peaked in the post-rebellion period.[12]

The central argument of this book is that stories flourished after the rebellion because of the radical changes experienced by contemporary scholar-officials going through the watershed reconfiguration of the Chinese elite. Specifically, storytelling enabled late medieval scholar-officials to create communal discourses for defining themselves in response to the new reality of literati life. Officialdom, the administrative system of state and local officials, ceased to be the option it had been for early medieval aristocrats; bureaucratic service instead became the livelihood for an expanding community of educated men, marking a new pattern of officialdom-centered literati life that foreshadowed the future examination societies. The social function of late medieval literati storytelling provides the key to understanding not only the communal adjustment of contemporary scholar-officials to the profound changes in literati life, but also the development of traditional Chinese literati culture for the millennium that followed.

LATE MEDIEVAL LITERATI STORYTELLING

I use the term "literati storytelling" as a way to expand our perspectives on late medieval stories and reframe debates central to the study of medieval Chinese literature and culture. By this term, I refer to the literati tradition of sharing accounts about characters and events of the past in casual conversations, as well as the gathering and transmitting of such narratives in writing. Leo Tak-hung Chan first coined the term in his discussion of a famous eighteenth-century collection of classical-language short stories. In line with the customary meaning of "storytelling" as "the action of telling stories," Chan emphasizes the oral provenance of these stories, and sees them originating in casual conversations among educated elite and serving to convey arguments and inform contemporary intellectual debates.[13] Others, such as William H. Nienhauser Jr., have used "storytelling" to refer to Tang writers' skillful, even creative ways of literary narration in prose.[14] Building on these earlier usages, I would like to emphasize on one hand that literati storytelling encompassed both oral and written modes, and, on the other, that the oral world is no longer available to us and we have access only to written accounts, which necessarily limits and tilts our discussions toward the literary aspects of this story-sharing culture.

Literati storytelling was an integral part of the medieval world of vibrant, extensive story exchange across social spectrums. Scholar-officials were not the only ones to tell stories, nor did the diverse stories that circulated among them reflect their concerns alone. Usually cast as historically accurate records of events, these short narratives covered a wide array of topics, recounting incidents about historical emperors, well-known or obscure scholar-officials, Buddhists, Daoists, soldiers, merchants, foreigners, servants, respectable women, courtesans, maids, gods, ghosts, animal spirits, and so on. Modern scholars often turn to these stories as a treasure trove for research on popular religions and beliefs.[15] What have yet to be examined closely, however, are the particular meanings of those stories by and for contemporary scholar-officials, or the crucial social function of literati storytelling for the elite community at large.

Discursive in nature, literati storytelling was vital to the social life of educated men. References to this story-sharing culture among scholar-officials were common. In his epilogue to the story "Miss Ren" (Ren shi zhuan), Shen Jiji (ca. 750–ca. 800) describes in detail the practice of trading stories as entertainment at informal gatherings:

> In the second year of the Jianzhong reign [781], I was demoted from the position of Left Reminder to serve in southeast China, along with General of the Imperial Insignia Pei Ji, Metropolitan Vice Governor Sun Cheng, Director in the Ministry of Revenue Cui Xu, and Right Reminder Lu Chun. We went the same way by land and water from Qin to Wu. At that time, former Reminder Zhu Fang also traveled along with us. Together we floated down the Ying River and crossed the Huai River, in a string of boats along the waterways. We feasted during the day and gathered for conversations at night, each of us sharing extraordinary stories. After these gentlemen heard the story of Miss Ren, they were all deeply moved and astonished. They asked me to write an account of her to commemorate her extraordinariness.[16]

The exchange of stories clearly provided these exiled officials much-needed diversion, comfort, and mutual support on an otherwise dull journey. One of numerous extant references to occasions of story sharing, this passage illustrates the close connection between oral and written modes of literati storytelling and its important role in creating and solidifying social relationships among scholar-officials.

While writing down stories and compiling collections was a continuous literati tradition, late medieval scholar-officials were particularly avid in collecting them. In his preface to *The Missing History* (Que shi), Gao Yanxiu (b. 854) explained that since his youth he had liked to write down what he had heard from elders, and had thus accumulated numerous entries over time. By editing out the doubtful and frivolous, he tried to align his collection with those of his predecessors:

> Thus since the Wude [618–627] and Zhenguan [627–650]
> reigns, people who have taken up the writing brush to write
> "minor discourses," "minor records," "petty histories," "unofficial
> histories," "miscellaneous records," or "miscellaneous accounts"
> indeed have been many. There is not any anecdote left unrecorded
> before the Zhenyuan [785–805] and Dali [766–780] periods. But
> there are still some from the Dazhong [847–860] and Xiantong
> [860–874] reigns and later [about people and events] that are worth
> commendation and promotion, can provide materials for entertaining
> conversations, or can impart lessons and warnings. It is a pity that
> they have not been documented in official records. Therefore I have
> recorded them here.[17]

Gao's words indicate that scholar-officials regarded the gathering and compilation of such stories from the past as a minor type of writing, less estimable than poetry, official historiography, and the like.[18] Nonetheless, these unofficial accounts were educative and entertaining and thus served the important social function of binding the literati community together. Gao's comments also represent a late-ninth-century perspective on how widespread these writing practices were among his contemporaries and predecessors.

Gao does not appear to have exaggerated the volume of such compilations in that the post-rebellion era was indeed a particularly prolific period. Although many collections are now lost or have survived only in part, a quick glance at the rough number of medieval titles under the broad rubric of the so-called "minor discourses in classical language" (wenyan xiaoshuo) can be useful, despite scholars' disagreements over the dating, nature, and classification of listed works. From the third to the early seventh century, about a hundred and thirty titles in total are known. They were mostly collections of *zhiguai* (records of the strange), along with a few single, relatively lengthy accounts and more than twenty collections of often apocryphal anecdotes on historical or legendary figures. The pre-rebellion period from 618 to 755 can be said to be sporadic. Around fifteen *zhiguai* collections appeared, along with roughly five single accounts and five collections of historical anecdotes. The two centuries after the An Lushan Rebellion, however, witnessed a spike in the overall production, with over one hundred *zhiguai* collections and approximately seventy single accounts and one hundred collections of historical anecdotes.[19] These numbers indicate that, compared to their early medieval and pre-rebellion predecessors, more late medieval scholar-officials were committed to story gathering and compilation. Their interests had also expanded beyond earlier preoccupations with wonders of the cosmos to focus on the allegedly historical experiences of past scholar-officials and their world. More than half of the late medieval single stories and story collections are extant in entirety or in part, albeit often with complicated textual history. Written in classical Chinese, the narratives vary in length from dozens to several thousand characters and are diverse in both form and content.

This rich corpus has not received sufficient critical attention because of our entrenched generic and disciplinary preoccupations. For one thing, the poetic genres of the Tang have commanded the most attention from literary scholars, eclipsing in effect other types of contemporary literary productions. For another, many collections of historical anecdotes, termed "historical miscellanies" (*zashi*), have been considered more trustworthy and the purview of historians, while critics of narrative literature are mainly concerned with examples with stronger literary features such as complex plots, sophisticated characterization, and refined language.

This preoccupation with the literariness of certain writers, single stories, collections, or story types can be traced to Lu Xun (1881–1936), the father of modern Chinese literature and literary studies. Lu Xun pioneered the now widely held belief in the longer, more complex "tales of the marvelous" (*chuanqi*) from the Tang as the first flourishing of mature fiction in Chinese literary history.[20] This interpretation highlights the individual writer's originality in creating a new story or adapting an existing one, and dismisses references to oral origins and transmission as fictional devices for bolstering the veracity of an account.[21] Because tales of the marvelous represent only a handful of stories, the majority of shorter and "cruder" narratives remain unaccounted for: the ambiguity of the term *xiaoshuo* (literally, "minor discourses") has proven a convenient way to finesse the gap. Now used in modern Chinese to refer to the genre of "fiction," *xiaoshuo* is also traditionally a flexible bibliographic category for writings that fall outside the established genres (such as poetry, historiography, and literary essays) and is characterized by miscellaneous, heterogeneous, and unorthodox content.[22] Conflating these two meanings under the rubric of *xiaoshuo*, critics have analyzed the literary artistry of tales of the marvelous in terms of fictionality, while discussing other "lesser" stories in terms of their proto- and non-fictional features.[23]

From various angles, scholars who have challenged this predominant approach argue against what they see as an anachronistic projection of modern assumptions about fiction writing onto medieval times. Glen Dudbridge, for instance, contends that Tang stories were not fiction but "a literature of record," which revealed contemporary beliefs, practices, and memories.[24] Likewise, Sarah Allen provides evidence of story retelling and transmission to demonstrate that Tang writers did not invent stories like modern fiction writers, but were rather "bound by a fundamental fidelity" in recounting existing stories.[25] The debate also draws in critics working on similar materials from other periods. Both Alister Inglis and Leo Tak-hung Chan refused to label these stories "fiction," underscoring instead their nature as products of active story exchange among literati and as indices of contemporary beliefs in the Song and the Qing (1644–1911) dynasties.[26] Robert Campany contends that early medieval stories of transcendence-seekers are "artifacts of social memory" that reveal collective constructions of the "immortals" (*xian*) as a social role.[27]

These opposing scholarly interpretations can be attributed to the very hybrid nature of literati storytelling itself. As a communal pastime, literati storytelling was part of an oral world in which stories circulated across the social spectrum. At the same time, it was also a significant mode of elite literary production and thus deeply immersed in a long-standing written tradition. An eclectic approach is necessary—one which takes into account both social and literary dimensions, collective and individual creativity, and which draws from critical insights across the scholarly divide between fiction critics and their opponents. In other words, we need to attend to what historian Gabrielle Spiegel has called the "social logic of the text," with an analysis of both "a text's social site—its location within an embedded social environment of which it is a product and in which it acts as an agent—and its own discursive character as 'logos,' that is, as itself a literary artifact composed of language and thus demanding literary (formal) analysis."[28]

To that end, I argue that literati storytelling is better understood as both a mode of discourse—encompassing casual conversations, narrative poems, and prose accounts—and as a medium of social culture formation, rather than as simply a conventional literary prose genre. Expressed in different forms, stories produced by and circulated among late medieval scholar-officials were not mere pastimes or pure fantasies, but rather articulations of social anxieties among the contemporary literati community. A more complete image of late medieval stories must combine careful analysis of their literary features with an in-depth examination of the crucial social role that these stories played for the literati community in a time of upheaval, most notably the breakup of the aristocracy as a locus of political power.

This new approach entails four methodological shifts. First, we leave behind the question of whether an author was a disguised fiction writer who invented a story or a sincere transmitter of a previously heard account and focus instead on his authorial function as a storyteller. Debates over a writer's creative intent cannot be resolved because "there is no litmus test for intentional fictionality."[29] We can say, however, that in offering a particular rendition of a story, the writer as a storyteller contributes to the communal discourses of his time with a narrative representation that was of interest to him and to his community.

Second, instead of focusing on canonized "tales of the marvelous" alone, a cross-genre approach is useful, extending the discussion to narrative poems, *zhiguai*, historical miscellanies, and the so-called transformation texts (*bianwen*, medieval manuscripts discovered at Dunhuang in China's northwestern borderlands at the turn of the twentieth century). By virtue of its breadth, this analysis takes into account both the different features of various narrative forms and their overlapping themes, thereby revealing a more comprehensive picture of literati storytelling in the late medieval milieu. For instance, although Dunhuang transformation texts have usually been studied as the earliest direct evidence for Chinese popular storytelling, the way in which they overlap with little-studied historical miscellanies compiled by elite writers suggests that popular and literati storytelling represented not two different worlds but two points on the same social and geographical continuum.

Third, this approach shifts attention from textual histories of individual stories and collections to the dialogic relations among them. Despite the impressive work that scholars have done to determine precise authorship and dates and to reconstruct the original forms of late medieval stories, such information remains speculative or vague in many cases. In fact, poetic texts in the Tang were subjected to many changes when they were produced and circulated.[30] The situation is even more complicated for Tang stories because they were in effect "public narrative properties" that could be reused and modified.[31] Although a quest for original, authentic late medieval stories is futile, extensive analysis of the extant versions can shine useful light on how late medieval literati storytellers participated in the shared discourses of their community.

Fourth, in a move away from reading these stories for topical references or as direct reflections of sociohistorical details, they may be seen as narrativizing the desires, anxieties, and perspectives of late medieval scholar-officials. Since writers routinely adopted the persona of a self-appointed historian and claimed that their writings meaningfully supplemented state-sponsored official histories, modern scholars have looked to these stories for specific historical information on contemporary political events, popular religious beliefs, and social life. The fundamental social function of stories for literati storytellers and their circles, however, merits examination as well.

In this regard, studies of similar issues in different historical contexts can offer useful guidance. Based on her study of how middle-class Americans tell stories of their loves and marriages, sociologist Ann Swidler points out that "culture is elaborated where there is active work to be done."[32] Literary and media representations of love flourish because of the institutional demands and dilemmas of marriage in modern life; individuals use these ideas as "tool kits" or "cultural repertoire" to address specific issues in their personal lives. Stories thus describe the psychic realities of people within the institutional matrices of their worlds.[33] If Swidler's research sheds light on the meanings of stories for their contemporary recounters, writers, and other producers, historian Robert Darnton asserts the possibility of understanding those meanings for a past community by reconstructing its cultural history. He shows, for instance, that the "ways of thinking" of French peasants in the fifteenth through eighteenth centuries can be discerned by analyzing their folktales "on the level of structure, noting the way the narrative is framed and the motifs are combined."[34] In the Chinese case, the "ways of thinking" or "cultural repertoire" that late medieval scholar-officials developed through storytelling can only be illuminated in light of the broader historical context, the reconfiguration of the Chinese elite that occurred during the Tang-Song Transition.

COMMUNAL CONSTRUCTION OF LITERATI IDENTITY

This study analyzes late medieval stories as samples of communal literati discourse to show how scholar-officials delineated the political, social, sexual, and cosmic dimensions of their identity. Late medieval literati storytellers included famous and little-known literati as well as those whose names are now lost. Some of them came from great aristocratic clans, and others from lesser families. Some were examination participants and Presented Scholar degree holders, while many others were not. Although most held bureaucratic positions at some point in their lives, some did not. Because of their diverse backgrounds, these storytellers represented the wide spectrum of social compositions and perspectives among members of the late medieval literati community.

Taken together, stories told by famous, little-known, and anonymous post-rebellion literati storytellers constituted unofficial, dialogic attempts to construct their shared identity. If culture, birth, and office-holding marked their social distinctions from non-scholar-officials,[35] storytelling was a fundamental medium through which the late medieval literati community constructed a multifaceted identity for itself. Such a literati identity centered not on an interiorized, divided self of the sort that would later characterize modern constructions of subjectivity, but rather on social roles that constituted different dimensions of a shared pattern of life. "Identity" here refers to particular domains of action for scholar-officials and the power relations in which they were embedded. Late medieval literati storytellers were preoccupied with a wide variety of topics, such as the careers of court officials, pedigree, morality, poetry, civil service examinations, supernatural encounters, and sexual adventures. These varying topics converged or clustered around certain poles, revealing thematizations that delineate the different aspects of literati identity formation.

"Thematization" is the discursive process by which literati storytellers engaged in a communal discourse through their different representations of and solutions to common sets of topics. Thematization occurred at the level of direct interpersonal communication. In one of his entries in the *Miscellaneous Morsels from the South Side of Mount You* (Youyang zazu), for instance, Duan Chengshi (ca. 803–863) describes a night banquet that he held during which a courtesan revealed her aversion to roasted fish, prompting all present to talk about their personal phobias and what they had heard on related topics.[36] Thematization also occurred in more general communal discourse: through their idiosyncratic narrative representations, storytellers became involved in dialogues that thematized and addressed the pressing concerns of their communities, even if they did not personally belong to the same circle or their stories did not have any direct bearing on other stories except in their overlapping topics. Thematization, while not necessarily leading to any unified understanding, delineated a shared but contested field of discourse.

Because of the nature of thematization as a mechanism of discourse formation, themes offer a crucial interpretive lens for us to understand the literary and social power of literati storytelling. A "theme" is not simply the subject of a story but a crucial topical nexus among clusters of stories.[37] This nexus enables us to see how literati storytellers participated in a common field of discourse through their divergent treatments of a common topic, or through their explorations of the different dimensions and problematics of a topic. Even if we do not know much about storytellers as historical individuals and cannot establish the precise chronological order of extant stories or the patterns of influence among them, it is still possible to show how these storytellers contributed to the thematization of shared topics important to their circles. In other words, thematic connections across stories denoted dialogic contestations among late medieval literati storytellers, shedding light on the shared identities they constructed in a time of transition and transformation.

A close reading of the diverse corpus of extant late medieval stories reveals four dominant themes: sovereignty, literati sociality, sexuality, and cosmic mobility. Although late medieval literati storytellers did not use precisely these terms, most of their surviving stories feature these themes; this is so because the stories provided a visible expression of the literatus's relations to the principal groups in his world—monarchs, fellow scholar-officials, and women—as well as to supernatural forces in the greater scheme of the cosmos. In other words, because the power relations that governed literati life in the institutional matrix of officialdom underlay the production and circulation of these stories, storytelling could offer vicarious experiences and symbolic fulfillments that made possible a rhetorical reiteration, negotiation, displacement, or even disruption of those dominant relations. Analysis of these four themes illustrates the fundamental facets—the political, social, sexual, and cosmic dimensions—of literati identity as constructed in late medieval literati storytelling.

Stories of sovereignty recount the words and actions of past monarchs, conveying literati storytellers' perspectives on the essence and parameters of royal authority and on their relationship to it. Sovereignty represents the vertical dimension in which scholar-officials defined their political power and role in relation to their emperor. By contrast, stories of literati sociality commemorate and pass judgment on past generations of scholar-officials: in doing so, they construct an unofficial history of the literati community. Literati sociality denotes the horizontal dimension in which scholar-officials envision the different bonds that would bind individuals into a strong community that was irresistibly oriented toward officialdom.

While sovereignty and literati sociality represent the central domains of literati life, sexuality embodies a peripheral dimension vis-à-vis the center. Stories of nonmarital bonds describe the affairs of literati heroes with women of various social backgrounds outside the institution of arranged marriage. The sexual dimension is vital because it does not simply evoke the literati fantasy of winning the hearts and bodies of women through their personal charms (rather than through the institution of marriage); more importantly, it turns nonmarital bonds into instruments for contesting the power relations that dominated the lives of literati in the central domains.

Beyond these worldly spheres, the cosmos offers fantastic possibilities for dealing with the structural constraints of literati life. Stories of cosmic mobility represent literati experiences of the supernatural in which scholar-officials are cast as privileged citizens of the universe, a portrayal that is often given in bureaucratic terms and yet simultaneously offers the magic and wonder of overcoming the constraints of officialdom. Cosmic mobility extends the domains of action for scholar-officials by relativizing the world of officialdom in the expansive cosmic dimension.

The communal construction of literati identity in these interconnected areas of thematization is characterized by diversity, contradiction, and ambivalence. The voices of famous, little-known, and anonymous literati storytellers epitomize the extensive and dialogic contestations among late medieval scholar-officials regarding their shared destiny of officialdom. Permeating these diverse explorations are contradictions and underlying ambivalences that exist at different levels, not only within single narratives but also between stories and across themes. Such diversity, contradiction, and ambivalence bespeak the very power of storytelling and its wide range of perspectives, providing flexible alternatives as "tool kits" or a cultural repertoire that could be appropriated by individual storytellers, audiences, and readers.

At the same time, contradiction and ambivalence also manifest a central paradox: the construction and subversion of the myth that the officialdom-centered literati life empowered scholar-officials. Like any myth, this one ironically suggested the way things should or could be, and was compelling precisely for its wishful nature. This myth of empowerment arose from the reality of officialdom as the institutional matrix of late medieval literati life. Although early medieval aristocrats did hold office, they were entitled to it by virtue of their pedigrees and could afford not to serve. As a matter of fact, "Disdain for practical administrative service was almost a hallmark of the early medieval elite"; reclusion, or withdrawal from an official career as a lifestyle, was highly esteemed, so much so that "a gesture (at least) in the direction of lofty reclusion became almost obligatory even for those with political ambitions."[38] By contrast, mainstream late medieval scholar-officials embraced reclusion more as a poetic ideal, while delineating as its counterpart a private space that was compatible with officialdom.[39] In a sardonic anecdote, when Prefect Wei Dan (fl. 779–806) conveys his poetic aspirations to retire to the mountains, the monk Lingche (ca. 746–816) mocks the hypocrisy of people like him with the following lines: "Everyone I have met said, 'I shall abandon my office and leave.' / When have I ever seen someone in the forests?"[40]

Late medieval scholar-officials could not afford to abandon their careers because they and their families depended on official income and privileges more than ever before. At the same time, entry into officialdom was more competitive because positions were far from enough for the growing population.[41] After obtaining the Presented Scholar degree in 792, which conferred only an eligibility for office, Han Yu (768–824), for instance, repeatedly tried and failed to get an appointment. When he eventually secured a position to work for a military governor in 796, he wrote about his sense of relief at having a salary to support his household of over thirty individuals.[42] As a matter of fact, the famous poet Bai Juyi (772–846) wrote so much about his official salaries, material possessions, and estates that they became a defining feature of his poetry.[43]

In its many facets, the literati identity that late medieval scholar-officials constructed through storytelling affirms the positive meaning of this officialdom-centered literati life. Stories about sovereignty and about literati sociality endorsed scholar-officials as major players in the political realm and their solidarity and collective power as a community. Because literati life centered on these two domains, storytellers sought historical authenticity and legitimacy for their idealized visions by recounting stories of those whom they believed to be recent exemplars. At the same time, narratives of sexuality and of cosmic mobility envisioned ways for individuals to overcome the limitations of these central domains of literati life. Tales of a youthful hero who temporarily deviates from his prescribed course in life to develop nonmarital bonds constituted a platform for challenging the domination of individuals by the patriarchal family (the embodiment of sovereignty) and the social senior (the personification of literati sociality). Meanwhile, stories of cosmic mobility endorsed efforts to rationalize or move beyond officialdom as the epitome of the structural constraints of literati life.

Yet the myth of empowerment is also destabilized or subverted, not simply by negation but by the contradiction and ambivalence in the voices of literati storytellers.[44] While stories about sovereignty conveyed strong literati identifications with sovereign power, they also revealed a self-conscious distancing from it. Although compilers of historical miscellanies on past generations of scholar-officials enthusiastically envisioned a diachronically unified literati community, their accounts also betrayed brutal competition and violence within that community. At the same time, sexual adventures were represented as only temporary deviations: the literati hero is bound to return and resubmit to the social authorities. Furthermore, there was no real escape from the institutional structure of officialdom since it was portrayed as extending into the supernatural sphere. These subversive undercurrents indicate that late medieval scholar-officials were aware of the limits to their empowerment and the negative implications of their embrace of officialdom.

The very construction of the empowerment myth, however, indicates that these scholar-officials were more optimistic than pessimistic.

Such optimism marked this era of transition and transformation, a time when literati saw and believed in the possibility of better times ahead. While it was harder to become an official in the late medieval period than it had been before, bureaucratic service was still feasible and was the primary means of livelihood. Even though only twenty to thirty people passed the Presented Scholar examination in an average year (a low success rate of 2 to 5 percent at the national competition), the overall pool of candidates was small, estimated at no more than 800 at the national level. In fact, the total number of candidates for the annual recruitment examinations that conferred the Presented Scholar and other degrees is believed to be roughly 2,000–3,000.[45] Moreover, there were many avenues into the Tang bureaucracy other than examinations, including hereditary privileges, service in the guards, financial management, clerical ranks, and recommendations; these accounted for at least 90 percent of the new entrants.[46] In addition, many men chose to serve military governors, making this a respectable option for those who could not find employment at court, as was the case with Han Yu at the beginning of his career.[47] Late medieval scholar-officials certainly did not foresee that with the centralization of the Song state and population growth, the number of examination participants would grow drastically to about 400,000 by the mid-thirteenth century.[48] Throughout the late imperial period, from the fourteenth to the nineteenth century, as more and more people took the examinations, it would become in effect a marker of elite status for most men rather than a realistic point of entry to a bureaucratic career.

The optimism of late medieval scholar-officials stemmed not only from the feasibility of officialdom for them but also from their confidence that they could rally themselves against rivals (such as eunuchs and military men) for influence and power. Post-rebellion intellectual and literary trends advocating the efficacy of *wen* (literature, culture, civil values) asserted the central role of scholar-officials, the very avatars of the values of *wen*, in solving contemporary political and cultural crises.[49] A good example was the Archaic Prose (*guwen*) movement championed by Han Yu, who envisioned a unity between one's literary writing, moral cultivation, and the power to transform society.[50] While the leading figures of these intellectual and literary trends were well-known scholar-officials of the time (most of whom were Presented Scholar degree holders), the construction of the myth of empowerment by famous, little-known, and anonymous literati storytellers alike indicates a broad picture of consensus formation in the literati community around their collective ascendancy.

By showing how late medieval scholar-officials adjusted to the changing conditions of literati life, this broader picture provides missing links in our understanding of the transformation of the Chinese elite in the Tang-Song Transition. Historians have tried to posit shifts in ideological foundation and sociopolitical pressures to explain the dissolution of the aristocratic mentality in the late medieval period.[51] The communal construction of literati identity in late medieval stories allows us to see the missing half of the picture: how bureaucratic life and meritocratic ideology came to be accepted as the norm. This missing half illuminates both the uncertainties and the exuberance of late medieval literati social life, which centered on officialdom but not yet on examinations, as examinations constituted only one of the many paths to an official career. The diverse voices of late medieval scholar-officials and the spectrum of possibilities they explored show how the newly intensified gravitational pull of officialdom in literati life enabled the advent of the examination society in the Song dynasty. In other words, the formation of consensus about the myth of empowerment explains why scholar-officials embraced the Song centralization, which has been seen by modern scholars as marking the onset of autocratic rulership in China.[52] Meanwhile, the deep ambivalences of late medieval scholar-officials also reveal that they were more than "willing subordinates" to the sovereign,[53] for they had explored, however wishfully by our standard, the various possibilities of empowering themselves in and beyond the political sphere.

Moreover, the examination of how storytelling crucially produced the identity of late medieval scholar-officials illuminates the inextricable connections between the literary and social dimensions of stories. These connections expand our visions of the contemporary literary landscape by showing how a story's literariness was not a matter of aesthetic constructions insulated within the text but was imbued with social significance through the complex ways it thematized social desires and anxieties of the time. Rather than being socially deterministic, this important aspect reveals the inherent links underlying the seemingly random or disparate stories and the communal discourses that they produced, that is, the very meanings of these stories for late medieval scholar-officials. The shared literary nature and social relevance of stories in their diverse forms thus shed fresh light on a vital but understudied part of medieval Chinese literature.

Such an extensive analysis of late medieval literati storytelling greatly enriches our understanding of the literati culture, for educated men of the time were not only part of poetry-writing communities but storytelling communities as well.

The study of the literary and social significance of late medieval literati storytelling also elucidates the historical origins of later literary production and cultural development. As products of their sociohistorical context, late medieval stories did not merely reflect reality but played an active role in fashioning that reality for storytellers and their communities. In this sense, late medieval literati storytelling created lasting literary and cultural legacies. Late medieval stories became the source of many later rewritings. The well-known love story "The Story of Yingying" (Yingying zhuan), for instance, appeared in at least seventy adaptations. The continuing relevance of late medieval stories points to the formative influence of identity-construction strategies developed by late medieval scholar-officials through storytelling. The tensions and ambiguities in this process are particularly valuable for understanding how key components of later identity paradigms were first constructed in the formative stage of literati culture.

STRUCTURE, SOURCES, AND TERMS

This study consists of four main chapters. They focus on the four thematized domains that I have enumerated above: sovereignty, literati sociality, sexuality, and cosmic mobility. Each chapter examines the formation of a major dimension of literati identity in late medieval literati storytelling.

To examine literati conceptions of their relationship to sovereignty, chapter 1 focuses on stories about the Illustrious Emperor (Minghuang) of the Tang, also known as Emperor Xuánzong (685–762; r. 712–756).[54] While the emperor's long reign achieved unparalleled prosperity, it ended tragically when he placed his trust in the non-Chinese general An Lushan (703–757), whose rebellion in 755 plunged the country into chaos and marked the downturn of the dynasty. Featured in over three hundred accounts in various generic forms, including narrative poems, tales of the marvelous, historical miscellanies, and Dunhuang transformation texts, the Illustrious Emperor was the most talked-about monarch in the post-rebellion period. A careful analysis of the diverse and often ambivalent images of the emperor in different sample narratives demonstrates how late medieval scholar-officials grappled with the post-rebellion crisis of sovereignty in attempts to establish their own political identity and authority.

Chapter 2 discusses how compilers of historical miscellanies tried to define literati sociality by recounting stories of previous generations of scholar-officials, thereby creating a communal past. While these miscellanies have traditionally been regarded as repositories of random historical information, they perform an ignored yet essential function of literati storytelling, namely constructing a composite picture or an unofficial history of the literati community by recounting chitchat that circulated in the community about predecessors. Four collections by men of divergent family background and social position serve as the focal points of analysis. These are the *New Tales of the Great Tang* (Da Tang xinyu) by Liu Su (fl. 806–820), *Records Prompted by Conversations* (Yinhua lu) by Zhao Lin (ca. 802–ca. 872), *Master Cloud Creek's Discussions with Friends* (Yunxi youyi) by Fan Shu (fl. 875–888), and the *Collected Words* (Zhi yan) by Wang Dingbao (870–940), most of which have received scant critical attention. Because of the differences in their backgrounds, these storytellers articulate distinct visions of literati sociality based on morality, prestige, poetry composition and sharing, and examination participation, respectively. These divergences testify to the diversity of late medieval literati social life, which was not yet dominated by examination participation. Despite underlying ambivalences, these storytellers also share a confidence in the meritocratic nature of the officialdom-centered literati life, affirming in different ways the commitment of the late medieval literati community to officialdom. Their voices thus exemplify a coalescence of literati attempts to establish and promote communal bonds.

Chapter 3 analyzes stories of nonmarital affairs to illuminate the sexual dimension of literati identity. Late medieval stories effectively relocated sexual liaisons, shifting the action from the fantastic to the social domain by portraying mortal heroines instead of the supernatural women found in earlier accounts. The social identities of these heroines as maids, singing girls, courtesans, wives, concubines, and unmarried daughters crucially denote the gender and social parameters of literati sexual adventures. From quintessential love stories, including "The Story of Yingying," to narratives of adultery, such as "The Story of Hejian" (Hejian zhuan), literati storytellers construct literati sexual roles in nonmarital bonds as a peripheral site outside the domain of acceptability. This peripheral site was crucial for challenging the dominant power relations in literati life—sovereignty and literati sociality—and for containing such challenges. The youthful persona of a literati sexual adventurer, along with the contradictory representations of female sexuality, thus enabled a paradoxical subversion of and submission to social authorities.

Chapter 4 examines how stories about literati experiences of the supernatural delineate the places and mobility of scholar-officials in an immense but bureaucratized cosmos. Stories highlighting the inexorability of fate attribute the vicissitudes of official careers to an arbitrary but ineluctable design. "Fate" thus comes to embody and naturalize officialdom itself. In contrast to this passivity, stories of the underworld bureaucracy extend officialdom into the afterlife, affirming an activism in terms of exploiting the bureaucratic power. Meanwhile, stories in which scholar-officials leave the world in pursuit of transcendence hold out the possibility of physically overcoming the structural constraint of official life, just as tales in which literati experience official careers in their dreams turn waking from such dreams into an epistemic mechanism that destabilizes the control of officialdom. These different, even contradictory assertions of cosmic mobility justify the privileged status of scholar-officials in the cosmos, affirming their power to rationalize or transcend the normative pattern of literati life.

For my textual analysis of stories in this book, I rely heavily on versions in the *Extensive Records of the Taiping Reign* (Taiping guangji), originally compiled in 978. This compendium includes the early versions of many late medieval stories, and it is widely used by modern scholars. In addition to this primary source, I also use individual collections of stories when available, since the *Extensive Records of the Taiping Reign* is far from comprehensive. Because of my cross-genre approach, I also discuss samples from anthologies of poetry and Dunhuang transformation texts. Because any given story usually has a long history of textual transmission, there are often variant versions. My interest here, however, is not in the material life of a text, which requires treating variants as independent and equal, but in the dialogic relations across late medieval stories. As a rule, I have focused on one selected version in my discussion, while taking into consideration variants if necessary. Nonetheless, I do not assume that these specific sample versions are the writers' original, authentic renditions, which usually cannot be retrieved even if they did exist. Despite any

problematic textual history that these sample versions may have, they
provide valuable windows into contemporary communal discourses.
When discussing authorship, I follow traditional attributions and
note any controversies.

As for periodization, I have used the general designations "late
medieval period" and the "post-rebellion era" to refer to the critical
two-century interim bracketed by the outbreak of rebellions in the
750s and the reassertion of central authority in the 960s. This period
is often further divided into "mid-Tang," "late Tang," and the "Five
Dynasties" in the north and the "Ten Kingdoms" in the south. Literary trends, however, do not always neatly correspond to dynastic
periods. As Darnton puts it, "World views cannot be chronicled in
the manner of political events, but they are no less 'real.'"[55] Many late
medieval stories cannot be dated precisely. Even in cases when the
time of their passing into written form was noted, there are indica-
tions that these stories might have been circulating even earlier. While
I am not suggesting that political periodization is unimportant, nor
do I ignore differences between historical periods, the more general
period terms allow me to examine the extensive connections among
stories without being burdened by futile efforts to place these stories
on a precise linear timeline.

Reading stories that emerged during this time span in terms of
their dialogic contestations, however, may risk anachronism, since
I have juxtaposed earlier, later, and undatable narratives. Although
the extant evidence showing to what extent a storyteller was aware
of specific accounts offered by his predecessors is limited, I seek to
explore how the stories were collected and invested with meaning
during the post-rebellion period. Rather than charting the diachronic
evolution of a central theme, we can examine how key elements of
the theme are mapped out in overlapping explorations of literati storytellers. This does not mean a complete disregard of the timeline of
stories or collections, but rather a pragmatic approach that is sensitive to chronology where it is evident, and flexibility in dealing with
cases where it is not.

Critics have traditionally discussed the specific authorial identity
of a writer in terms of the genre in which he wrote, such as the poet
and the historian; for the sake of consistency, I refer to writers discussed in the book as literati storytellers. Since writers resorted to different genre forms in recounting their stories, the term "storyteller" is
useful in calling attention to these writers' shared authorial function

as chroniclers of stories and participants in communal discourses. This is not to negate or dispute the traditional labeling of authorial identities, but to facilitate a useful discussion of a wide range of texts and writers, without having to untangle the long-standing assumptions about the relations among them.

Although a complete understanding of the world of late medieval literati storytelling is theoretically and practically impossible, this study is one attempt to capture glimpses of it. By presenting a useful middle ground between fiction critics and their opponents, this eclectic mode of analysis also expands our perspective on both premodern literati storytelling as a tradition of its own and on the genesis of Chinese fiction. In addition to offering specialists a new perspective for reflecting on long-standing divisions between orality and writing, prose and poetry, fiction and non-fiction, the popular and the elite, this study also contributes to our knowledge of the genealogies, politics, and social functions of storytelling as a fundamental human pursuit.

CHAPTER I

Sovereignty

The Case of the Illustrious Emperor

The Illustrious Emperor was the most talked-about monarch in the period after the An Lushan Rebellion because he embodied a paradox of both brilliant success and catastrophic failure. His reign, during the Kaiyuan (713–742) and Tiaobao (742–756) eras, was a period of sustained peace and prosperity that marked the apogee of the Tang dynasty. It was interrupted in 755, however, by the rebellion of the non-Chinese general An Lushan, which devastated the country. During the emperor's flight to southwest China, his army mutinied, killed his chief minister Yang Guozhong (d. 756), and forced him to execute his favorite concubine Precious Consort Yang (Yang Guifei, 719–756). Soon he also had to abdicate in favor of his son.[1] The court never fully recovered from this weakening of central authority, in particular from the subsequent rise of military governors who originally helped to pacify the rebellion but later became alarmingly powerful; one such governor eventually brought down the dynasty in the early tenth century. The end of the Illustrious Emperor's reign thus marked a crisis in sovereignty, when erosions of sovereign power allowed various political players, including military men, eunuchs, and scholar-officials, to compete for dominance.

Stories about the Illustrious Emperor thus provided a perfect medium through which late medieval scholar-officials could reimagine sovereignty and define modes of engagement with the monarch that strengthened their own power and authority. As the supreme political power of the ruler, sovereignty had long been central to political discourses. Early in the Tang, Emperor Taizong (r. 626–649) wrote treatises that showed a monarch's perspective on his own roles and responsibilities; later, a little-known literatus named Zhao Rui (fl. 716) put together a compendium to synthesize theories of rulership, illustrating efforts on the part of scholar-officials.[2] Of course, political and ritual representations of sovereignty had always been essential to rulers in legitimizing and sustaining their imperial authority.[3] The Illustrious Emperor himself, for instance, performed grandiose rites to heaven and earth (*feng* and *shan*) on Mount Tai and its foothill, respectively, and erected a stele bearing an inscription that he personally composed and transcribed.[4] Poetry also provided a personal, literary medium for these monarchs that allowed them to shape the images of their empire and themselves.[5] Apart from such self-representations, the posthumous assessment of a ruler was an important subject of historiographical representations and open to controversy and manipulation.[6] The forces affecting such images in the popular imagination were broader and more diverse, however, with monarchs becoming typecast as "good" or "bad," or with other labels over time.[7]

While the images of the Illustrious Emperor as constructed in late medieval stories were part of popular representation, literati storytellers were not interested in sovereignty as political power *per se* but as a personal power of domination possessed and wielded by the monarch. By recounting stories of the Illustrious Emperor, post-rebellion scholar-officials tried to augment their privileged access to that power by envisioning special personal relationships that they could develop with the monarch. While sovereignty by definition dictated a subservient relationship for scholar-officials, and the focus of literati life on officialdom marked their dependence on that sovereignty, these special relationships with the monarch empowered scholar-officials by allowing them to position themselves as major players in the political sphere. In different genre forms, late medieval literati storytellers portrayed the Illustrious Emperor as a lover, a ruler, an emblem of dynastic apogee, and a mortal man: through such stories, they respectively asserted cultural and political modes of their intimate identification with the monarch, their sociohistorical instrumentality to his reign, and their belief in restraining his power.

Stories of the Illustrious Emperor do not really reflect what "actually" happened during his reign; rather, they constitute a flexible medium for post-rebellion scholar-officials to project visions of sovereignty best suited to their interests and agendas. This is similar to the posthumous cult of Elizabeth I that thrived in Stuart England:

the cult offered a "representational flexibility" that allowed constituencies across a wide political spectrum to promote divergent models of sovereignty and to make sense of turbulent political conditions.[8] Analogously, the Illustrious Emperor became a symbol for late medieval scholar-officials. A symbol encompasses a rich diversity of meanings and can be understood in different ways: the flexible, ambiguous nature of the symbol is important for building solidarity without the requirement of unified opinions.[9] Late medieval literati storytellers clearly sought to construct a range of images of the Illustrious Emperor in order to define their own roles and powers in the political domain.

CULTURAL INTIMACY: THE ILLUSTRIOUS EMPEROR AS LOVER

By recounting stories about the relationship of the Illustrious Emperor with Precious Consort Yang, late medieval literati storytellers transfigure him into a lover, and hence a literati hero. In other words, by imagining the emperor as a lover, storytellers integrate him into a shared cultural sphere of sentimentality and sexual desire—the emergent literati culture of romance. This transfiguration represents a new, intimate mode of cultural identification with the monarch as "one of us."

The "Ballad of Eternal Sorrow" (Changhen ge) by Bai Juyi and its companion work, "An Account of the 'Ballad of Eternal Sorrow'" (Changhen ge zhuan) by Chen Hong (fl. 785–830), played a central role in the transfiguration of the Illustrious Emperor into a lover.[10] Bai Juyi wrote his ballad after he had embarked on a promising career, passing the Presented Scholar examination in 800, a special examination at the Ministry of Personnel in 803, and a decree examination (zhiju) held by the new Emperor Xianzong (r. 805–820) in 806.[11] Over the next four decades Bai became a leading literary figure and rose to the upper echelons of Tang bureaucracy. His poetic reputation extended far beyond his time and beyond the Tang Empire.[12] Less is known about Chen Hong, who obtained the Presented Scholar degree in 805 and seems to have served only in low- and middle-rank positions. He aspired to be a historian and compiled a thirty-fascicle history that is no longer extant.[13]

The collaboration between Bai Juyi and Chen Hong occurred in the context of Xianzong's successful military campaigns, which restored the political dignity of sovereignty. After half a century of rampant warlordism, the new emperor demonstrated that he was willing and able to assert central authority. In 806–7, right after his ascension, Xianzong's campaigns defeated the unruly military governors Liu Pi (d. 806) in the southwest and Li Qi (d. 807) in the Yangzi region. Loyalists extolled Xianzong's accomplishments, as we see in the poem "On the Sagacious Virtue of the Emperor of the Yuanhe Reign" (Yuanhe shengde shi) written in 807 by Han Yu, then Erudite of the National University.[14] Bai Juyi's poetic rendition and Chen Hong's prose account constituted a literary-historical project to restore the dignity of the image of Xianzong's great-grandfather, the Illustrious Emperor.

This image had been tarnished by his favoring of Precious Consort Yang and the subsequent outbreak of rebellions, a detail that made him fit the stereotype of the debauched last ruler only too well. Floral Purity Palace (Huaqing gong), the hot spring resort that the emperor frequented with Precious Consort Yang, became one of the popular sites for Tang writers to reflect on historical cause and effect. The poem "Passing Floral Purity Palace" (Guo Huaqing gong) by Li Yue (fl. mid-to late eighth century), for instance, was explicit in its criticism of the emperor: "The lord amused himself and made light of the myriad state affairs. / [After] the melody 'Rainbow Skirts,' warfare arose within the four seas."[15] Even those who were sympathetic to the emperor were prone to make damaging historical analogies. The famous poet Du Fu (712–770), for instance, wrote in the poem "Northern Journey" (Bei zheng): "I have never heard that the fall of the Shang and Xia dynasties / is traced to the execution of [the bewitching consorts] Bao Si and Da Ji."[16] Du Fu believed that the death of Precious Consort Yang signified a Tang revival because her execution by the Illustrious Emperor proved his sagacity, thus distinguishing him from those earlier rulers who were unable to change their self-destructive trajectory. Yet by comparing her to the notorious femmes fatales Da Ji and Bao Si, Du Fu perhaps inadvertently suggested similarities between the emperor and the rulers destroyed by these women. The moralism linking the emperor's political downfall to his sexual obsession with Precious Consort Yang emanated from the long-standing belief that indulgence of excessive sexual desire marks moral deficiency on the part of men in general and monarchs in particular.[17]

The twin compositions of Bai Juyi and Chen Hong aimed precisely to salvage the image of the Illustrious Emperor by redefining his sexual obsession as romantic devotion. Glossing over inconvenient details, such as that Precious Consort Yang was originally the emperor's daughter-in-law and that he gave her a makeover by turning her into a Daoist priestess before taking her into his harem,[18] Bai and Chen portray the emperor simply discovering and falling in love with a beautiful woman from the Yang family. He and Precious Consort Yang enjoy a blissful life, but it is cut short by the rebellion and her consequent execution. The inconsolable emperor enlists the help of a Daoist wizard, who finds out that Precious Consort Yang has become an immortal on a faraway island. When she receives the wizard, she not only reveals a secret pledge of eternal love between her and the emperor, but also conveys her loyalty to him and her longing for their future reunion.

In line with the melodramatic convention of the ballad (*ge*), a subgenre of Music Bureau poetry (*yuefu*), Bai Juyi's poetic version movingly describes the Illustrious Emperor's emotional journey from happiness to pain and longing, and concludes with climactic lines evoking the pledge of love between him and his consort as well as their eternal devotion and sorrow:

> On the seventh day of the seventh month in the Palace of Eternal Life,
> At midnight, when no one was around, they whispered to each other:
> In heaven, we wish to become two birds with paired wings;
> On earth, we wish to be twin trees with branches interlocked.
> There will be a time when the long-lasting heaven and earth cease to exist;
> Yet this sorrow will linger on and on, never ending.[19]

Despite such sympathetic portrayals, modern scholars have debated extensively over how serious Bai Juyi was in his romanticization of the emperor, as he also includes lines that seem critical, such as "Spring nights were unfortunately too short and the sun rose high; / From then on, the monarch stopped attending his morning court."[20] The perceived conflict between sentimentalism and moralism in Bai Juyi's ballad stems, however, from the fact that by presenting the emperor as a devoted lover, Bai creates a split in his identity: the emperor's romantic role contradicts and destabilizes his political one.

In the verisimilar style of the "biography" (*zhuan*) form that originated in historiography, Chen Hong's complementary prose account aims precisely to resolve this paradox by splitting Precious Consort Yang's persona. On one hand, Chen Hong labels her a "creature of bewitching beauty" (*youwu*),[21] embodying a feminine vice that is the source of the Illustrious Emperor's political troubles. The first half of the story supports this image by describing how her ingenuity in monopolizing the emperor's sexual attention leads her family to gain tremendous influence, especially her cousin Yang Guozhong, who abuses his power as a chief minister. Thus, "When An Lushan led his troops toward the imperial palace, he used punishing the Yangs as his pretext."[22] The execution of Precious Consort Yang thus not only appeases the mutinous soldiers but also redeems the emperor's political failure. On the other hand, after her resurrection as an immortal in the second half of the story, Chen Hong turns her into a paragon of feminine virtue, particularly loyalty.[23] Referred to as the Jade Consort, she vows with a single-minded determination to reunite with the emperor: "Whether we are immortals or mortals, we will certainly meet again and resume our happy union as before."[24] Her reincarnation as a devoted lover serves to absolve the emperor's guilt for failing to protect her and to reward his persistent devotion.

By depicting Precious Consort Yang as both a bad and a good lover in the story, Chen Hong tries to present the Illustrious Emperor as a good monarch as well as a dedicated romantic hero. The prose account opens with the statement "During the Kaiyuan reign, the court was peaceful and in all lands within the four seas there was no trouble."[25] As the country has become so peaceful, according to Chen Hong, there is nothing for the emperor to worry about, and, since he must have worked very hard to achieve this success, he certainly deserves romance as a diversion. Although he has thousands of palace women available to him, he sets his heart on a single one and showers her with his attention and gifts. Even when the Illustrious Emperor is perilously close to losing his political stature during the mutiny, Chen Hong emphasizes the emperor's devotion to his beloved: "His Majesty knew that there was no way she could avoid [her end], but he could not bear to see her die. Turning his sleeve to cover his face, he had the attendants lead her away."[26] The narration here does not focus on his political helplessness under duress, but rather confirms his love by showing his reluctance to abandon her. After her death he is shown wholeheartedly lamenting his romantic loss rather than his own miseries and disgrace as a retired sovereign deprived of power. The emperor's romantic identity humanizes him: despite all of his powers as head of the empire, he has the mundane desire to be with his beloved for eternity, and in that sense he is as vulnerable as any man in the face of death and loss.

Chen Hong's agenda to make the emperor's dual roles consistent is filled with contradictions, however. If the death of Precious Consort Yang illustrates the price that a femme fatale must pay for the abuse of her sexual power, her rebirth as an immortal significantly undermines such an interpretation: it implies that after punishment can come redemption. Moreover, this contradiction in Precious Consort Yang's image is detrimental to that of the emperor. When she is cast in an unflattering light, the emperor's devotion to such a woman makes him seem foolish and ridiculous. Although she may be said to deserve execution, her dual roles as a political culprit and a romantic heroine turn the incident into a moment of powerful irony that reveals the emperor's failure as a romantic hero. Even though he is ostensibly the most powerful man in the world, he is not able to protect his love; instead, he gives her up in exchange for his own safety and the endurance of the dynasty.

Despite such tensions, Bai Juyi and Chen Hong succeeded in popularizing the love story and redefining the Illustrious Emperor as a lover; Bai's poetic version became particularly well known. The transformation of the emperor into a lover turned him into a literati celebrity, making him part of what Stephen Owen has termed a "culture of romance," marked by increasing literati interest in poems and stories on love and romantic sentiments.[27] In such representations, the male role as a lover, defined by romantic passion for and devotion to a woman other than one's principal wife, started to be cast in a positive light, although traditional moralism against sexual obsession with women continued to hold sway.[28] If the "poetry of seductive allure" (yanshi) by Bai Juyi's best friend Yuan Zhen (779–831) illustrated a new poetic trend of constructing male romantic subjectivity in poetic terms,[29] stories about literati liaisons explored the social conditions of such relationships, as in "The Story of Li Zhangwu" (Li Zhangwu zhuan) by Li Jingliang (fl. 794–821), "The Story of Li Wa" (Li Wa zhuan) by Bai Juyi's younger brother Bai Xingjian (776–826), and "The Story of Yingying" attributed to Yuan Zhen. Although the status of the Illustrious Emperor sets him apart from other literati romantic heroes, it also turns him into the most melodramatic lover of them all: supported by imperial resources, with the entire empire as its grandiose stage, his romantic relationship involves the most beautiful woman in the world.

The Illustrious Emperor as lover represents for scholar-officials an unprecedented, intimate mode of cultural identification with the monarch as "one of us." The epilogue to Chen Hong's prose account not only explains the circumstances and agendas that informed his collaboration with Bai Juyi, but also illustrates how such a cultural intimacy worked:

> In the twelfth month, during the winter of the first year of the Yuan-he reign [807], Bai Juyi of Taiyuan was transferred from the post of Editor in the Imperial Library to serve as a sheriff in Zhouzhi. I, Chen Hong, and Wang Zhifu of Langye had settled in that county. In our spare time, we went together to visit the Celestial Roaming Monastery. When our conversation touched upon this story, we were moved and our sighs echoed each other. Wang Zhifu raised a wine cup and toasted Bai Juyi, saying, "If there is no outstanding talent to polish it, a story so rare over time will gradually disappear and eventually become unknown to the world. Since you are one who has the consummate skill of poetry and the sensibility for emotions, please compose a ballad for the story. What do you think?" Bai Juyi thus wrote the "Ballad of Eternal Sorrow." We were not only moved by the story, but also wanted to castigate the creature of bewitching beauty [i.e., Precious Consort Yang], block the path of [future] troubles, and pass on the lesson to posterity. After Bai Juyi completed his ballad, he asked me to provide a prose account. As to things that the world has never heard of, I, not being a survivor of the Kaiyuan era, have no way of knowing; as to things that the world has known, the annals of the Illustrious Emperor are extant. Here I am simply presenting a prose account of the "Ballad of Eternal Sorrow."[30]

Chen's disclaimer that his account does not provide any new, authoritative information on the Illustrious Emperor is a tacit admission of the dubious authenticity of the story, which had circulated orally up until that point. The statement that he and his friends were deeply moved by the story, however, indicates the strong empathy of the literati audience for the emperor as a lover, reinforced by a shared hostility toward the danger of female beauty. As a matter of fact, this empathy prompts them to become self-appointed guardians of the emperor's cultural memory, aiming not just to preserve his image as a lover but also to polish and enhance it. That Bai takes up that task at the request of his friend indicates, moreover, a belief that as an outstanding poet he is able to understand and reimagine the personal, emotional journey of the emperor and to represent it convincingly to a broader audience.[31] Social hierarchy notwithstanding, the literati storyteller, the sovereign-lover, and the literati audience share the same cultural status as men of sophisticated feeling and sensibility. This image of the emperor is reinforced by other stories portraying him as an accomplished musician, calligrapher, and a true connoisseur of arts and literature in general, qualities that mark a refined literatus.[32]

Cultural intimacy with the Illustrious Emperor allowed casual and even playful comparisons between him and individual scholar-officials. A good example is the following story about the poet Zhang Baoyin, then chief secretary on the staff of the Surveillance Commissioner of Lingnan Circuit, which is included in *Master Cloud Creek's Discussions with Friends* by Fan Shu:

> It was said at that time that secretary Zhang was comparable to He Xun in terms of his unbridled literary talent and to the Illustrious Emperor in terms of his outstanding physique. When Zhang was about to return north [to the capital] after the end of his appointment [in Guangzhou], he left a poem as a joke for his colleagues. Everyone who heard it could not help laughing. The poem reads as follows:

> I have tried to recall the former times when I was rich and noble;
> Even now I can still [picture them] dimly in my mind.
> After my cotton robe was tattered, I thought of women in the palace;
> When my silk pants were worn through, I remembered my royal garments.
> The falcon crouching on my back was my Gao Lishi;
> The lovely lady that I had painted was my Precious Consort Yang.
> Thin and pallid, I now take leave of Nanhai [i.e., Guangzhou];
> It seems just like the moment when the emperor returned from taking refuge in Shu.[33]

The comparisons by scholar-officials of chief secretary Zhang to the Illustrious Emperor—as well as Zhang's own comparisons of himself in the story—reiterate the emperor's status as a literati celebrity, just like the famous literary genius He Xun (480–520). By picturing himself in the persona of the Illustrious Emperor in his poem, however, Zhang playfully subverts as well as reinforces the analogy. On one hand, he calls attention to the comic incongruities between himself and his royal analogue. He can only pretend that the falcon on his back is Gao Lishi (684–762), the Illustrious Emperor's eunuch confidant, or that the lady in the painting is Precious Consort Yang. Such pretentions, to say nothing of his shabby clothing, expose the absurdity of a comparison between him, a poor and low-ranking scholar-official, and the sovereign. On the other hand, this discrepancy does not necessarily invalidate the wishful nature of the performance. Now that he is exhausted as he leaves his minor position on the staff of the Surveillance Commissioner, he can at least still hang on to the comforting illusion that he is like the emperor returning from royal exile in southwest China. Filled with layers of irony, Zhang's poem is invigorated by the self-conscious mockery of his own performance. The laughter of his colleagues conveys their consensus in recognizing his humor and ingenuity in positing himself as an inferior comic double of the emperor in order to identify and associate with him.

Secretary Zhang's mock performance of the role of the Illustrious Emperor also points to an important implication of cultural intimacy in terms of diminished social hierarchy. As the image of the emperor as a lover was established, his sexual relationship with Precious Consort Yang became the subject of public discussion and imagination, as we see in many Tang writings.[34] After the end of the Tang, these erotic undercurrents became even more obvious. Entries from the *Surviving Anecdotes from Kaiyuan and Tianbao* (Kaiyuan Tianbao yishi) by Wang Renyu (880–956) recount, for example, how the emperor enjoys sex-enhancing pills and how he uses the metaphor of mandarin ducks in bed to describe their lovemaking.[35] Voyeuristic fantasies of the emperor's sex life symbolically impinge upon the emperor's exclusive sexual claim to Precious Consort Yang. In his *Supplements to the State History* (Guoshi bu), Li Zhao (fl. 785–829) includes a telling story about an old shop-mistress who retrieves Precious Consort Yang's silk stocking after the execution and makes a fortune by lending it to visitors and charging one hundred coins per sitting.[36] With its presumed authenticity, the stocking is, in the words of Paul Kroll, "an apt symbol for the remains of the past."[37] Fondling it provides not only a momentary connection with the past, but also imaginary access to the sensual body of Precious Consort Yang.

These vicarious identifications with the Illustrious Emperor as lover imply a symbolic access to sovereign power, along with subversive political innuendoes. As a matter of fact, another entry from Li Zhao's collection claims that the rebel general An Lushan started his rebellion because of his desire for Precious Consort Yang.[38] While the story provides a simplified explanation for the cause of the rebellion by substituting sexual motives for political ones, it also makes clear the transgressive nature of such a desire, for the availability of Precious Consort Yang signifies the accessibility and vulnerability of sovereign power. Post-rebellion scholar-officials' sense of cultural intimacy with the Illustrious Emperor thus horrified their counterparts in the Song, an era of successful imperial centralization that made such intimacy unthinkable. The literatus Che Ruoshui (1210–1279) severely criticized his Tang predecessors, commenting, "Poets [of the Tang] elaborated extensively on events related to the Illustrious Emperor during his Tianbao reign. The 'Ballad of Eternal Sorrow,' for example, makes a complete mockery of the Sovereign-Father and expresses no sadness or grief for him."[39] To the likes of Che Ruoshui, cultural intimacy amounts to a breakdown of social hierarchy, hence the charge that Tang writers were "disrespectful" (*wuli*) toward the Illustrious Emperor, the Sovereign-Father. The perceived audacity of post-rebellion scholar-officials, however, indicates precisely their confidence in and optimism about their unique cultural identity with the monarch.

POLITICAL INTIMACY: THE ILLUSTRIOUS EMPEROR AS RULER OF HIS COURT

In stories about the Illustrious Emperor's political governance, late medieval literati storytellers cast scholar-officials as the closest allies of the sovereign. If advocates of literary and intellectual movements asserted the centrality of scholar-officials on the post-rebellion political stage by promoting the revitalization of *wen* as prerequisite to the recovery of a unified social and moral order,[40] literati storytellers did so by evoking concrete "historical" examples. They linked the Illustrious Emperor's earlier successes to his intimate personal and political bonds with scholar-officials, and his later downfall to his abandonment of such commitments. In promoting this theme of political intimacy, they highlighted scholar-officials as the real force behind successful governance, elevating these representatives of cultural power above other contenders to be the exclusive partners with whom the monarch should share his sovereign power. Although stories about political intimacy appear in many collections, analysis of collections devoted to the memory of the emperor's Kaiyuan and Tianbao reigns is particularly useful because they consistently foreground this theme, revealing not only each storyteller's individual agenda but also overlapping visions among the collections.[41]

A chief minister from one of the great clans, Li Deyu (787–849) compiled his *Jottings of Tales Heard from the Lius* (Ci Liu shi jiuwen) in 834 to present to Emperor Wenzong (r. 827–840). According to his preface, Li first heard the seventeen anecdotes in this collection from his father, Li Jifu (758–814), who in turn had heard them from his colleague Liu Mian (d. 805). Liu Mian was the son of Liu Fang (fl. 741–760), a court historian who had become acquainted in exile with Gao Lishi, the Illustrious Emperor's most trusted eunuch and the original narrator of these stories. Along with this collection of anecdotes, Li submitted another book to the throne entitled *Outline of Strategies for Reining in Court Officials* (Yuchen yaolüe), likely a treatise on how to control subordinates, although the book is not extant. The presentation occurred just one year before the tragic Sweet Dew Incident (Ganlu zhi bian) in which officials who were secretly allied with Wenzong failed to purge a coterie of powerful eunuchs and were met with bloody retaliation.[42] In this regard, Li Deyu's decision to combine a book of disquisition with a collection of historical examples suggests that he probably anticipated Wenzong's desire to reassert his royal authority.

Since Li Deyu's intended reading audience was primarily Wenzong himself, he was interested in presenting the Illustrious Emperor as a role model. Li casts the Illustrious Emperor as a loving brother and caring father (and grandfather) who attracts the service of extraordinary Daoist and Buddhist figures and takes the interests of his people to heart. Among the monarchic ways of conduct that the Illustrious Emperor exemplifies, Li emphasizes the intimacy he had with his early chief ministers: six entries (one-third of the whole collection) focus on the emperor's interactions with or appointments of chief ministers. The following entry is representative:

> When the [future] Illustrious Emperor was Crown Prince, [his aunt] Princess Taiping felt threatened by him. She spied on him from morning to night and reported his slightest mistakes to [his father] Emperor Ruizong [r. 684–690; 710–712]. The attendants of the palace secretly straddled the two sides in deference to her power. At that time, [the future] Empress Yuanxian was favored by the Illustrious Emperor and had just become pregnant. Afraid of Princess Taiping, the emperor wanted Yuanxian to take medicine to abort the fetus, but there was no one for him to speak with [about the matter].[43] Zhang Yue was able to enter the palace of the Crown Prince in his role as a Grand Tutor. When the emperor casually brought up the issue with him, Zhang offered clandestine support. On another day, when Zhang again entered the palace, he hid three doses of abortifacient within his robe and presented them to the emperor. The emperor was glad to get the medicine and, dismissing all of his attendants, lit a brazier in the hall in order to prepare it himself. Before the medicine was ready, he became tired and began to doze off. Then he caught a glimpse of a god who was more than ten feet

tall and wearing golden armor. With a dagger-axe in hand, the god
circled three times, then upended the pot, spilling all of the medicine. The emperor rose to check it and was amazed. After he stoked
the fire and put in another dose, he returned to his couch and waited,
pretending to close his eyes. He saw the god turn over the pot again.
All three doses were overturned. The next day when Zhang arrived,
the emperor told him the entire story. Zhang descended the stairs [to
the courtyard] to do obeisance and offer congratulations. He said,
"This fetus is ordained by Heaven and cannot be eliminated." Later
on, when the pregnant mother had a craving for something sour, the
emperor again told Zhang, who then hid quinces in his sleeves whenever he came to deliver lectures on the classics. As a result, no one
could rival the favor that Zhang enjoyed during the Kaiyuan reign.
It is said that [the future] Emperor Suzong [who was the child born
from this pregnancy] treated Zhang's sons Jun and Ji like his own
relatives and brothers. Liu Fang was recommended to office by Zhang
and personally heard him relate this story, which was consistent with
the account of Gao Lishi.[44]

Although in this anecdote Zhang Yue (667–731) is still just a tutor,
the Illustrious Emperor as yet is still a crown prince, and Emperor
Suzong (r. 756–762) is an unborn child, the dynamics of the story
are built upon their future identities as chief minister, emperor, and
heir apparent. The account projects an idealized vision of intimacy
between ruler and chief minister. The confinement of the crown
prince in the palace and the key role of Zhang as his only contact
with the outside world illustrate their symbiotic relationship: the
lord depends on the minister to carry out his intentions and rule the
empire. The prince also relies on Zhang's intellectual authority: by
proclaiming that the guardian god's actions represent the Mandate
of Heaven, Zhang asserts the confident voice of political wisdom.
Ritually, his performance of obeisance fulfills and validates the prediction by treating the crown prince formally as an emperor. Moreover, Zhang's contribution of first the abortifacient and later the
quince is highly symbolic in that the medicine to kill and the food
to nurture represent the power to eliminate and to preserve the heir
to the throne. In other words, Zhang wields the power to shape the
political future of the dynasty. Zhang Yue's critical role in the preg-
nancy of the crown prince's consort thus exemplifies an ideal fusion
of the personal and political intimacy that could develop between a
minister and his monarch. This intimate bond, as the story suggests,
deepens and undergirds the political success of both Zhang and the
Illustrious Emperor.

This thematic emphasis pervades other anecdotes concerning the emperor and his chief ministers. We are told that when he first ascends the throne, the emperor pays special respect to Yao Chong (650–721) and Song Jing (663–737), rising up to meet them when they arrive and personally seeing them off at the veranda; he even entrusts Yao with the power to monopolize the promotion and demotion of lower-ranking officials.[45] In another story, when Xiao Song (ca. 668–749) requests retirement, the emperor instead gives him the post of the Right Minister, wrapping two new tribute oranges with white silk to bestow on him.[46] Elsewhere, the emperor is said to always write the names of chief ministers he is about to appoint by hand: this intimacy is not physical, but the emphasis on his personal care in making the appointments remains constant.[47] By foregrounding the intimate terms between the emperor and his chief ministers in these stories, Li Deyu systematically reiterates the special bond between the two parties.

Li's case illustrates how intimate fragments of casual conversations between colleagues, friends, and family members could be repackaged and turned into political capital. His book presentation to Wenzong was an unmistakable gesture meant to cultivate a similar bond of intimacy with the emperor.[48] By putting together this collection, Li strategically positioned himself as a devoted advisor who offers a model of imperial conduct, an intimate insider who shares privileged knowledge that is missing from official records, and a key transmitter who passes on information valuable to the emperor's family and to state history. Although we do not know the effect the book's submission had on the relationship between Wenzong and Li Deyu, it is interesting to note that after Wenzong's brother Emperor Wuzong (r. 840–846) ascended the throne, Li became the ruler's most trusted chief minister.[49] Perhaps in this new relationship, Li fulfilled the idealized vision that he propagated in his collection.

Although Zheng Chuhui (d. 867) reiterates the theme of intimacy between the Illustrious Emperor and his officials in the *Miscellaneous Records of the Illustrious Emperor* (Minghuang zalu), he substitutes a gifted literary writer for Li Deyu's ideal chief minister. Unlike Li Deyu, who entered officialdom through hereditary privilege, Zheng Chuhui chose to take the Presented Scholar examination and passed in 834, despite his prominent pedigree as the grandson of the famous chief minister Zheng Yuqing (748–820).[50] Although a preface attributed to Zheng Chuhui has not survived, Song historians believed that his collection was prompted by his dissatisfaction with the limited scope of Li Deyu's version.[51] Zheng's motivations may, however, have been expressly political, for he seems to have belonged to the faction of Li Deyu's enemies.[52]

Zheng Chuhui's anecdotes about the Illustrious Emperor's appointments of chief ministers tellingly shift their focus to the performance of edict writers. For instance, in the story of the appointment of Zhang Jiazhen (665–729), Wei Kang's (667–726) instant composition of an elegant edict wins the emperor's praise; Wei is also able to swiftly compose a second edict after the emperor realizes that he mistakes another official for Zhang in the first one.[53] The following entry on Su Ting (670–727) is another case in point:

Su Ting far surpassed others in intelligence and could recite [from memory] several thousand words in a day. Although his memory was superb, his father Su Gui still disciplined him strictly; he was often ordered to prostrate himself in front of his bed wearing a black cotton robe with his legs uncovered to be beaten. After Ting grew up, his erudition in literature and learning ranked foremost among his contemporaries, but he was unrestrained in his behavior and addicted to drinking. After the Illustrious Emperor had overcome the enemies of the state, he was troubled by the difficult choice of the right candidate to draft his edicts. He turned to ask Gui: "Who can write edicts well? Please think about it for me." Gui answered, "I, your servant, don't know of others, but my son Ting is rather quick-minded and could wait on Your Majesty's orders. He is prone to drinking, but if fortunately he can avoid getting drunk, he can get the work done." The emperor immediately summoned Ting. When he arrived, he had a hangover and could only make rough obeisance. [Earlier] he had vomited outside the hall, [so now] the emperor ordered the attendants to support him and lay him down in the imperial presence, and then personally covered him with a comforter. After Ting woke up, he picked up the paper and brush that had been provided and instantly finished the composition; its brilliant embellishments were unhindered and its diction was elegant. Greatly pleased, the emperor gave him a pat on the back and said, "No one knows the son better than the father. Could there be another case like this?" From this point on he thought highly of Ting and intended to put him in important positions.[54]

The physical intimacy between the emperor and Su Ting not only represents an idealized vision of literary talent hewing a shortcut through the social thicket to the center of power, but also makes the ideal bond between emperor and literary genius parallel to the relationship between parent and child. The story emphasizes the resemblance of Su Ting in his drunken stupor to a child fast asleep, and makes paternal the Illustrious Emperor's loving gesture of covering him with a comforter. Su Ting's drunkenness shows him in a moment of self-indulgence and, implicitly, of self-confidence and pride—thus the image highlights the right of literary talent to claim a temporary independence from political hierarchy.[55] Yet this momentary freedom is meant to be an expression of subjectivity and individuality, not a serious challenge to the political structure, just as the impressive performance of the sober Su Ting proves his effective and indispensable role within the political system. Unlike the conventional idealizations of drunkenness as the avenue for personal escape and freedom, the story emphasizes the political condition of this independence: it is contingent upon the emperor's elegant accommodation in the mode of a doting father.

The entry on Su Ting's success resonates with other stories that reveal Zheng Chuhui's persistent concerns about the efficacy of literary talent in officialdom. By conveying that he will not compete for power with Li Linfu (683–752), the most powerful chief minister during the second half of the Illustrious Emperor's reign, the presentation of a poem on returning swallows by the official Zhang Jiuling (678–740) appeases Li's anger.[56] The story of Li Linfu's slander and murder of Li Shizhi (d. 746), however, shows Zheng Chuhui's awareness of the limits of poetic power in the face of vehement political attack, as well as his effort to achieve a sense of poetic justice. At the end of the account, Zheng Chuhui appends Li Shizhi's two poems on the contentment found in drinking, one composed before and one after he is removed from the position of chief minister.[57] Although these two poems do not seem to have any direct bearing on the political event recounted, their inclusion underscores Li Shizhi's admirable spirit, seemingly untouched by political ups and downs.[58] Showing sympathy for Li Shizhi's victimization, Zheng also offers a kind of poetic vindication by honoring Li's poetic voice as a triumphant last note to his tragic life story.

Compared to his predecessors, such as Li Deyu and Zheng Chuhui,[59] Wang Renyu gives the theme of political intimacy a new spin in his *Surviving Anecdotes from Kaiyuan and Tianbao* by foregrounding the figure of the Hanlin Academician (*Hanlin xueshi*). Wang lived through the last years of the Tang and served at the court of Former Shu, one of several regimes that emerged after the demise of the Tang. According to him, after the army of the Later Tang destroyed the Former Shu regime, he passed through the old Tang capital area in 925 en route to an audience with Emperor Zhuangzong (r. 923–926).[60] The journey inspired his collection, which was meant to complement existing records, presenting, he said, "what the previous writings do not have."[61]

Because Wang Renyu himself had held the position of Hanlin Academician, he promoted intimate relationships between the Illustrious Emperor and the academicians. The following story provides an example of his thematic emphasis:

> The Illustrious Emperor was in a side hall of the palace and wanted very much to discuss state affairs with Yao Chong. It was the fifteenth of the seventh month. Hard rain fell incessantly, and mud on the road was over a foot deep. The emperor ordered his attendants to hoist his royal sedan chair and go summon Yao, who was a Hanlin Academician at that time. People inside and outside the palace saw this [courtesy] as a great honor. Among the emperors who were eager for and respectful of worthy scholar-officials, there had been none like this since ancient times.[62]

The emperor's gesture of having Yao Chong carried into the palace in the imperial sedan chair underscores his strong, intimate relationship with the Hanlin Academician. Members of the Hanlin Academy (est. 738) helped to draft imperial edicts and were selected for their literary talent, but they do not seem to have played a major role in politics during the Illustrious Emperor's reign. During the post-rebellion era, however, thanks to being on call in an office right next to the inner palace, some academicians were able to develop a close relationship with the monarch out of this privileged proximity and influence major political decisions, so much so that they acquired the nickname "inner chief minister" (*neixiang*).[63] Given that Yao Chong's biographies do not indicate that he held such a post, it is unclear whether Wang Renyu manipulated the account or simply recorded a shared misconception. Whatever the case, the twists in Wang's version show a new shift in the intimacy theme, an emphasis that reveals his self-projection.[64]

In addition, Wang Renyu also consistently foregrounds the identity of other famous officials at the Illustrious Emperor's court as academicians in his collection. He refers to Su Ting and Zhang Jiuling as academicians, for example, who in previous collections were both better known by their highest rank as chief minister. Likewise, Wang indicates that the poet Li Bai (701–762?) served as an academician, although Li Bai's position was actually academician-in-attendance (*Hanlin gongfeng*), which did not involve edict composition.[65] Whether or not Wang Renyu was personally responsible for these discrepancies, the concentration of these stories demonstrates Wang's persistent promotion of the academician as the most visible figure in the Illustrious Emperor's court. Wang thus conflated Li Deyu's exaltation of the chief minister and Zheng Chuhui's stress on literary talent by turning the academician into a new elite icon, the epitome of both political and literary genius.

Attributing the Illustrious Emperor's legendary success to his personal and political intimacy with his civil officials, these storytellers promoted the scholar-official as the key to a strong, prosperous rule. Most of the positive characters in the collections belong to the first half of the Illustrious Emperor's reign and relate to his earlier success. By contrast, counterexamples account for his later failure: the literati storytellers attribute the emperor's tragic fall to the eventually rebellious general An Lushan's ingenious deceptions, the emperor's misplaced trust in Li Linfu, his squandering of power, wealth, and attention on Precious Consort Yang and her family, and so on.[66] None of these power players in the later court represent positive literati figures: An Lushan is cast as a barbarian general; Precious Consort Yang as a beautiful, superficial woman; her cousin Yang Guozhong as a vulgar upstart with little education; and Li Linfu as a power-hungry man known for persecuting righteous scholar-officials such as the poet Li Shizhi. Exacerbating the emperor's unfortunate relationships with these figures is his rejection of Zhang Jiuling, presented in various stories as a prominent scholar-official who wisely advises the emperor against doting on military governors, appointing Li Linfu as chief minister, or exonerating An Lushan.[67]

Through such positive and negative "historical" examples, late medieval literati storytellers conveyed great optimism about the political power of scholar-officials as representatives of *wen* and their intimate political bonds with the monarch. From Li Deyu's chief minister to Zheng Chuhui's literary genius to Wang Renyu's Hanlin Academician, we see a growing emphasis on the seamless fusion of the literary and political potency of *wen* in the role of the scholar-official. The optimism of late medieval scholar-officials is nowhere clearer than in Wang Renyu's story of the Illustrious Emperor bringing Hanlin Academician Yao Chong to the palace in the royal sedan-chair: as an agent of intellectual authority, the scholar-official becomes a co-occupant of the sovereign's seat. Against other power contenders in the late medieval political landscape, scholar-officials advocate such idealized visions of their exclusive political intimacy with the monarch in order to justify and boost their collective political ascendancy. Their confidence, however, also betrays a sense of wishful thinking or even anxiety that such power-sharing is, ultimately, the imperial prerogative and might just as well not happen.

SOCIOHISTORICAL INSTRUMENTALITY: THE ILLUSTRIOUS EMPEROR AS AN EMBLEM OF DYNASTIC APOGEE REMEMBERED

Featuring a talkative old man as a survivor of the Kaiyuan-Tianbao era, the narratives of late medieval literati storytellers emphasize the sociohistorical instrumentality of scholar-officials as mediators both between the people and their reigning monarch, and between the past and the present. As a living eyewitness who compares the reigning monarch to the Illustrious Emperor, the old man represents both the voice of the people and that of the past; by posing as the putative old man's spokesmen, literati storytellers assert the crucial role of scholar-officials as distant political commentators informed by social conscience and historical memory, figures who can ensure the reigning emperor's connections to the illiterate populace as well as the bygone past. Modern scholars tend to question the authenticity of these storied old men because of their unrealistically advanced age, seeing them as a "fictional device" used by writers to justify the veracity of their accounts.[68] Whether or not encounters between old men and literati storytellers actually occurred, the old-man persona allows the Illustrious Emperor to be used as a flexible emblem of dynastic apogee, and also allows the articulation of potentially dangerous political commentaries.

By airing criticisms of the reigning monarch in particular and the human weaknesses of sovereigns in general, the lengthy prose narrative "Story of the Old Man of the Eastern Part of the City"(Dongcheng laofu zhuan) shows in distinctive ways the sociohistorical instrumentality of the scholar-official. This piece has been attributed to Chen Hong, the author of "An Account of the 'Ballad of Eternal Sorrow,'" or to Chen Hongzu, who appears as the old man's interlocutor in the story and about whom we have no biographical information.[69] According to the story, Jia Chang, born in the first year of the Kaiyuan reign, is in charge of gamecocks for the Illustrious Emperor and enjoys royal favor for decades until the An Lushan Rebellion. Unable to follow the emperor into exile, he hides in the mountains. After the capital is recaptured, Jia abandons his family and becomes a pious Buddhist monk. When Chen Hongzu, a scholar-official, visits his temple, Jia embarks on a long monologue in which he enumerates the Illustrious Emperor's political achievements and criticizes the reign of the current emperor, Xianzong. His literatus interlocutor Chen Hongzu silently leaves, not daring to make any comment.[70]

The story carefully establishes the narrative authority of Jia Chang in order to ensure the validity of his political commentaries. We are told that neither his sight nor his hearing has failed and that his strength of mind is unimpaired. Moreover, his closeness to the emperor for four decades affords him a privileged vantage point as a court insider, while his new identity as a devout Buddhist monk gives him a detached and supposedly impartial perspective from which to look at recent events. When prompted by Chen Hongzu's question about the Illustrious Emperor, the old man cites examples of the emperor's effective control of military governors, his successful economic policies, his elevation of officials with local administrative experience, his recruitment of talent on the basis of moral character rather than literary performance, and his subjugation of foreign states and the exclusion of barbarian influences. Contrasting these accomplishments to the present conditions of Xianzong's reign, the old man decries the alarming deteriorations of the past model. As Robert Joe Cutter has rightly pointed out, the monologue is "a social and political commentary" that, in its effort to criticize the present, idealizes the Kaiyuan reign period.[71]

While the idealization is fitting on the part of the old man, a beneficiary of the Illustrious Emperor's favor, the story as a whole conveys an unsettling view of sovereignty as a power exercised by fallible rulers. Jia Chang's court career demonstrates the Illustrious Emperor's talent, compassion, and generosity as a capable monarch. Jia comes to royal attention when he is seen as a little boy playing with a wooden gamecock by the road; the emperor summons him into the palace and makes him a lad of the Gamecock Quarter. After he proves his skills in understanding and ordering the gamecocks, the emperor promotes him to be head of the five hundred lads. Throughout his reign, the emperor showers Jia with gifts, arranges for his marriage, and even sponsors his father's funeral. Jia reciprocates with loyalty and

devotion: the performances of his gamecocks outshine those of wres-
tlers, sword jugglers, tightrope walkers and others, and he refuses to
submit to the rebel leader and later renounces the world rather than
serve the new emperor. The Illustrious Emperor's ability to recognize
and employ Jia's talent and Jia's loyalty to the throne thus embody an
ideal relationship between monarch and minister, echoing the theme
of political intimacy seen above.

However, Jia Chang's successful career as a gamecock fighter also
ironically reveals the emperor's blindness to the serious implications
of his apparently trivial pastime. Cockfighting had long been associated with profligacy, along with other notorious leisure sports such as
dog and horse racing.[72] The emperor's pursuit of this hobby leads him
to employ Jia Chang's talent only for the purpose of entertainment,
although Jia is said to have been exceptionally strong and nimble. By
implication, Jia could have had a more influential career like his father
Jia Zhong, who is said to have helped the Illustrious Emperor, then
still a prince, raise an army against Empress Wei (Wei hou, d. 710),
the widow of his uncle Emperor Zhongzong (r. 684; 705–710), and
install his own father, Emperor Ruizong, on the throne.[73] Moreover,
the Illustrious Emperor remains oblivious to the unintended effects of
his hobby, which creates a popular craze for cockfighting. We are told
that well-to-do people spend their fortunes on gamecocks, and that
even the poor play with mock ones. In addition, Jia Chang's enjoyment of imperial favor sends the wrong message about the court's
estimation of talent. The popular ditty about Jia's example, while
it argues that cockfighting and horseracing ensure riches and honor
more effectively than studying, is laden with sarcasm and resentment.

Most fatefully, the emperor's weakness lies in his failure to understand fully the implications of his role as Son of Heaven and to act
accordingly. The correlations between human activity and cosmic
mechanism in cosmological theories of *yinyang* and "five phases"
(*wuxing*) require that he discern the social and cosmic significance
of his personal actions and political decisions, interpret portents, and
make necessary adjustments in order to avert disasters and ensure
prosperity.[74] According to the storyteller, however, "His Majesty was
born in the hour of the rooster in the rooster year *yiyou*, and yet
he appointed court officials to fight cocks. In a time of peace, this
portended chaos."[75] Because the rooster is his symbol, the emperor's
endorsement of cockfighting signifies that he condones challenges
to his sovereignty; rebellions are the inevitable outcome. If even a

brilliant sovereign like the Illustrious Emperor is still fallible and is destroyed as a result, what is to be expected of lesser rulers? The story thus conveys a dark vision of the precariousness of sovereignty and its inevitable decline. Precisely because of the unsettling nature of this view, the storyteller ends the story with the ambiguous silence of the literatus interlocutor in response to the old man's personal complaints about historical decline.

While the "Story of the Old Man of the Eastern Part of the City" illustrates the role of the scholar-official as a critic of monarchs, the poem "Song of Continuous Prosperity Palace" (Lianchang gong ci) by the famous poet Yuan Zhen offers an alternative model of subtle didacticism couched in flattering terms. After obtaining the degree of Canonical Expert (*mingjing*) at the age of fifteen,[76] Yuan Zhen took and passed the decree examination held by the newly enthroned Xianzong in 806. Ranked a top candidate, Yuan Zhen was promoted to the position of censor. Along with his friends Bai Juyi and Li Shen (772–846), he championed "new Music Bureau poetry" (*xin yuefu*), a poetic movement that aimed to revive the function of poetry as a medium for social commentary.[77] According to legends on the origins of the *Book of Songs* (Shi jing) and Music Bureau poetry, officials gathered folk songs from around the country so that the monarch could understand the thoughts of his people and the effect of his governance. The poets of "new Music Bureau poetry" appointed themselves spokesmen for the populace, exposing what they saw as the social problems of the day in plain, straightforward poetic language.[78] Yuan Zhen was exiled in 810 presumably because of his conflict with eunuchs. Bai Juyi was also demoted, and he attributed part of the reason to the new Music Bureau poetry, which he believed was offensive to those in power.[79]

Yuan Zhen composed the "Song of Continuous Prosperity Palace" in 817–18, when he served as an assistant administrator in Tongzhou, toward the end of nearly a decade of exile. The poem describes the narrator's fortuitous encounter with a survivor of the Illustrious Emperor's era who lives near Continuous Prosperity Palace (Lianchang gong), one of the temporary royal residences. The garrulous old man reminisces about the past of the palace, enlivened by banquets, singing, and music from the emperor's grand entourage. After the rebellions, the deserted palace retains traces of the happy past, such as the couch of the emperor and the dressing table of Precious Consort Yang. But, overtaken by weeds, the place has been invaded by nature and become the residence of snakes, foxes, rabbits, and birds. Prompted by the poet's question of who is to blame, the old man is able to identify the culprits, despite his pretense of ignorance:

> At the end of the Kaiyuan reign, Yao Chong and Song Jing passed away;
> Gradually, the court was swayed by the influence of Precious Consort
>   Yang.
> In the palace, she adopted An Lushan as her foster son;
> The front gate of [her sister] Lady Guoguo was as noisy as a
>   marketplace.
> I cannot remember the [given] names of chief ministers who abused
>   power;
> Vaguely I can recall they were Yang [Guozhong] and Li [Linfu].[80]

Although the old man is saddened by half a century of subsequent political instability, he is pleased with Xianzong's military success and optimistic about the future:

> The reigning emperor [Xianzong] is sagacious and his chief ministers
>   intelligent;
> The areas of Wu and Shu were immediately pacified after his decree was
>   announced.
> The imperial army again targeted the renegade in western Huai;
> Since his fall, peace has reigned in the world once again.[81]

Anticipating Xianzong's return to Continuous Prosperity Palace, the old man ends his lengthy monologue by expressing his hope for an ideal time when armies will become completely obsolete.

This poem testifies to Yuan Zhen's strategic reinvention of the poetic didacticism underlying the earlier new Music Bureau poetry. The old man's seemingly straightforward commendation of Xianzong is complicated by his reference to the Illustrious Emperor as a model of both success and failure. Although the clear identification of the "bad guys" around the Illustrious Emperor seems to absolve him of responsibility, he is still implicated because he fails to tell the good from the bad. Moreover, while the Illustrious Emperor's pleasure seeking at Continuous Prosperity Palace marks the peace and success of his reign in the old man's account, such monarchial indulgence has also been taken as the cause of his downfall by others. While the advent of peace as a result of Xianzong's current military victories should lead him back to the palace to celebrate and enjoy himself, as did the Illustrious Emperor, the royal return may also adumbrate another fall from success to failure. The comparison of the reigning emperor to his illustrious ancestor can thus be understood not just as a compliment but also as a warning and even an implicit criticism. The restoration of past glory potentially slides into the repetition of past mistakes.

Such subtle didacticism—without the pointed critique of the reigning emperor or the Illustrious Emperor, as in the "Story of the Old Man of the Eastern Part of the City"—could be advantageous, as is suggested by the positive reception of Yuan Zhen's poem. According to Yuan Zhen's biography, Xianzong's son Emperor Muzong (r. 820–824) was greatly pleased by the "Song of Continuous Prosperity Palace," apparently embracing only its surface meaning. Muzong summoned Yuan from his exile and made him his edict drafter. His royal favor was so great that within the next few years, Yuan was advanced to the office of chief minister, although his political ascendancy was unfortunately cut short by the emperor's premature death.[82] Whether or not Muzong was a naïve reader, Yuan Zhen's conscious modification of poetic didacticism demonstrates a distinctive vision of the connection between past and present. If the "Story of the Old Man of the Eastern Part of the City" envisions the present as an inevitable deviation from the past, Yuan Zhen's poem conceives of the relationship as an irresistible return.

While the "Story of the Old Man of the Eastern Part of the City" and the "Song of Continuous Prosperity Palace" present the ventriloquizing scholar-official as a critic and as a eulogist-cum-remonstrator, respectively, the "Poem of the Northford Gate" (Jinyang men shi) by Zheng Yu (fl. 836–855) offers another alternative, this time, as nostalgic optimist. Zheng Yu, who belonged to the prestigious great clan of the Xingyang Zhengs, composed this two-hundred-line verse (one of the longest extant Tang poems) in late 851 or early 852, soon after he passed the Presented Scholar examination.[83] Similar to the narratives of his predecessors, Zheng Yu's poem features a loquacious old innkeeper living near the Northford Gate (Jinyang men) outside the Illustrious Emperor's hot spring resort, Floral Purity Palace. Rather than giving a coherent narrative, however, the old man recounts various anecdotes about the Illustrious Emperor's reign. In addition to offering poetic renditions of these stories, Zheng Yu also includes close to thirty interlinear explanatory notes in narrative prose. Echoing the cross-genre collaboration of Bai Juyi and Chen Hong, Zheng Yu uses these prose passages to contextualize shifting poetic images and to make the old man's monologue more comprehensible.

By elaborating on the old man's nostalgia for the Illustrious Emperor's reign, Zheng Yu's poem illuminates a different problem surrounding the link between past and present—not in terms of deviation or repetition, but of disconnection. The old man's reminiscences present a multifaceted picture of the Illustrious Emperor's reign in the familiar images of prosperity, extravagance, and destruction. The destructive forces, however, do not just come from the rebel armies of An Lushan but also from the recent past of Wuzong's reign. Wuzong, a Daoist-inclined monarch, was infamous for presiding over the unprecedented destruction of the Buddhist establishment. He ordered the secularization of monks and nuns and the confiscation of monastic properties across the country.[84] In the poem, the old man is critical of Wuzong's policy, specifically casting the Buddhist persecution as the destruction of a link between the Illustrious Emperor's era and the present:

> The wall paintings of [Wang] Mojie were broken into pieces amidst the smoke;
> The handwriting of the Illustrious Emperor's poems disappeared into the clouds.
>
> ([Note:] The Stone Urn Monastery was built with the materials left from the construction of Floral Purity Palace during the Kaiyuan reign. The jade statues in the main hall were all tribute from Youzhou and they arrived on the same date as the statue of Laozi [enshrined] in the Pavilion for Worshipping the Genesis. There was nothing like their exquisite charm, and if struck, they made the sounds of chime stones. The rest of the statues were carved by Yang Huizhi in person, and those with hollow limbs were all made by Yuan Jia'er. Expertly refined and delicately beautiful, they were unequaled from time immemorial. The Red Tower was located on a cliff to the west of the main hall, facing a precipice below. In the tower, there were poems inscribed by the Illustrious Emperor, one transcribed in the cursive style and the other in the bafen style; there were also two walls with landscape paintings by Wang Wei. These were all lost after the monastery was destroyed. Mojie was Wang Wei's style name.)[85]

To the old man, the authentic traces of the Illustrious Emperor's era testify to its accomplishments, epitomized by the statues carved by the famous artisans Yang Huizhi and Yuan Jia'er, paintings by the well-known literatus Wang Wei (701–761), and the calligraphy of the emperor himself. The Illustrious Emperor's past reign thus does not simply represent useful historical lessons; its artistic aura highlights its status as the political and cultural high point of the dynasty. Wuzong's destruction of Buddhist monasteries is thus a synecdoche for the destruction of the precious accomplishments of the past. The old man's hostility toward Wuzong likely reflected Zheng's personal bias. As indicated by another interlinear note, the Stone Urn Monastery, where Wang Wei's paintings and the Illustrious Emperor's poems were inscribed, was also the place where Zheng Yu had studied in preparation for his examination. Wuzong's anti-Buddhist movement thus destroyed a place with which Zheng had personal connections. Moreover, Zheng Yu also probably tried to keep in line with the efforts of the reigning emperor, Xuānzong (r. 846–859), to distance himself from his predecessor and nephew Wuzong; Xuānzong restored Buddhism within five years of his ascendance to the throne.[86] Regardless of Zheng Yu's personal motives, his poem indicates a strong concern with the symbolic meaning of maintaining historical continuity with the apogee of the dynasty.

Moreover, Zheng Yu also optimistically envisions the political possibility of restoring the glories of the past. The literatus interlocutor and narrator in the poem reassures the old man that the reigning emperor Xuānzong will usher in a new era of peace and prosperity:

> It will not be hard to see the Yellow River's water become clear and the Eastern Sea's waves become subdued;
> Our Majesty has established a foundation of peace and prosperity.
> In the past the lands of the Huang River valley were lost [to the Tibetans];
> Last night they were recovered, no longer subject to damage and disaster.
> The barbarian king fled north and abandoned the borderlands [he seized from the Tang];
> His caitiff steeds ran west, leaving the Yuezhi region abandoned.
> It is not easy to encounter two sagely eras;
> I hope you take good care of yourself and nurture your body.[87]

The optimism about the reigning emperor Xuānzong in Zheng Yu's poem seems contrived, however, because the court was not directly involved in reclaiming the Gansu Corridor from the Tibetans. The local leader Zhang Yichao (799–872) recovered the lost territory under his own initiative and pledged allegiance to the Tang court in 851. He was later awarded a military governorship that legitimated his control in the area.[88] Zheng Yu's poem thus inadvertently reveals a perceived crisis in sovereignty that was acute in the mid-ninth century: the present is disconnected from a projected sublime past, embedded in the reality of military separatism, religious conflicts, and foreign invasions. Despite this challenging reality, Zheng Yu's poem demonstrates his staunch loyalism by encouraging the reigning emperor to strive for greater success. Although it is not clear whether Zheng Yu benefited in any way from his poem, as Yuan Zhen did, his mode of political commentary as a nostalgic optimist underscores his political devotion.

From the criticisms in the "Story of the Old Man of the Eastern Part of the City" to the commendations in "Poem of the Northford Gate," the purported transmission of popular wisdom shows how late medieval literati storytellers explored and affirmed ways to articulate sensitive political opinions by using the persona of an old man. While the ventriloquism emphasizes the instrumental role of the scholar-official as political commentator and mediator, it also suggests a tendency to avoid direct, politically dangerous confrontations with the monarch. Indeed, it takes a Daoist adept with magical powers to really confront, challenge, and even set a limit to the authority of the monarch.

SUPERNATURAL RESTRAINT: THE ILLUSTRIOUS EMPEROR AS A MORTAL MAN

In stories about the Illustrious Emperor's relationship with Daoist figures, literati storytellers underscored the nature of sovereignty as a secular power confined to the world of mortals. Since Daoist priests had traditionally claimed access to the world beyond and their independence from society and its secular authorities, these stories dramatize their problematic relationship with the ruler, foregrounding their power to compete for and circumscribe sovereignty. The Daoist adept, featured in stories from literati collections as well as Dunhuang transformation texts, can be said to represent the alter ego of the scholar-official. Although literati figures do not appear in these narratives, scholar-officials were the storytellers, compilers, and members of the audience who enjoyed such stories.

The Illustrious Emperor was certainly not the only monarch whose image was closely associated with religious figures in the popular imagination. Emperor Wu of the Liang dynasty (Liang Wudi, r. 502–549), for instance, was widely considered a Buddhist ruler, while the First Emperor of Qin (Qin Shihuang, 259–220 BCE) and Emperor Wu of the Han dynasty (Han Wudi, r. 140–87 BCE) were known for their obsession with the cult of immortality and their patronage of Daoist masters of alchemy and esoterica.[89] Although the historical

Illustrious Emperor promoted Daoism and elevated Laozi, the Daoist patriarch to whom the Tang royal house traced its imperial lineage,[90] late medieval stories dramatize his interactions with both Buddhist and Daoist figures.

These stories are preoccupied with the explicit and implicit competitions among Buddhists, Daoists, and the monarch. In stories about a contest held before the Illustrious Emperor, for example, a Buddhist monk and a Daoist priest try to outdo each other in magic displays to demonstrate the superiority of their respective religions.[91] In other stories, Buddhist and Daoist characters show off their extraordinary powers to impress the emperor without the presence of opponents. Foreign monks—for instance, Shanwuwei (Śubhākarasiṃha, 637–735), Bukong (Amoghavajra, 705–774), and Jingangzhi (Vajrabodhi, ca. 669–741)—demonstrate their ability to induce rain at the emperor's request.[92] Meanwhile, Daoist Zhang Guo shows off his foreknowledge, immunity to poison, and ability to destroy and regrow parts of his body, among other feats of magic; another adept, Ye Fashan, takes the emperor on fantastic trips to the moon and remote parts of the country.[93] Such displays, in the words of Robert Campany, not only indicate the "adepts' bid for imperial and official-class patronage," but also amount to "the staking of a claim to a separate domain of power that was beyond the control of rulers and officials."[94]

In stories about the explicit power competition between the adept and the ruler, the adept (usually a Daoist figure) embodies the character type of a rebellious trickster whose superior power emanates from his transcendent status. Although Buddhists and Daoists as historical individuals were competitors of scholar-officials for the monarch's patronage in the political sphere, and could be denounced by the literati for their efforts to monopolize the imperial favor, medieval scholar-officials also developed close relationships with religious figures and institutions in their personal lives, becoming admirers, lay practitioners, and even official converts.[95] As we shall see in chapter 4, late medieval literati storytellers saw the pursuit of transcendence or becoming an immortal as a path of cosmic mobility open to scholar-officials in particular. The literati thus identified with and in theory could assume the role of the Daoist adept. This is a more powerful alternative to and substitute for the scholar-official's conventional persona of a recluse who expresses political defiance solely through noncooperation.

The Daoist trickster adept represents a consistent tradition in medieval stories. In earlier accounts, characters such as the River-Dwelling

Sire (Heshang gong), who literally rises into the air to confute the des-
ignation of him as an imperial subject, and Zuo Ci, who mocks contemporary Chinese rulers, assert that as envoys from another realm,
adepts like themselves are beyond imperial control.[96] In late medieval
stories, the figure of Luo Gongyuan represents a new addition to the
lineage of tricksters. In one account, Luo sniffs at tribute oranges,
causing each to lose a segment, which the Illustrious Emperor only
discovers after he peels them open to eat.[97] In another story, Luo
refuses to fully divulge the secrets of his magic to the emperor. After
the emperor executes Luo, he appears to a royal messenger, sound and
well, and comments tauntingly, "How cruel is His Majesty's play at
the game [of killing me]!"[98] Luo's excision of the tribute fruit as well
as his escape from the emperor's death penalty unscathed underscore
his transcendent status and his superior power.

Although most anecdotes of the Illustrious Emperor's interactions
with Daoist adepts are dispersed among a number of literati collections, the Dunhuang transformation text "The Story of Ye Jingneng"
(Ye Jingneng shi) is a synthetic story that incorporates many of those
scattered themes.[99] Transformation texts have traditionally been seen
as the earliest examples of Chinese popular literature,[100] and like
many other Dunhuang manuscripts, "The Story of Ye Jingneng" was
written in a language with vernacular characteristics. Because the
story features a Daoist priest and makes pro-Daoist statements, it has
been regarded as one of the few Daoist texts among the corpus of
Dunhuang manuscripts.[101] Whoever wrote down or copied this story
seems to have had a lower level of education than the literati writers
we have seen—such as Bai Juyi, Chen Hong, Yuan Zhen, and others—because the text shows frequent orthographic mistakes. These
differences notwithstanding, as Zhang Hongxun has shown, almost
every episode in the text has variants that appear in seventeen collections of anecdotes compiled by elite writers.[102]

Rather than suggesting that the elite collections were the source of
the Dunhuang story or vice versa, these overlaps indicate that stories
in general, and those about the Illustrious Emperor and Daoist figures
in particular, enjoyed wide circulation across the social spectrum.
While the literati collections testify to the ongoing appeal of these
stories across time, spanning close to two centuries, the Dunhuang
version, discovered in the borderlands of northwest China, demonstrates the extent of their spatial dissemination. Thus, insofar as "The
Story of Ye Jingneng" can be taken to indicate popular sensibilities,

such sensibilities by no means exclude the elite. As a matter of fact, by combining disparate anecdotes of Daoist figures to make a coherent narrative featuring a single hero, the Dunhuang story actually brings subversive elements of literati discourse to the fore that have been overshadowed by the much greater number of stories promoting the intimacy between the monarch and the scholar-official.

The protagonist Ye Jingneng in the Dunhuang transformation text is a composite character. In official history, Ye Jingneng (d. 710) appears as a favorite thaumaturge of Emperor Zhongzong and Empress Wei. He was executed by the Illustrious Emperor when he, then still a prince, eliminated his widowed aunt Empress Wei and installed his father on the throne.[103] In the transformation text, however, the protagonist Ye Jingneng is a synthesis of the Daoist figures associated with the Illustrious Emperor, including Ye Fashan, Zhang Guo, Luo Gongyuan, Ming Chongyan, and Shen Tianshi.[104] Confusion over the identities of such Daoist adepts among late medieval scholar-officials was not at all unusual. The ninth-century writer Zhao Lin complained that his contemporaries circulated anachronistic stories of Ye Jingneng serving at the court of the Illustrious Emperor. In Zhao's eyes, they had clearly mistaken Ye Fashan for Ye Jingneng.[105] Historicity, however, is beside the point here, as the protagonist Ye Jingneng in the Dunhuang story represents the archetypal Daoist adept who has a tense relationship with the ruler, exemplified here by the Illustrious Emperor.

Although "The Story of Ye Jingneng" is incomplete, missing the beginning portion, it is a long narrative recounting this adept's attainment of magic powers, his service at court, and his departure from it. Ye Jingneng learns the secrets of incantations from a scroll of spells sent to him by the god Indra in the All-Encompassing Heaven.[106] He then decides to make a name for himself at court. On his way to the capital, he stops the god of Mount Tai from taking the wife of a certain Magistrate Zhang. After his arrival in Chang'an, he publicly executes a fox spirit that has possessed a girl. The Illustrious Emperor hears about this and invites him to court, treating him as a master. Ye performs various feats of magic, such as transforming a wine jar into a Daoist priest who serves as drinking companion, bringing down rains to relieve the drought, taking the emperor to southwest China to see lantern displays, and transporting him into space to tour the palaces of immortals on the moon. The relationship, however, turns sour not only because of the evil machinations of the eunuch Gao Lishi

but, more importantly, because Ye steals the emperor's favorite concubine and impregnates her. After the emperor fails in an attempt to
kill Ye, the latter departs for the All-Encompassing Heaven, passing
on a message to the emperor through an envoy. The story ends with
the emperor's tearful regrets over losing Ye.[107]

Ye Jingneng's relationship with the Illustrious Emperor is ambivalent because he is willing to serve the emperor as a subject, on one
hand, but on the other he is also an esoteric master who is independent from imperial jurisdiction. After Ye passes a test set by the god
Indra, he demonstrates his complete mastery of magical incantations
and becomes the counterpart of the Illustrious Emperor in the realm
of spirits: "All the ghosts and spirits under heaven could be summoned by Ye Jingneng, and no gods would ever defy his orders."[108] By
stopping the god of Mount Tai from taking Magistrate Zhang's wife
and by killing the fox spirit possessing the girl, Ye Jingneng demonstrates his sovereign power over the spirits. In the beginning, Ye and
the Illustrious Emperor are on good terms, a relationship predicated
on mutual deference and collaboration. The emperor positions himself as a disciple of Ye and visits him regularly to pay his respects. At
the same time, Ye uses his magic powers to do the emperor's bidding.

Beneath the surface of this apparent harmony between the two,
however, tensions abound because of their competition for control.
The emperor's distrust of the elixir of immortality brought by Ye indicates his unwillingness to submit to Ye's esoteric authority. Moreover,
his insistence on learning the art of incantation from Ye demonstrates
his desire to expropriate the secret of Ye's powers. By having Ye
carry out fantastic tasks for him, the emperor shows his authority as
supreme head of state as well as his virtue in attracting talented men
to his service. Hence, after Ye showcases his powers, we are told that
court officials congratulate the emperor for being a ruler who sur-
passes all others before.

Meanwhile, because of the dualistic nature of his role, Ye Jingneng's performance of magical feats is both a deferential service to
the emperor and a display of his own superiority over him. As a matter of fact, Ye's impressive performances often come at a cost to the
emperor's authority. In the episode in which Ye takes the emperor to
southwest China to view lanterns, for example, the emperor depends
on Ye's magical power to travel three thousand miles in an instant;
he also follows Ye's every instruction, including leaving his undergar-
ment in the temple of the King of Shu so that local officials and people

would know about his incognito visit to the area. In other words, the emperor plays the role of a puppet while Ye assumes full control of the whole process. Although the Shu people are in awe of the emperor after this unannounced visit, so much so that officials no longer dare to give orders without his authorization, this strengthening of central authority stems from Ye's design. As a matter of fact, the change implies that the area had previously been beyond the emperor's control, a poignant reference to the regional autonomy of post-rebellion military governors.

If the lantern episode reveals the deficiency in the emperor's political power, the trip to the moon exposes the weakness in his mortal body. Although the emperor follows Ye's advice and dons a cotton-quilted jacket, the cold of the moon proves too much for him and prevents his enjoyment of the spectacular sights. When the emperor repeatedly beseeches Ye to return him to the human world, we are told that Ye "could not help smiling."[109] The emperor's failure to withstand the cold and Ye's knowing smile are highly symbolic: the visit to the immortal world may elevate the emperor above previous rulers, as evidenced by his courtiers' congratulations, but it also underscores his inferiority to Ye and his status as a mere mortal.

The story further highlights the Illustrious Emperor's mortal and hence inferior status by revealing his infertility. In stark contrast to the historical Illustrious Emperor, who had a number of sons, this story depicts him as a barren man worried about having no successor. When the emperor and his empress seek Ye Jingneng's help in divining whether they will ever have children, Ye checks the records in the bureaucracies of heaven and the underworld and provides them with a disappointing negative answer. Because lineage is inseparable from dynastic continuity for the emperor, his infertility becomes the ultimate sign of his personal weakness and of a crisis in sovereignty. If predetermination of male heirs symbolizes the supernatural endorsement of sovereignty, the withholding of such an endorsement signals the imminent loss of the Mandate of Heaven. This crisis of sovereignty spawns opportunities for encroachment and subversion.

By stealing and impregnating the emperor's favorite concubine, Ye challenges and usurps the emperor's sovereign power. "To cuckold the ruler," as Jack Chen puts it, "is an arrogation of the privileges of the emperor that strikes at the domestic—and sexual—metaphor of sovereignty itself."[110] Although the emperor's favorite woman in the story calls Precious Consort Yang readily to mind, she remains

anonymous throughout, personifying the sexual and political vulnerability of sovereignty. If supernatural endorsement gives sovereign
power its legitimacy, its efficacy in the mortal world depends on the
emperor's maintenance of a sexual-political order—the monarch's
power to monopolize and impregnate high-ranking, beautiful women
represents his power to enforce a political hierarchy that keeps other
men, his competitors, in check. This may bring to mind the anecdote
that conflates the rebel general An Lushan's desire for the throne with
his desire for Precious Consort Yang. Moreover, Ye Jingneng himself embodies a successful example of sovereign control: earlier in the
story Ye has policed and punished the sexual transgressions of the
god of Mount Tai and the fox spirit.

The irony of Ye Jingneng's own sexual transgression does not necessarily indicate an inconsistency in his character, however, but rather
the very instability of sovereignty as an autocratic power of domination: it is available to any man of superior force. While Ye is able to
assert his sovereignty over gods and spirits, the emperor does not suc-
ceed in subordinating Ye, who instead usurps his sexual and hence
political status. The emperor's failure in his efforts to execute Ye further underscores the limits of his sovereign power. Instead of directly
proclaiming Ye's guilt, the emperor stages a meeting to entrap him:
he asks Ye to divulge his secrets of incantations, which Ye predict-
ably refuses, and then the emperor orders Ye's execution on grounds
of insubordination. The emperor's hypocritical maneuver helps him
save face, but his attack on Ye is foolish because Ye has consistently
demonstrated his superior power throughout the story. When soldiers
rush to kill Ye, he simply walks into a pillar to protect himself and
eventually flies up to heaven, beyond the reach of the emperor's control, like many trickster adepts before him.

It is highly significant that the story ends with the emperor's concession and remorse. Realizing that he cannot defeat Ye, he tries to
appease him and repair their relationship by blaming the eunuch Gao
Lishi for everything. Through his message to the emperor, however,
Ye makes it clear that they will never see each other again. In tears,
the emperor sings Ye's praises, acknowledging his wondrous magical
powers, and expresses his regret at losing him:

> We indeed have been unfair to you, Sir.
> We hope that you understand Our thought.
> Looking afar at the Shu area,
> Our two eyes shed tears in vain.

Since the creation of heaven and earth,
There has been no one like Ye.
Write down his deeds for Us,
And honor him in the official history.[111]

The emperor's admission of fault indicates his painful recognition
that by jealously guarding his women, or the sexual expression of
his sovereignty, he has destroyed his collaborative relationship with
Ye. The Shu area that he gazes longingly toward is the place where
Ye had taken him to view lanterns as well as where Ye is last seen in
the story. Most poignantly, Shu was the very place in which the historical Illustrious Emperor sought refuge after the outbreak of the
An Lushan Rebellion. This evocation of Shu conveys a cautionary
message against autocracy: had the emperor been willing to share
his sovereignty with Ye, he would have benefited from Ye's powerful assistance and would not have found himself in serious trouble.
This negative lesson thus echoes and reiterates the theme of political
intimacy and partnership between the emperor and scholar-officials
that we discussed above.

Thus "The Story of Ye Jingneng" can be seen as a fantastic refrac-
tion of the mundane monarch-minister relationship. If Ye's magical
powers represent the minister's knowledge and skills, which are indispensable to the emperor, his sexual transgression signifies how those
powers can also come into conflict with the monarch's interests and
threaten his autocratic rule. If in normal circumstances the minister
would have been vulnerable to the emperor's vengeful violence, as
numerous examples in Chinese history have shown, "The Story of
Ye Jingneng" inverts the power relationship and makes the emperor
look like a fool.[112] Despite its subversive nature, the story is not rebellious. Instead of taking over the Illustrious Emperor's position, Ye
Jingneng goes off to a realm beyond his reach, much like a recluse. In
this way, Ye resembles the hermit praised by Confucius: "[A gentle-
man] goes out to serve when the world is ruled by the Way and goes
into hiding when it is not."[113] By his departure Ye exposes the nature
of sovereignty as a temporal power that can be challenged, mocked,
and rejected.

"The Story of Ye Jingneng" also provides a valuable window into
the continuity between popular and elite storytelling. Modern scholars have underscored the poor literacy and social marginality of the
scribes who produced Dunhuang transformation texts in the bor-
derland, assuming that they only played the limited role of copying.

Although this assumption may be valid in many cases, the overlaps between the Dunhuang "Story of Ye Jingneng" and variant versions in literati collections also suggest another possibility: the role of the scribes as storytellers might not have differed in nature from that of their more educated counterparts in the empire's heartland. At the very least, the case of "The Story of Ye Jingneng" reminds us to keep an open mind. Even though such scribes were marginal members of the literati community, they were uniquely situated at the liminal nexus between the high elite and the illiterate populace, and their active cultural roles have yet to be properly studied. Popular and literati storytelling, after all, were not mutually exclusive but constituted interconnected parts of late medieval everyday life.

From a sentimental, dedicated lover to a weak, ridiculous cuckold, images of the Illustrious Emperor, as represented by late medieval literati storytellers, are diverse and even contradictory. In other words, the Illustrious Emperor is such a compelling character precisely because, as a symbol, he is able to stand for so many meanings at once. Employing various genre forms and different narrative strategies, storytellers delineate these meanings to convey their idealized visions of the relationship between scholar-official and monarch. They affirm the possibility of developing special, exclusive bonds with the monarch as his cultural peers, political partners, and sociohistorical mediators. In the context of the post-rebellion sovereignty crisis, the promotion of these beliefs not only showed the strong identification of scholar-officials with the sovereign as men of comparable cultural sensitivity, but also the persistent efforts to bolster their political relevance and justify their ascendancy over other competitors for power and influence. By constructing the Daoist adept as the literati alter ego, late medieval scholar-officials also assert the necessity and possibility of restraining sovereign power. These visions thus affirm the various modes of empowerment for scholar-officials in the political domain.

This myth of literati political empowerment, however, is filled with tensions and ambivalences. On one hand, storytellers reiterate the cultural and political intimacy of scholar-officials with the ruler, positioning themselves as his closest and strongest allies. On the other hand, the personae of the old man and the Daoist adept also affirm the possibility that scholar-officials might distance themselves from and even challenge sovereignty. This tension between intimacy and distance contains another layer of ambivalence: while the themes of political intimacy and sociohistorical instrumentality highlight the literati respect for the political hierarchy, the themes of cultural intimacy and the supernatural restraint of sovereignty indicate the audacity of literati in envisioning potential subversions of that hierarchy.

These different and contradictory modes of empowerment ultimately betray an implicit sense of vulnerability about the subservience of scholar-officials to the monarch. Although featuring a Daoist adept as the restrainer of sovereignty indicates scholar-officials' awareness of the ruler's autocratic tendencies, the wish-fulfilling nature of the solution reveals a recognition of their own powerlessness in curtailing him. The myth of political empowerment serves precisely to counter this vulnerability by affirming the active roles and powers of scholar-officials in their relationship with the monarch. Late medieval scholar-officials were optimistic because the post-rebellion crisis of sovereignty created a milieu in which they imagined that they could set the terms and conditions of their engagement with the monarch. This optimism was also grounded in a belief in the collective power of the literati as a community, defined and bound by enduring communal bonds.

Literati Sociality

*Remembering Individuals and Community
in Historical Miscellanies*

If sovereignty represents the vertical, political axis of literati life, its horizontal counterpart was literati sociality, which bound scholar-officials into a strong community. By gathering anecdotes about past generations of scholar-officials and compiling them into historical miscellanies, late medieval literati storytellers constructed unofficial histories of their community. Establishing a range of positive and negative exemplars, they defined social bonds that they believed would ensure present solidarity and future continuity for their community. In doing so, they delineated various modes of belonging for individual scholar-officials as well as their collective social roles.

This chapter shifts attention from narratives in different generic forms to focus on a particular type, historical miscellanies, which contain diverse, disparate stories about famous or obscure figures—mostly previous generations of scholar-officials. Gleaned from oral and written sources, anecdotes in these collections have an aura of historicity because of their references to historical figures, times, places, and circumstances, and they are thus often taken as historical accounts. By cross-examining sources, however, modern scholars have shown that many are apocryphal.[1] As stories, these vignettes are no different in nature from other more literary narratives, for historical miscellanies represent a little-studied mode of literati storytelling. In fact, recounting and compiling anecdotes of earlier scholar-officials offered a distinctive way for literati storytellers to commemorate their predecessors and envision their communal past.

Literati storytelling in historical miscellanies produced in effect an unofficial historiography of the literati community. Although anecdotes in these collections could occasionally be accepted by court historians and incorporated into official records, most were excluded because they were deemed insignificant or unfit.[2] These vignettes actually feature discourses produced by and for the literati community: for example, they often refer to characters by official titles or nicknames and provide only snapshots of their lives. In contrast to biographies of the same figures in official or state-sponsored histories, these accounts presume an audience of insiders who already know about those figures. Moreover, historical miscellanies cover many more literati figures than official histories do. By recounting and putting together such vignettes, literati storytellers created a composite picture of the past, or a distinctive mosaic style of cultural memory alternative to official history, even as they claimed goals such as "to supplement what official historians have missed" and "to contribute to topics of conversation."[3]

Compiling historical miscellanies was particularly popular among late medieval scholar-officials. The practice was visible during the early medieval period, the most famous example of which was *A New Account of the Tales of the World* (Shishuo xinyu) by Liu Yiqing (403–444). In stark contrast to the over twenty collections in the pre-Tang era and no more than five during the pre-rebellion period, late medieval literati brought the genre to new heights by producing roughly one hundred titles, as noted in the introductory chapter. This unprecedented outpouring indicates that late medieval scholar-officials were much more motivated in constructing unofficial histories of their community and defining their shared communal bonds. Compared to the few pre-rebellion compilations, such as the *Fine Anecdotes from the Sui and the Tang* (Sui Tang jiahua) by Liu Su (fl. 728–742) and *Complete Records of Court and Country* (Chaoye qianzai) by Zhang Zhuo (ca. 650–730), post-rebellion collections show a much wider spectrum in terms of storytellers' personal predilections in choice and arrangement of entries, revealing their diverse, even contending, views of literati sociality.

The discussion below focuses on four collections to illustrate the most prominent modes of literati sociality articulated by late medieval literati storytellers: morality, prestige, the composition and sharing of poetry, and examination participation. Although stories in many other collections had certainly contributed to such thematizations in

the communal discourse, these four examples serve as focal points
of analysis, since it is impossible to cover the full array of late medieval historical miscellanies. Given the diverse nature of entries in such
compilations, it is perhaps not surprising that the four selected collections also contain stories that fit better under one of the other three
types of literati sociality. Each of these literati storytellers, however,
had emphasized preeminently a particular type, a preoccupation that
emanated from his background and agenda. They thus represent different subgroups in the late medieval literati community, specifically,
those from lesser backgrounds who preferred morality as the para-
mount value and fair yardstick, members of great clans who strived
for all forms of social prestige, practitioners and aficionados of poetry
who worshipped poetic talent, and examination participants who
tried to promote themselves as an ultra-elite.

Although these subgroups by no means excluded each other,
their different visions of literati sociality show the diversity of late
medieval literati social life, which was not yet examination-cen-
tered, since examination success was only one of many avenues of
entry into officialdom. The Tang examination system and culture,
due to its significance as the forerunner of later institutions, has
dominated modern critics' attention.[4] In addition, since examination aspirants and degree holders were the most prolific writers
of the time, their voices are prominent in extant writings, which
inevitably influence our understanding of the contemporary literati
community. Nonetheless, we should not, as Denis Twitchett has
cautioned, "read into [the Tang examination system] an importance, a place in society, a basis in Confucian orthodoxy, and a
sophistication of method that it had not yet acquired."[5] As we shall
see below, examinees were only one of the subgroups of late medieval scholar-officials who tried to promote themselves and advance
their own interests. In other words, late medieval literati were not
a homogeneous group but consisted of people whose experiences
and outlooks diverged significantly. The differences notwithstanding, various subgroups embraced the transformations of literati
life because they saw them as opportunities for empowering the
literati community in general and their own groups in particular.
Although modern historians have described the big picture of these
changes, the voices of late medieval literati storytellers allow us
to better understand the perspectives of people who were actually
going through the historical process at ground level.

THE MORAL COMMUNITY

In his *New Tales of the Great Tang* (Da Tang xinyu), Liu Su (fl. 806–820), who held one of the lowest-ranking offices in the Tang bureaucracy, envisioned a community of scholar-officials committed to moral values. His miscellany conveys his strong conviction that one could establish oneself as a member of the literati community through moral choices and actions, regardless of rank or pedigree. In his eyes, the collective power of scholar-officials as moral agents also turned them into independent arbiters who could ensure the meritocratic nature of officialdom-centered literati life by resisting and even curtailing political abuses.

Liu Su's interest in defining literati sociality in moral terms has to do with his status as an obscure scholar-official without rank or pedigree. His preface indicates that he was an assistant magistrate in Xunyang County (in modern Jiangxi). The earliest biographic reference mentions that he served an assistant magistrate in Jiangdu County (in modern Jiangsu) during the Yuanhe reign (806–821).[6] He compiled his collection in 807, in the context of Emperor Xianzong's political restoration, meaning that his work was contemporaneous with Bai Juyi's and Chen Hong's renditions of the love story of the Illustrious Emperor. Apparently encouraged by Xianzong's success in quelling warlords, Liu Su celebrated the legacy of the Great Tang by commemorating its luminaries: his collection includes more than three hundred anecdotes and features over five hundred historical figures from the beginning of the dynasty to the reign of Emperor Daizong (r. 762–779). It is no coincidence that Liu Su identified himself with Xun Shuang (128–190), the compiler of the *Tales of the Han* (Han yu), no longer extant, which commemorates the first long-unified imperial dynasty. Although modern scholars believe that Liu Su imitated Liu Yiqing's *A New Account of the Tales of the World*,[7] a collection that focuses on an age of disunion, he himself made no mention of this.

In fact, Liu Su's collection is quite different from Liu Yiqing's. The world of the *New Tales of the Great Tang* is one of scholar-officials devoted to officialdom, not aristocrats who were entitled to power and prestige by virtue of birth and who, as in Liu Yiqing's collection, showed a characteristic disdain for political office. In the words of Paul Rouzer, although early medieval aristocrats "continued to hold office, office holding contributed much less to their sense of worth, their sense of *identity*" than the closed, competitive exchange among themselves.[8] In stark contrast, even hermits who rejected officialdom are presented in Liu Su's collection in terms of their endorsement by the court. We are told, for instance, that the recluse Lu Hong is summoned to the court and given an official position, which he declines; he then goes back to Mount Lu, along with the Illustrious Emperor's generous gifts of rice and silk.[9] Liu Su's recluse essentially strikes a peace contract with the emperor, much like a tribute state. By traveling to the court and returning to his mountain, the recluse traces a geographical hierarchy between the center and the margin, underscoring Liu Su's vision of a political order in which the literati community gravitates toward the court.

By recounting stories of past scholar-officials, Liu Su endeavored to establish a set of moral values by which this community should abide. He divided his entries into thirty categories, each marked by a two-character phrase indicating his focus: most of the categories were designed to evaluate the performances of scholar-officials with respect to their obligations in the officialdom-centered literati life. Duties toward lords are covered in categories such as "Assistance [to Emperors]" (*kuangzan*), "Remonstrations" (*guijian*), "Extreme Remonstrations" (*jijian*), "Loyalty and Dedication" (*zhonglie*), and "Integrity and Righteousness" (*jieyi*). Responsibilities in official administration are illustrated in categories such as "Enforcement of Laws" (*chifa*), "Capability in Governance" (*zhengneng*), "Purity and Incorruptibility" (*qinglian*), and others. In addition to political roles, interactions with colleagues are also important, as we see in the categories "Tolerance and Forgiveness" (*rongshu*), "Recognition of [Talented People When They Were Still] Insignificant" (*zhiwei*), and so on. Moral conduct outside the bureaucratic context is also upheld, as in "Filial Conduct" (*xiaoxing*), "Brotherly Love" (*youdi*), and "Hermitic Reclusion" (*yinyi*). Liu Su also includes negative categories, but these are limited to three: "Flattery and Sycophancy" (*yuning*), "Cruelty and Hardheartedness" (*kuren*), and "Admonitions and Lessons" (*chengjie*).

The specific performances of past scholar-officials serve to define and substantiate these categories of virtue and vice. In the "Assistance [to Emperors]" category, for example, minister Wei Zheng (580–643) defeats a doubtful colleague with his eloquence and convinces Emperor Taizong of the feasibility of practicing the kingly way.[10] Another entry in the "Enforcement of Laws" describes how censor Xu Yougong (641–702) refuses to go along with his colleagues, who prove the efficiency of their work and advance their own careers by manipulating legal cases; his stubbornness and impartiality thus save the reputations and lives of many people.[11] Through vivid examples of men who lived up to high standards, these stories create inspiring models for present and future generations. By contrast, the negative examples instruct the audience how not to behave. For instance, in the category of "Flattery and Sycophancy," censor Guo Ba goes so far as to volunteer to taste the urine of his supervisor Wei Yuanzhong (d. 707) when Wei becomes sick.[12] In "Cruelty and Hardheartedness," we are told how the infamous official Lai Junchen (651–697) creates tools of torture to extract confessions from prisoners and implicate other people, destroying thousands of families.[13] These cautionary tales supplement the more numerous positive examples.

Although Liu Su's categories and examples overlap to some extent with those in official histories, they serve different moralizing interests. Official histories present and evaluate individuals as subjects of the state. Through selective representation of individuals' lives in the biographies and explicit comments in the encomia, historians offer praise and blame according to state-sanctioned ideologies and use these exemplars to reinforce the imperial authority and political hierarchy.[14] By contrast, Liu Su's unofficial history concerns individuals as members of the literati community, who are judged not simply by their political performances but also by their social interactions. Liu Su's categories of virtue and vice are thus much more comprehensive than those in official histories, including "Tolerance and Forgiveness," "Flattery and Sycophancy," and even "Humor and Jokes" (*xiexue*).[15] As character sketches, the vignettes convey the individuated images of literati figures on account of their particular words and actions, imparting lessons on how to be good members of the community.

The extensive scope of the moral scheme that Liu Su established underscores his belief in the autonomous ethical power of scholar-officials to make choices and judgments as a community. Liu Su was clearly a court loyalist. In his eyes, the accomplishments of the Great Tang derived from the level playing field of Tang bureaucracy, in which individuals could distinguish themselves through service to the state, regardless of their background. In his anecdotes, monarchs show their appreciation for righteous and devoted ministers by bestowing gifts of gold and silk, positions, emoluments, and salutary gestures. Grieving the death of Wei Zheng, for instance, Emperor Taizong composes a memorial stele inscription for him in his own calligraphy.

Liu Su's loyalism notwithstanding, his collection shows his conviction that the bureaucracy's system of punishment and reward is fundamentally flawed because it is determined by the personal will of the powerful. Even Wei Zheng, who enjoys Emperor Taizong's trust and respect when alive, posthumously suffers the consequences of the monarch's whims: believing slander, the emperor symbolically executes Wei by destroying the stele he had created, although he later realizes his mistake and restores the stele. In one entry, the five ministers who unseat Empress Wu Zetian (624–705; r. 690–705) and restore the Tang royal house are praised for their courage and wisdom; from other anecdotes, however, we learn that these outstanding statesmen later suffer the revenge of the empress's nephew, who destroys their families.[16] Within the treacherous realm of court politics, even minor frictions can have deadly repercussions. In the "Warnings and Lessons" category, we are told that censor-in-chief Su Weidao (648–705) slights his subordinate censor Zhou Ju, who thus feels resentful. When Su is implicated in a case, Zhou is appointed to try him and ensures that he receives the death penalty.[17] The irony and horror of the story lies in an easy turning of the tables: one's position in the bureaucratic hierarchy is never secure, and the institution allows ample opportunity for the indulgence of personal agendas and abuses of power.

The mismatch between merit and penalty in officialdom can even defy supernatural justice. Although Liu Su often evokes the popular belief in the working of retribution in stories where murderers suffer unnatural deaths, he also shows that supernatural influence may be limited. In the "Brotherly Love" category, for instance, minister Feng Yuanchang (fl. 650–687) is praised as a paragon of virtue, along with his exemplary brothers; however, because of his refusal to support Empress Wu's ambitions to usurp power, he is punished and executed. According to Liu Su, this case shows that "the divine principle of blessing the good is insignificant and cannot be relied upon."[18] Although such cynicism is rare in Liu Su's collection, the statement is a poignant recognition of the fundamental vulnerability of scholar-officials in officialdom.

According to Liu Su, only the independent moral power of the literati community can counter this vulnerability. In his eyes, individuals are moral agents who make choices for themselves and must bear the consequences. In his collection, the overwhelming number of positive examples provides strong evidence that scholar-officials form a moral community. As individuals, scholar-officials can stand up for their moral principles and refuse to bow to political manipulation and coercion, even though it may cost them their lives. Because of their collective moral power, they constitute the backbone of a social world that encompasses all under heaven. Throughout his collection, Liu Su refers to various groups that constitute this world in a wide range of terms, including "the court" (*chaoting*), "court and country" (*chaoye*), "the ranks of courtiers" (*chaolie*), "colleagues" (*tonglie*), "various ranks of officials" (*qungong*), "famous scholar-officials everywhere" (*tianxia mingshi*), "gentlemen" (*junzi*), "insightful scholar-officials" (*youshi zhi shi*), "people and minor officials" (*renli*), "common people"(*baixing*), "commoners at large" (*zhaoshu*), locals such as "people of Shu" (*Shuren*), "attendants" (*zuoyou*), "all those seated around" (*manzuo*), "observers" (*guanzhe*), "listeners" (*wenzhe*), "commentators" (*lunzhe*), "contemporary commentators" (*shiyi*), "contemporaries" (*shiren*), "people" (*ren*), "the masses" (*zhong*), "acquaintances and strangers" (*zhi yu buzhi*), "all within the four seas" (*hainei*), and "all under heaven" (*tianxia*).

While Liu Su evokes figures from all walks of life, he assumes that scholar-officials occupy a central position in this diverse public and command moral support as the representatives and leaders of the people. In one story, for instance, a county assistant magistrate named Pan Haoli comments that the impartial Xu Yougong is not only comparable but actually superior to the Han official Zhang Shizhi (fl. 179–156 BCE), known for his fairness in legal judgments.[19] In the entry on Xu Yougong mentioned above, we are also told that "contemporaries compared him to [another Han official] Yu Dingguo."[20] Although Liu Su does not spell it out, the contemporaries evoked in this entry are probably scholar-officials like Pan Haoli, who were familiar with the biographies of the two Han precedents in particular and the history of the Han in general. Even when Liu Su clearly invokes the less educated among the populace, they are presented in effect as the followers of scholar-officials. In another story, for example, two young, filial sons, Zhang Huang and Zhang Xiu, kill the official Yang Wanqing in revenge for his false accusation against and execution of their father; they are, however, executed for violating the law. Liu Su's narrative emphasizes the public sympathy for these two boys:

> After the death of Zhang Huang and Zhang Xiu, scholar-officials
> and commoners deplored their passing. [Scholar-officials] composed

eulogies and posted them at crossroads. People at the marketplace collected money to dig a charitable well at the locale of their execution [to commemorate them]. They were both buried on Mount Beimang. Afraid that their tombs would be destroyed by the family of Yang Wanqing, people created several false tombs nearby. In ways like these they were mourned with deep grief by their contemporaries.[21]

Liu Su emphasizes solidarity and consensus among scholar-officials and non-scholar-officials, especially the role of the former as leaders. In this case, literati composition and circulation of eulogies gives voice to public opinion, rallying people across the social spectrum to do what is within their power to honor these boys.

With literati at its center, the broader community plays the role of historical witness and judge in the eyes of Liu Su, sustaining a communal hall of fame and infamy that transcends the political reality of the moment. Even monarchs, the supreme rulers of the empire, are not immune to the ever-watchful "surveillance" of this community, as indicated by the following entry:

[Once] during the Zhenguan reign [627–650], Emperor Taizong said to Chu Suiliang: "You are in charge of Court Diaries. What have you recorded? May [I] the sovereign see them?" Chu Suiliang answered, "Today's Court Diarists correspond to the Left and Right Historians of ancient times, who were responsible for recording the sovereign's words and actions. Both the good and the bad are recorded to serve as lessons and warnings, so that sovereigns would refrain from doing anything unlawful. I have never heard of any monarch personally perusing the records [of his own reign]." Taizong asked, "When there is something bad, do you really have to record it?" Chu Suiliang answered, "Adhering to the Way is not like adhering to one's official duties. My responsibilities happen to be recording, so whatever you do will be put in writing." Liu Ji stepped forward and said, "Even if Chu Suiliang was ordered to not record it, everyone in the world would record it [in their memory]."[22]

Although Liu Su did not identify the source of this story, an earlier, more detailed version can be found in the *Essentials of the Zhenguan Administration* (Zhenguan zhengyao) by Wu Jing (670–749), who includes another anecdote about Taizong previewing drafts of the Veritable Records of his own reign.[23] Whether or not Liu Su was aware of the second story, what is relevant here is his clear preference for the story of Chu Suiliang (596–658) and Liu Ji's (d. 645) successful resistance to Taizong's attempt to infringe upon the historians' right of impartial recording. Chu Suiliang's rejection of

Taizong's request to see the Court Diaries resonates with accounts of heroic historians in the *Zuo Tradition* (Zuo zhuan), who would rather die than change the record to improve the image of those in power.[24] Even heroism such as this may not deter the monarch: after all, Taizong is in a position to punish anyone who displeases him, as implied by his ominous last question. It is Liu Ji's evocation of an omnipresent public, "all under heaven," that finally makes the emperor desist. This idealized, homogeneous public with an unimpeded network of information exchange represents a continuous, infinite group beyond imperial control, extending both spatially (to all under heaven) and temporally (to posterity).

Again, the literati community occupies the central position in this seemingly egalitarian group. Only through scholar-officials can all under heaven know what is actually going on at the court. Moreover, the literati monopoly on writing makes them the exclusive bearers of alternative memory through written transmission: Liu Su's own collection is precisely such an example. As a matter of fact, Taizong is hailed as an exemplary monarch in other entries of Liu Su's collection, where he is presented as a figure willing to submit to the wisdom and authority of his literati advisors. This story of him pushing limits indicates that late medieval scholar-officials such as Liu Su were aware of the real danger of despotism. They remained confident, nonetheless, about their collective power—as the mind and the mouthpiece of "all under heaven," or as the guardians of the communal hall of fame and infamy—to constrain the emperor and put him in his place.

For Liu Su, this communal hall of fame and infamy could compel the redress of historical wrongs by the court. In the entry about Feng Yuanchang, Liu Su describes a decree by Emperor Zhongzong that the entrance to Feng's house be named "Gate of a Loyal Minister" (Zhongchen men), a symbolic recognition of and reward for Feng's loyalty to the Tang. Posthumous reputations were not just symbolically significant, but also had real political and social implications for one's descendants. Liu Su's entry on the impartial and courageous judge Xu Yougong claims that Zhongzong not only awards the highest rank to Xu posthumously but also generously rewards his family; a high official even voluntarily offers his own position to Xu's son. By contrast, the progeny of an infamous official could be ostracized. A memorial to the throne in 725 recommended that the offspring of cruel officials from Empress Wu's reign be banned from officialdom permanently, while those of several others with lesser crimes be forbidden to hold positions close to the emperor.[25]

In the eyes of Liu Su, however, the communal hall of fame and infamy, sustained by the independent moral power of the literati community, offers the ultimate historical vindication, for it overrides immediate personal gains and losses. People who choose to advance themselves at the expense of others earn eternal infamy for themselves, while those who suffer in their lives for moral integrity receive places of honor. The question of whether to submit to the demands of political circumstance in order to receive benefits in the here and now or to disregard them for the sake of a good posthumous reputation was not new; canonical figures such as the sage Confucius (551–479 BCE), the poet Qu Yuan (ca. 339–ca. 278 BCE), and the historian Sima Qian (145 or 135–86 BCE) are known to have struggled with this dilemma. Liu Su's collection emphasizes such moral actions for all scholar-officials in the official and personal spheres of literati life. In his eyes, by making moral choices one will make a lasting name for oneself in the memory of a unified community of independent and unfailing arbiters.

Because the unity of the literati community is essential to Liu Su's vision, his collection rarely includes contradictory accounts. There is, however, one exception. In the "Honesty and Incorruptibility" section, the dying Emperor Gaozong (r. 649–684) entrusts the care of his heir to Pei Yan (d. 684), who is said to deliberately delay the military crackdown on rebels who rise up against Empress Wu when she dethrones the heir, her own son. The discerning empress discovers Pei's trick and executes him. The story concludes with the following statements: "Although Pei Yan rose to high ranks, he was rather poor. When his property was confiscated, [it became clear that] he did not have any savings. His contemporaries mourned his death."[26] This emphasis on Pei Yan's poverty and purity is consistent with the story's projection of him as a Tang loyalist. In the "Warnings and Lessons" section, however, Pei Yan is condemned in another story for siding with Empress Wu to dispose of the new emperor: "Pei Yan was at the helm of the state and he received the great trust of the dying emperor in person. He did not fulfill his duty to assist and protect the new emperor, but instead carried out the conspiracies of Yi Yin and Huo Guang,[27] resulting in the transfer of the throne to Empress Wu. He provided wings to a beast, and his later execution [by Empress Wu] was indeed his just desert."[28] The story emphasizes the disastrous consequence of Pei Yan's failure, which paves the way for Empress Wu to displace the ruling family of the Tang and establish her own dynasty. The contradictory images of Pei Yan as martyr and traitor indicate a disagreement over his role in Empress Wu's usurpation of power. Although this contradiction may be due to the different sources from which Liu Su drew entries for his collection, it reveals that the literati community might not always have agreed on what happened or on how to evaluate historical figures, further pointing to potential or real factionalism within the community. These two contradictory accounts in Liu Su's collection are thus exceptions that suggest his persistent efforts to represent a unitary vision of literati sociality.

By describing how one's predecessors responded to diverse circumstances of literati life, as well as the immediate and long-term consequences of their various choices, Liu Su tried to instill in his reader the dual perspectives of the individual and the collective. Readers are put in the shoes of historical figures in order to understand their responses to challenging situations, and they are also encouraged to identify with the posthumous judgments on those responses. By constructing a communal hall of fame and infamy, Liu Su's collection conveys his strong conviction that remembering a past moral community can ensure and strengthen its future, for only as a community of moral agents can scholar-officials maintain their solidarity and dominance.

THE PRESTIGE COMMUNITY

If the obscure official Liu Su pictured a broad moral community in which any literatus could participate, Zhao Lin (ca. 802–ca. 872), who belonged to one of the great clans, commemorated only a small circle of successful figures in his *Records Prompted by Conversations* (Yinhua lu). To Zhao Lin, literati sociality consisted of a network of prestige. In his view, individuals could earn prestige through all forms of social achievement, the most important of which was official rank. Such prestige could also be shared and enhanced by others with familial and social connections to these successful people. Using explanations within the main text as well as interlinear commentaries, Zhao Lin carefully inserted himself and his family into the center of this elite web of status and success.

A member of the Zhaos of Tianshui, an aristocratic clan with a long-standing history of office holding, Zhao Lin enjoyed a smooth official career. He passed the Presented Scholar examination in 834 and then a special examination held by the Ministry of Personnel in 838. He was appointed Editor in the Palace Library, a much coveted entry post reserved for men of great literary promise with a bright political future. He occupied the position of Left Rectifier of Omissions around 853 and later served as a prefect in various locations. He likely compiled his collection later in life.[29]

Because of his illustrious background, Zhao Lin's vision of literati sociality is defined by elitism. His collection envisions a strong commitment to social hierarchy, especially to the exclusive privilege of scholar-officials for court service. His collection adopts a unique set of categories based on the five musical tones: *gong, shang, jiao, zhi,* and *yu.* The harmony of these tones was traditionally attributed to their proper division and hierarchy, and thus the tones were often used as an analogy for social structure. The *Book of Rites* (Li ji) states: "The *gong* corresponds to the lord, *shang* to officials, *jiao* to commoners, *zhi* to matters, and *yu* to objects. If these five tones are in order, there will not be any stagnant sound."[30] Zhao Lin's rubric follows this prescription exactly. The *gong* section includes anecdotes about emperors, from the Illustrious Emperor to Emperor Xuānzong. The *shang* section is the most extensive, containing more than one third of the total entries. It is reserved for officials, as Zhao Lin explains, "Because 'the *shang* corresponds to officials,' those from princes and dukes to people who have come up through official ranks are put in this section."[31] Meanwhile, his explanatory note to the *jiao* section states, "Those who did not serve as officials are listed in this section."[32] Most of the entries in the *jiao* section are about Buddhist monks and Daoist priests. The *zhi* section covers miscellaneous historical information mostly on officialdom: "Because 'the *zhi* corresponds to matters,' anything discussed in general that does not pertain to people or objects is put in this section."[33] Zhao Lin reserves the last section, *yu,* for entries that concern the supernatural, such as omens and fortune-telling. Overall, this organizational scheme emphasizes the privileged status of scholar-officials within the social hierarchy.

Zhao Lin's elitism can also be seen in his rendition of specific accounts. He appears hostile to people who might threaten the interests of scholar-officials. For example, he criticizes some Daoists and Buddhists for impinging on the specialty of literati: "There were even some who claimed the title 'great virtue (*bhadanta*) in literature.' How can literature be an appropriate title for monks and priests? This is a gross misuse of language!"[34] In addition, he recounts how his friend collides with a drunken army man, who is reminded by bystanders that failure to pay due respect to scholar-officials would be met with severe punishment. With this example, Zhao tries to show the effective, commendable efforts of the metropolitan governor Liu Qichu (d. 827) to enforce proper social distinctions.[35] At the same time, Zhao Lin portrays emperors in terms of their strong affinities to and respect for scholar-officials. He emphasizes, for example, that his uncle Zhao Xiu, a successful candidate in both the Presented Scholar and decree examinations, is singled out by Emperor Dezong (r. 779–805) for a special appointment as a county magistrate.[36] Moreover, many entries in the last section focus on omens of official appointments. In Zhao Lin's eyes, these omens demonstrate that scholar-officials enjoy supernatural favor: "Thus we know that the positions of generals and ministers can hardly be random."[37]

Zhao Lin's elitism further translates into an admiration for the celebrities who constitute the upper echelons of the literati community, as well as a contempt for his community's lesser members. As noted in chapter 1, he criticizes those who confused the historical Daoist priest Ye Jingneng, active during Emperor Zhongzong's reign, with Ye Fashan, another Daoist associated with the Illustrious Emperor. He also conveys disdain for scholars who fail to understand words and characters correctly, eventually offering this advice, "The rhyme dictionary *Qieyun* is a common book. Why not put a copy on one's desk for the sake of easy consultation?"[38] Rather than commemorate such underachievers, whose names he never identifies, Zhao Lin only cites the successful who embody different kinds of prestige derived from office, imperial recognition, pedigree, examination, literary talent, moral virtue, and so forth. His sense of officialdom as a meritocratic field is thus drastically different from that of Liu Su. To Liu, the means to immediate social success is a moral issue: the index of one's virtue is the ability to sacrifice one's current personal interests for a larger moral good. By contrast, Zhao sees the status quo as meritocratic: the end result of success is not only the reward for merit but also the very measure and proof of it.

A case in point is Zhao Lin's entry on the former chief minister Zhao Zongru (746–832), a clansman of his grandfather's generation. He compares Zhao Zongru to two other chief ministers, Du Yuanying (769–832) and Song Shenxi (d. 833):

When Duke Zhao from Tianshui [Zhao Zongru], my senior clansman, was appointed Director of the Ministry of Personnel after serving as chief minister, he selected Du Yuanying, a Presented Scholar
degree holder, in the [special examination of] Erudite Learning and
Grand Composition. When he became a military governor in the
south, he recruited Du to be on his staff. Later, after Du became a
chief minister, Duke Zhao was made Director of the Ministry of Personnel again. When Du went to serve as military governor of Shu, he
requested to have Song Shenxi on his staff. A few years later, suffering the invasion of southern barbarians, Du was demoted to serve as
prefect of Xunzhou and subsequently died. Although Song Shenxi
became a chief minister, he was soon wronged and exiled to Kaizhou
[and died there]. Several more years passed before Duke Zhao finally
passed away.[39] Altogether he served as Director of the Ministry of
Personnel for eight terms. He was entrusted military governorship
three times, all with the honorific title of Minister in the Department
of State Affairs. The only agency in which he had never served was
Ministry of Works, but he was twice appointed to Ministry of War,
Ministry of Personnel, and Court of Imperial Sacrifices. He passed
away at the age of eighty-seven, before which he had never had any
serious illness. In terms of extraordinary honors and longevity, none
can surpass him at court.[40]

In order to highlight Zhao Zongru's accomplishments, Zhao Lin
compares him with two of his juniors and suppresses the historical violence raging in the background. Behind the careers of Du
Yuanying and Song Shenxi were the political storms of the 820s
and 830s, including the dramatic changes between the regimes of
emperors Muzong (r. 820–824), Jingzong (r. 824–827), and Wenzong (r. 827–840). Song Shenxi, for instance, was a confidant of
Wenzong, and his plan to wrest power away from powerful eunuchs
only earned him and many other officials ruthless persecution at the
hands of their enemies.[41] Song would have been featured as a righteous official and a martyr in Liu Su's collection, and he is indeed
presented as such in *The Lost History* (Yi shi) by Lu Zhao (fl. 827–
860).[42] Nevertheless, Zhao Lin uses Song Shenxi as a foil to Zhao
Zongru, admiring the latter's capacity to navigate the treacherous
political waters and his living to advanced age and high status. Because of Zhao Lin's preoccupation with celebrities, the literati community that he commemorates is marked by a conspicuous absence
of the violence seen in Liu Su's collection.

Zhao Lin's interest in successful people also indicates his belief in
the complementary nature of different forms of prestige. Official rank
is without doubt the fundamental sign of identity to him: characters

in his collection are usually referred to by their official titles, often the highest ones attained, either posthumously or during their lives.[43] Personal qualities and other merits further enhance the reputation of these personages. For instance, Guo Ziyi (697–781), enfeoffed as Prince of Fenyang for pacifying the An Lushan and other rebellions, is said to pay special respect to the mother of his secretary, Liu Fang, because he himself lost his parents early on.[44] Guo is commendable because of his humility and filial piety *despite* his extraordinary power and status, which could have made him arrogant and selfish. His positive personal attributes in turn help to explain and justify his political success.

Zhao Lin's accommodating approach to social prestige distinguishes him from other more conservative members of great clans. Chief minister Li Deyu, a member of the Lis of Zhaojun (and the compiler of *Jottings of Tales Heard from the Lius* discussed in chapter 1), for example, reportedly tried to convince Emperor Wuzong of the superiority of people with illustrious pedigree to those without. He argued that the courtly education of the sons and brothers of ministers (*gongqing zidi*) started right after their births, whereas poor scholars (*hanshi*) did not have access to the court culture until after passing examinations.[45] By contrast, Zhao Lin embraced the prestige of examinations and pedigree with equal enthusiasm. A holder of the Presented Scholar degree himself, he compiled the *Integrated Records of Degree Holders* (Zhujia kemu ji), a no longer extant register of successful examination candidates that combined and updated previous versions.[46] In his *Records Prompted by Conversations*, Zhao Lin describes his own examination successes and carefully noted those of others, showing his high regard for this avenue of personal advancement. At the same time, he was also proud of his own pedigree, as indicated by his praise for another clansman who compiled a genealogy boasting of the accomplished members in their clan. Unlike Liu Su, who mentions no choronyms (commandery names prefixed to aristocratic family names to mark pedigree) for the officials he features, Zhao Lin pays close attention to the family backgrounds of the figures in his collection. In the entry on the important mid-Tang writer and thinker Xiao Yingshi (707–758), for instance, he details the Xiao family's lineage, tracing twelve generations (including personal names and official titles) to the father of Emperor Wu of the Liang dynasty (r. 502–549).[47]

Zhao Lin's stance thus represents a pragmatic attitude within great clans of the late medieval period: he recognized that the prestige of pedigree had come to depend upon the success of clan members in officialdom, rather than the reverse, as had been the case in the early medieval period.[48] He greatly admired the Lis of Zhaojun because their three branches had produced a total of six chief ministers, a phenomenon that was, in his words, "rare among all clans."[49] In stark contrast, Xiao Yingshi's lineage was a perfect example of decline. According to Zhao Lin, after Xiao Yingshi's son gave up a career as an official to become a recluse, his grandsons and great grandsons failed to make a comeback, becoming mere county clerks whose names were either unknown to Zhao Lin or not worth recording. Implicit in his awe of the Lis is an acknowledgement of the fierce, unpredictable competition inherent to officialdom, which made such success seem extraordinary and even miraculous.[50] At the same time, Zhao Lin also respected those without pedigree who had established a name for themselves. His entry on the Instructor of the Heir Apparent Lu Yu (733–ca. 804), for example, emphasizes that despite being abandoned at birth and raised by a monk, Lu became a famous scholar-official. For inventing the method of decocting tea, he had come to be deified and worshipped by tea merchants across the country.[51]

In his collection, Zhao Lin does not show any sense of insecurity about literati competitors from lesser backgrounds, a confidence that stems from his vision of literati sociality as a network of shared and mutually enhanced prestige. Unlike Liu Su's attention to the conflict between the good and the bad in officialdom, Zhao Lin underscores solidarity and mutual support among scholar-officials. For instance, while Zhao Lin praises Liu Qichu for his harsh measures against army men and commoners who fail to show respect toward scholar-officials, as we have seen above, he also commends Liu for his friendliness toward his own kind: "When [Liu Qichu] spoke with his subordinate officials, he never hurt their feelings, nor scolded any of them."[52] In addition to official selections and recommendations, Zhao Lin also takes note of how social interactions in general help to strengthen the bonds between members of the community. In another story, the newly appointed military governor Hu Zheng (758–828) passes his hometown Hezhong on the way to his post. He pays a courtesy call to the local official, Zhao Lin's clansman Zhao Zongru, by presenting himself as a commoner under Zhao's jurisdiction.[53] Hu's flamboyant gesture shows off his loyalty to his native place and his respect for Zhao Zongru despite his own higher official status. Zhao gains prestige for being honored, but by playing his part he also enables Hu to gain prestige as well. By contrast, a similar attempt by Liu Xuanzuo (730–787), another military governor, fails because of an unappreciative county magistrate who is so intimidated by the gap between his rank and Liu's that he dares not receive Liu according to the protocols of a commoner's visit. We are told that his refusal makes Liu sigh and regret deeply.[54] Understandably, this magistrate is doomed to anonymity in Zhao Lin's collection because his failure to play his expected role is symptomatic of his incapacity to rise to prominence in elite circles.

Zhao Lin puts himself and his family squarely at the center of this network of prestige undergirded by familial and social bonds; indeed, entries about others often serve as vehicles for self-promotion. His description of Emperor Xuānzong's high regard for censors is a good example. In Zhao Lin's account, his own memorial recommending that the locale of the New Year ceremony be moved to a different palace makes a great impression on the emperor, so much so that the emperor later mentions him, along with two others, as exemplary censors.[55] Carefully including the whole memorial in an interlinear note as evidence of his own outstanding performance, Zhao Lin makes sure that the reader understands why he deserves this imperial favor. In addition to such direct, personal connections, he also emphasizes indirect links. A concubine of the Illustrious Emperor, for instance, turns out to be a great-great-aunt of Zhao Lin's mother, and the prince she bears is said to be a favorite brother of Emperor Suzong.[56] In various ways, Zhao Lin thus manages to link himself and his family to the monarchs featured in his collection, who are, after all, the biggest celebrities in the empire.

Zhao Lin likewise makes extensive use of interlinear notes to provide background information and link himself to other scholar-officials featured in his collection. This can be seen in the following entry:

In the sixth year of the Taihe Reign [832], Director Tang Te, then a sheriff in Weinan County, served as the official for selecting metropolitan candidates for the Presented Scholar examination. Chief minister Du Cong was the metropolitan governor at the time and wanted to ask Tang to insert his relatives and friends into the selection list. *([Note:]At that time the top ten candidates were singled out and other candidates were also ranked on the pass list).* He summoned Tang for a casual conversation and ordered tea and wine to be prepared. As soon as he mentioned candidates, Tang hastened down the stairs to the courtyard and prostrated himself, without anything in response. Du did not dare to bring up the issue again and eventually

> let it go. There were over thirty candidates on the selection list that
> year and all of them passed the Presented Scholar examination in the
> following several years. There was nothing like this before or after.
> *([Note:] By mere chance, I was on this list).*[57]

Zhao Lin relates the story to extol Tang Te's courage and integrity in ensuring the fair selection of candidates from the Chang'an prefecture. Although Du Cong initially harbors selfish intentions, he becomes commendable by abandoning his original plan to pressure Tang Te by means of his power and authority. The quality of Tang Te's candidates is proved by their success in the subsequent Presented Scholar examination. This entry confirms that candidates from the metropolitan area had higher chances of passing the Presented Scholar examination than those from other parts of the country, because these candidates not only represented the largest group in the pool, but also were well connected.[58] Despite his disingenuous rhetoric of self-depreciation, however, Zhao Lin is concerned to prove the worthiness of his own Presented Scholar degree, as well as his privileged connection to Tang Te and Du Cong, both of whom had successful careers.

By citing familial and social bonds, Zhao Lin effectively establishes for himself a web of connections with luminaries. In addition to the explicit network seen above, there are also less obvious ones. We are told, for example, that Pei Wu (d. 826), director in the Department of State Affairs, is exemplary in his devotion to his family because he takes good care of his widowed sister-in-law and her children; like a reward for his virtues, generations of his family have risen to important positions at court.[59] By cross-reference, we know that this Pei Wu is a colleague of Zhao Lin's uncle Zhao Xiu, both special appointees of Emperor Dezong. Liu Fang, the secretary that Prince of Fenyang Guo Ziyi holds in especially high regard, turns out to be Zhao Lin's maternal granduncle, while Lu Yu, the vaunted progenitor of tea culture, is a close friend of Liu Dan, Zhao Lin's maternal grandfather. By these various means of making connections with the luminaries in his collection, Zhao Lin conveys his belief that he and his family are centrally and securely situated in the upper echelons of the literati community.

Zhao Lin's commitments to different forms of prestige are not free from tensions that subvert the rosy picture of the literati community he constructs. His admission that the year in which he passed the Presented Scholar examination was exceptional indicates that unfair manipulations were the norm and that social success was far from meritocratic. In other words, celebrities might not simply look after the orphans in the clan, as Pei Wu did, but might instead use their influence to secure advantageous positions for their kinsmen and friends, in the manner attempted by Du Cong. Thus, through implication and contrast, Zhao Lin cannot help but reveal the dark side of the communal network of prestige, particularly the abuse of power.

Understandably, Zhao Lin contradicts himself on this issue. On one hand, he clearly disapproves of Du Cong's effort to interfere with the selection list of the metropolitan candidates; on the other, he also praises men, such as the military governor Liu Xuanzuo, for giving their relatives supernumerary staff positions in order to ensure their livelihood. The contradiction indicates Zhao Lin's dilemma: as a member of one of the great clans, Zhao Lin is committed to the continuity and prosperity of his family and relations; as a capable man of letters, he is also drawn to the ideal of personal advancement based on talent and fair competition. Although both are equally legitimate for him, they are logically and ideologically opposed.

For Zhao Lin, however, the gap can be bridged. This is exemplified by his story about the Presented Scholar degree holder and the famous chief minister Pei Du (765–839). We are told that when an old friend's son seeks Pei's help, Pei gives him the post of entrance guard after some observation, realizing that he can sit quietly for a long time with little need of company. The man turns out to be an excellent gate watcher.[60] This story reveals Zhao Lin's bottom line: talent and pedigree are complementary means for success, but only a truly outstanding scholar-official can rise to the top of the bureaucratic ladders or achieve other forms of prestige in the competitive literati world. While an established official is obligated to use his position of power to help his family and friends, there is an ethical way of doing so—by helping them secure positions best suited to their abilities, just as Pei Du did with the appointment of his friend's son to be a gate watcher. Officialdom, as Zhao Lin insisted, represents a network of prestige in which both individual scholar-officials and their relations should prosper without compromising meritocracy, at least in theory.

THE POETRY COMMUNITY

If, in the eyes of Liu Su and Zhao Lin, the literati community was primarily defined by officialdom, Fan Shu (fl. 875–888), a recluse throughout his life, envisioned a more expansive mode of literati sociality predicated on a shared culture of poetry. Although officials also figure prominently in his collection *Master Cloud Creek's Discussions with Friends* (Yunxi youyi), his focal point is not their performance or status in officialdom, but their role as poetic writers and readers. By commemorating past poetic writers and readers, Fan Shu reveals his faith in the power of poetry as a cultural bond that creates an enduring literati community beyond the limited sphere of officialdom.

We know very little about Fan Shu's life. He lived near the Creek of Five-Colored Clouds in the Wu region, hence his self-chosen name Master of the Creek of Five-Colored Clouds (Wuyun xi ren) and the title of his collection.[61] His preface to the collection indicates that he traveled extensively to visit famous sites and meet with other scholar-officials. Upon his death, his friend Li Xianyong wrote a commemorative poem, "Grieving [the Death of] the Recluse Fan Shu" (Dao Fan Shu chushi), praising his reputation and lamenting that he did not have support from high officials to help him start a political career.[62]

Fan Shu's compilation represents the intersection between the post-rebellion poetic culture and storytelling culture. Mid- and late-Tang poets not only were innovative in thematic explorations, but they also developed new obsessions with poetic craft, in particular, the construction of parallel couplets. For some dedicated practitioners, poetry became a vocation in its own right.[63] These shifts in poetic culture went hand in hand with an intensified interest in stories about poets. While many other collections included anecdotes on poets, there emerged two historical miscellanies focusing entirely or mostly on poets, the *Original Occasions of Poems* (Benshi shi) by Meng Qi (fl. 841–886) and *Master Cloud Creek's Discussions with Friends* by Fan Shu. Although such anecdotes can be seen sporadically in pre-Tang collections, such as Liu Yiqing's *A New Account of the Tales of the World,* and in pre-rebellion ones, including Liu Su's (fl. 728–742) *Fine Anecdotes from the Sui and Tang* and Zhang Zhuo's *Complete Records of Court and Country*, the emphasis is usually on the wit, spontaneity, and refinement of the talented poet. By contrast, stories in Meng Qi's collection convey a more synthetic vision of poetic competence: in the words of Graham Sanders, "The political savvy and erudition of the *Zuo Tradition*, the apparent sincerity of the *Han History,* and the polished wit and talent of *Topical Tales* come together to produce a powerful mode of discourse that can yield great benefits to those who have the competence to deploy it at the right time and place for the right person."[64] Unlike Meng Qi's entries, which focus on specific circumstances of poetic composition, Fan Shu's are often much lengthier and portray the complex dynamics of interactions among poets and aficionados, revealing his vision of a poetry community.

While Zhao Lin's prestige community is predicated on sociopolitical hierarchy, Fan Shu's poetry community encompasses an implicit gender hierarchy. Although Tang women are known to have played active roles in poetic culture,[65] Fan Shu presents them as lesser counterparts of literati poets. To him, women who write poetry are admirable because they are unexpected. In his words, "The wife of Cao Shu wrote about her journey to the east; the wife of Liu Ling composed an advisory poem about giving up drinking. They were truly rare in terms of what women can do."[66] Female poets are thus regarded as extraordinary because they are judged in relation to women without poetic skills or even literacy, unlike male poets who are considered talented because they write better than other literati.

Moreover, the poetic voices and power of women poets are much more circumscribed. In the story of Lady Shen, who is divorced by her husband for failing to bear children, she composes a poem upon her departure which so moves her husband that he takes her back.[67] The persuasive power of Shen's poem lies in her animation of the conventional abandoned woman persona with emotional sincerity and intensity, presumably arising from her personal experience.[68] The story does not necessarily reflect the poetic voice of a historical woman, because it is, after all, a narrative construction on the poetic efficacy of a woman writing in the traditional female poetic persona.[69] In Fan Shu's collection, wife-poets such as Lady Shen can be said to embody the classic dictum "Poetry expresses intent" (*shi yan zhi*) in its most basic, straightforward sense. While women poets directly articulate their life experiences, their restricted social roles are matched by an equally limited scope of composition: women are supposed to write only on certain subjects and in certain voices. Furthermore, the presumed transparency of their self-expression suggests naiveté, because their autobiographical tendency also implies an inability to fully wield the poetic power of performativity.[70]

In stark contrast, Fan Shu presents male literati poetry as a sophisticated art form that fulfills complex social functions and allows for a wide range of performances. In one entry, for instance, Fan Shu emphasizes the gap between male poetic persona and real-life identity as a source of humor and irony. We are told that vice director Lu Lun (ca. 748–ca. 798) writes in the voice of a monk, whereas the celibate Buddhist monk Qingjiang describes the romantic reunion of the Cowherd and the Weaving Maid on the seventh evening of the seventh month. The sighted literatus Liu Changqing (?–ca. 789) composes lines about the senses of a blind person, while the blind Song Yong envisions beautiful scenery.[71] In many other entries, Fan Shu shows how male poets use poetry to mock, threaten, tease, encourage, comfort, befriend, and commemorate others. To him, only male literati have full command of such poetic competence.

As he sees it, the key mode of interaction among literati poets is competition for originality. The following story illustrates the fundamental dynamic:

> Wang Xuan practiced the art of poetry from his youth. He composed poems to give expression to feelings stirred by things, and his works, on a par with "The Inlet of the Qi River" [from the *Book of Songs*], were well known. [Once] he visited the Western Little Stream and, mooring by the Zhuluo Mountain, he inscribed a poem on the Xi Shi Stone:
>
> In the mountains, the thousand peaks are beautiful;
> By the river, tender grasses flourish in the spring.
> Having encountered the silk-washing stone,
> I do not see the silk-washing lady.
>
> A little while after he finished writing, he saw a girl with jingling jade earrings leaning against a stone. She lingered and made the following apology:
>
> Ever since I returned to Yue from the palace of Wu,
> Recognized by no one, I wore mourning clothes for a thousand years.
> At that time my heart was even firmer than metal and stone.
> Today because of you, it can no longer be hard.
>
> Uniting in love like mandarin ducks, they also exchanged poems on their sad separation. Later, Guo Ningsu from Xiaoshan heard about Wang Xuan's experience. He often visited Silk-Washing Creek and chanted poems day and night. He inscribed poems on the Stone many times but all was quiet and nothing happened. Disappointed, he returned home. The Presented Scholar examinee Zhu Ze mocked him, and no one who heard Zhu's poem could help laughing. Ningsu was so ashamed that he never visited the place again. Zhu Ze's poem was as follows:

> The peach and plum blossoms of the spring are speechless by nature.
> But they are greatly annoyed by the noise of birds in the setting sun.
> Let me ask: how does the Eastern Neighbor's imitation of Xi Shi,
> compare to Guo Ningsu's emulation of Wang Xuan?"[72]

This story puts a new spin on the legend of the femme fatale Xi Shi, who is said to have bewitched King Fuchai (fl. fourth century BCE) and thereby brought down the state of Wu in order to avenge his conquest of Yue, her home state.[73] The poet Wang Xuan's encounter with the ghost of Xi Shi is mediated by the Silk-Washing Stone, which, like the Drunken Stone associated with the iconic recluse-poet Tao Yuanming (ca. 365–427), serves as hard evidence that authenticates and reinforces the existing legend.[74] Although we do not know exactly how the Xi Shi Stone came into being, its production must have been similar to that of the Drunken Stone: a stone by the Silk-Washing Creek was identified as the actual one on which Xi Shi had once washed her silk every day before she was sent to the Wu palace. Meanwhile, the figure of the Eastern Neighbor is a comic double of Xi Shi: despite her ugliness, she tries to imitate Xi Shi's charming habit of knitting her eyebrows but only ends up making herself even more repulsive.[75] Fan Shu's story amplifies these legends, following the same mechanisms of materialization and the production of a comic double. By inscribing a poem of longing on the Stone, Wang succeeds in evoking Xi Shi's spirit and even achieves physical consummation with her, literalizing and sexualizing the poetic trope of "meditation on the past" (*huaigu*).[76] By contrast, Guo Ningsu's futile effort to imitate Wang Xuan makes him a particularly ludicrous figure because he is not only a gullible, comic double of Wang Xuan, but also calls to mind an earlier foolish imitator, the Eastern Neighbor. If materialization affirms the legend proper by authenticating it, the comic double does so by highlighting the impossibility of replication.

The story also shows how a chain of poetic discourse—its production, reception, and reaction—serves as the central mechanism of poetic meritocracy in the literati community. Although the story describes Xi Shi's poetic reply, the focus is on her role not as a poet but rather as a lover and sexual reward for the talented poet Wang Xuan. The narrative assumes an extensive web of poetic circulation and storytelling among male literati. Within the story, news of Wang Xuan's success becomes publicly known and inspires Guo Ningsu's clumsy imitations; the account of Guo's failure leads to Zhu Ze's

mockery, which further circulates as a communal amusement. Within
this web, poetic originality is a matter of efficacy and social consensus. Wang's poem, which is a rather conventional work of meditation
on the past and certainly not the first inscribed on the Xi Shi Stone, is
considered superior by the internal audience because it strikes a mysterious chord with its intended reader, the spirit of Xi Shi. Guo's many
imitations are inferior simply because they fail to move her. Zhu's
poem is applauded as witty because it exposes the inherent ironies of
Guo's behavior. The winner, loser, and clever commentator, as judged
by an audience, thus constitute a range of roles available to individuals on account of their own poetic talent within a competitive poetry
community.

Not every poem a writer composes can be expected to be outstanding; instead, small specimens of poetic works—"outstanding lines"
(*mingju*), mostly parallel couplets, or "outstanding poems" (*mingshi*)—became the signature evidence of poetic excellence.[77] While
Tang poets' obsession with parallel couplets has been explained in
terms of poetic aesthetics and Chinese cosmogony,[78] contemporary
stories were concerned with social tensions surrounding these poetic
artifacts as intellectual property. In one story from Fan Shu's collection, for example, the poet Bai Juyi, then prefect of Suzhou, evaluates
the best couplets by Xu Ning (fl. 806–826) and Zhang Hu (fl. 821–
847) in order to decide which one to nominate as the top candidate
for the Presented Scholar examination. Being ranked lower than Xu,
the proud and indignant Zhang takes his leave. Later he finds another
famous poet, Du Mu (803–ca. 853), who truly appreciates him.[79] The
same Du Mu is said to be so impressed by one of Zhao Gu's (fl. 830–
847) couplets that he nicknames him "Tower-Leaning Zhao" (Zhao
yilou), for the couplet reads: "Specks of morning stars in the sky, the
geese flew past the frontier fortress; / As soon as the long flute started
playing, one leaned against the tower."[80]

Because outstanding couplets epitomize personal poetic achievement and identity, they are also presented as objects of manipulation and even deadly struggle in Fan Shu's stories. In another
entry, for instance, scholar Feng manages to curry the favor of the
Presented Scholar degree holder and prefect Yong Tao (b. 805) by
claiming to be his admirer and reciting Yong's couplets right in
front of him.[81] This story represents an ironic inversion of a normal scroll presentation, in which an examination candidate would
submit samples of his writing to a potential patron in order to win

the latter's recognition and support.[82] Outstanding couplets are not only open to such exploitation, but could also lead to fatal violence. *Advisor Liu's Fine Anecdotes* (Liu Binke jiahua lu) by Wei Xuan (ca. 801–ca. 866), for example, includes a story in which the poet Liu Xiyi (ca. 651–ca. 679) is murdered by Song Zhiwen (ca. 656–712) because he refuses to cede to Song his couplet, "Year after year, the flowers seem the same;/ Yet with each passing year, people all change."[83] It is fitting that the couplet is one that sentimentalizes human mortality, the source of the anxiety that motivates such fierce competition. The premature death of Liu Xiyi also perpetuates the myth of cultural immortality: although his young talented life is cut short, the couplet has the power to extend it in a transcendental, eternal form.

More than personal intellectual property, outstanding lines or poems are a cultural heritage; thus, according to Fan Shu, they also define the literati poetry community diachronically. In one lengthy story, Fan Shu tells us that when a local county magistrate hears that the famous poet Bai Juyi is passing through the area, he paints a wall in the temple of the Goddess of Mount Wu and invites Bai to inscribe poems there. Bai tells the magistrate that his friend Liu Yuxi (772–842) was unable to compose any new poem on the Goddess during his three-year term of office in the area and, in the end, chose to destroy more than one thousand existing inscriptions, leaving only the four best. Without trying his own hand in any new composition, Bai departs reciting those four poems singled out by Liu Yuxi.[84] Composing poems while passing famous sites such as the Goddess's temple was not only an important part of travel writing and landscape inscription, but also created and sustained a poetry community localized around these sites and across time.[85] Latecomers activated and spoke back to the poetic voices of their predecessors—which were frozen in inscriptions on stones, walls, wooden boards, and paper— in order to find their own new voices and in anticipation of the voices of future generations.

Since each generation is essentially required to write on the same set topics, this diachronic community is defined by a fundamental tension between innovation and tradition. In another story in Fan Shu's collection, for example, the examination candidate Tan Zhu stands out because his poetic inscription on the tomb of a famous courtesan exposes an irony: his predecessors have paid no attention to the numerous graves nearby and only to that of a beautiful woman.[86] Tan's poem thus proves its superiority over others with its fresh, critical perspective.

At the same time, there is a limit to outdoing one's predecessors. Liu Yuxi and Bai Juyi's inability to produce new poems on the Goddess of Mount Wu, whether real or feigned, is a concession to the artistic achievements of their poetic forerunners. If the chain of poetic proliferation defines a poet's relationship with the poetic tradition in terms of innovation, the perfection of outstanding lines and poems represents the canonical aspect of the tradition that signals the limit of such innovation. Paradoxically, a good poet needs to be both an innovator and a worshipper of the tradition, one who knows the acceptable bounds of his inventiveness. Just as poetic originality defines for one a legitimate, distinctive position in the community, paying tribute to the masters of the past fulfills one's "filial" duty.

Yet the poet-worshippers are not merely submissive and powerless. By acknowledging their inability to surpass previous poetic masters, Liu Yuxi and Bai Juyi also demonstrate their authority as arbiters of the poetic art, of which they are experts as outstanding poets in their own right. Liu Yuxi's elimination of more than one thousand existing inscriptions is shocking not just because of the scale of the destruction, but also because it reveals the power of latecomers over their predecessors in this diachronic community. Far from living passively in the shadow of their predecessors, latecomers actually determine the shape of that very shadow. Liu Yuxi's action corresponds in this way to the practice of anthologizing literature, the principle of which is to preserve the fine blossoms of the literary garden and get rid of weeds.[87] The story, however, also reveals the extreme consequences of such weeding: the physical destruction of "mediocre" poems allows no alternative to Liu Yuxi's judgment, symbolizing the irreversible effect that latecomers have in molding the tradition. By reciting the four best poems chosen by Liu, Bai Juyi pays tribute to Liu as the best poetic arbiter before him, extending the lineage of poetic worshippers and judges who shape the tastes of future readerships.

In Fan Shu's poetry community, readers not only admire outstanding lines and poems but also put them to practical use. In one entry, we are told that when officials recommend the strategy of marriage alliance with northern tribes as a solution to their invasions, Emperor Xuānzong responds by quoting a poem of Rong Yu (744–800) that criticized such a policy. For Fan Shu, the royal reader's familiarity with the works of a literatus poet is "an honor for the community of scholar-officials" (*shilin zhi rong*).[88] The emperor's evocation also echoes the Eastern Zhou practice of "citing poems" (*yinshi*) from the *Book of Songs* to lend moral authority to one's speech, as depicted in the *Zuo Tradition*.[89] By contrast, the characters in Fan Shu's stories evoke poems because of their presumed poetic perfection. The recitation thus turns the original author into a substitute for the reciter, because the poem articulates exactly what one would want to say and how one would want to say it in a particular circumstance, so much so that one does not need to compose a new poem.

In the eyes of Fan Shu, the cultural heritage of outstanding lines and poems can thus create an important mode of bonding among readers of the poetry community. The story of a young examinee named Li Huizheng stopping by the villa of the old hermit Wei Siming is a good example. The two discuss literature for days and play a drinking game of exchanging memorized poems. Wei's recitation of the couplet "The playful young man from Chang'an, / was riding a white horse with a golden bridle," for example, ridicules Li for his youth and self-indulgence. Li responds by citing another couplet to call attention to Wei's advanced age: "The handsome young man of yesterday, / has turned into an ugly old man today."[90] Such exchanges recall another Eastern Zhou practice, "offering poems" (*fushi*), in which rulers and ministers recited passages from the *Book of Songs* as part of ritual protocol at a formal banquet. The game was challenging because, by being taken out of their original context and given new messages for the current occasion, the reenacted poetic segments lost their particularities and demanded proper decoding and response.[91] Despite formal similarities with "offering poems," the Tang counterpart to this practice no longer entails any diplomatic or political consequence for the performers, but becomes a playful, culturally sophisticated way for them to articulate personal opinions and poetic sensibilities.

As a matter of fact, the competition between Wei Siming and Li Huizheng represents an important mode of bonding between them as poetic aficionados. Among the couplets they exchange, the authorship of only one is known to us today; this is the very couplet for which Song Zhiwen allegedly murdered Liu Xiyi. The story of Wei and Li thus portrays a world of extensive poetic circulation in which outstanding couplets and poems are shared knowledge,[92] so much so that two strangers can debate and even banter with each other by drawing from memory what appears to be a large poetic repertoire. If the old Wei Siming and the young Li Huizheng have tied in their competition for superior poetic understanding and taste, the former wins by his privileged status within the "fan club." Wei Siming had once been a bandit chief; after realizing that his gang was about to rob the poet Li She (fl. 806–827), he demanded only an impromptu poem, the content of which led him to mend his ways and become a hermit. As the one-time acquaintance of Li She, the subject of one of Li's poems, and the recipient of a poetic gift in Li's handwriting, Wei asserts his seniority and superiority as a poetic fan over Li Huizheng, a latecomer who does not enjoy the luxury of physical contact with his beloved poetic icon. Yet by hearing Wei's story of his encounter with Li She and examining the evidence in the form of Li's handwritten copy of the poem to Wei, Li Huizheng also becomes an important part in the lineage of fandom. He is now well positioned to pass on his own eyewitness account, and he does so to none other than the compiler Fan Shu. This lineage of storytelling enables bonding between successive generations of poetic aficionados and strengthens the ties between them and their poetic icons. Poets of the past represent not merely the abstract, invisible hands behind outstanding couplets and poems, but flesh-and-blood human beings with whom one could connect. To Fan Shu, poetry, along with the stories of poetic authors and readers, became the ideal, enduring bond of literati sociality, binding scholar-officials synchronically and diachronically into a homogeneous cultural elite.

THE EXAMINATION COMMUNITY

In contrast to the works of other compilers we have seen, the *Collected Words* (Zhi yan) by Wang Dingbao (870–940) is distinguished by its tight focus on the culture of civil service examinations, in particular the prestigious and competitive Presented Scholar examination. During the Tang, passing examinations was only one route to an official career: it was actually more common to enter officialdom through hereditary privilege, clerical service, service in the guards, recommendations, and so on. Wang Dingbao's collection provides evidence of the fetishization of examination culture even before examinations became the predominant route to official preferment. His vision of examination participation as a fundamental mode of literati sociality, imbued with meanings and tensions, thus anticipated a major shift in literati life under the Song and subsequent dynasties.

Wang Dingbao strongly identified with the examination culture because of his own participation and success in it. He claimed to be related to the illustrious Wangs of Taiyuan, and he passed the Presented Scholar examination in 900 after three failed attempts. Just like other promising examination graduates, who were sought after as sons-in-law in expectation of their bright futures, Wang Dingbao married the daughter of his chief examiner Wu Rong (d. 904), although the couple is said to have separated later for unknown reasons. He completed his collection sometime between his escape to Guangzhou following the demise of the Tang in 907 and the founding of the Southern Han there in 917. He was active as a member of the coterie of ex-Tang officials and became an important figure at the new court.[93]

The Tang examination culture that Wang Dingbao commemorated in his collection centered around the prestigious Presented Scholar examination. While the Ministry of Personnel offered annual assessment and selection (*quanxuan*) of people who became eligible for new or reappointments to positions of the sixth rank or lower (including Canonical Expert, Presented Scholar, and other degree holders at the end of their wait period), there were two types of examinations for recruiting new blood in the Tang. The emperor held decree examinations (*zhiju*) irregularly to recruit special talents as needed by the court. By contrast, the annual recruitment examinations (*gongju* or *changke*) consisted of a two-tier structure: prefectures across the country chose their best candidates, often according to quotas, and sent them to the capital to participate in national competitions held by the Ministry of Rites. These candidates competed for degrees in specialized branches of expertise, such as mathematics, law, ritual, history, and orthography. The degree of the Canonical Expert, which certified expertise in Confucian classics, and that of the Presented Scholar were both popular, but the latter became the most coveted title from the eighth century.[94]

The Presented Scholar degree was the most prestigious for several reasons. After poetic composition was made a central requirement in the late seventh century, the Presented Scholar examination became an official avenue for recognizing the most talented literary men in the empire. It was also the most competitive contest, with a success rate of only 2 to 5 percent and no more than thirty graduates annually. Since the degree conferred only eligibility for office, successful candidates, such as Bai Juyi, often took the special examinations of the Ministry of Personnel and the decree examinations to bypass the mandatory wait period, further proving their outstanding status.

They were thus able to secure prestigious entry posts that paved the way to the upper echelons of the Tang bureaucracy. As a matter of fact, many major post-rebellion political and cultural figures held the Presented Scholar degree.

Historians have shown that participants in the Presented Scholar examination created an examination culture to distinguish themselves as a special group in the broader literati community. The pool of examinees was fairly small. It was stipulated in 845 that candidates for the Presented Scholar examination be kept at fewer than 700 per year nationwide; although the precise figure might have varied by year, the average was probably no more than 800.[95] While the number of candidates at the prefectural level cannot be known for sure, it is clear that most people chose other avenues than the examinations. The fewer than thirty successful graduates of the Presented Scholar examination comprised only a tiny fraction of new entrants into the Tang bureaucracy. Many candidates were life-long devotees of the examination, since it was rare to pass on one's first attempt. In his collection, Wang Dingbao notes the year 901 in particular because five elderly men passed; three were more than sixty years old, and two were over seventy.[96] The annual examination cycle set the rhythm for the lives of examinees: presenting scrolls of sample writings to potential patrons, studying with friends to sharpen literary skills, seeking prefectural nominations, and congregating in the capital and taking the tests. Moreover, celebratory rituals for newly minted graduates evolved into an elaborate system that sealed the bonds among them and showcased them to residents of the capital. A register or honor list of these annual graduates was maintained and circulated; Zhao Lin's compilation, mentioned earlier in this chapter, was one example.[97] As examinees frequented pleasure quarters as an alternative sphere of social interaction, examination culture also extended into courtesan culture.[98]

Although the stories of his predecessors that Wang Dingbao includes in his collection have usually been taken as historical by modern scholars in their efforts to reconstruct the history of the Tang examination community, of concern here is Wang's own understanding and construction of that history. His recounting of stories illustrates a late medieval perspective on the meanings and tensions of examination participation as a fundamental mode of literati sociality. Tracing the institutional origins and development of the Presented Scholar examination, Wang Dingbao includes an anecdote that shows his identification with the collective meaning of examination participation:

> [The Presented Scholar examination] became prominent during the Wude reign [618–627] and fully flourished during the Zhenguan reign [627–650]. This was because Emperor Wen [i.e., Taizong] cultivated civil powers [*wen*] and ceased martial ones [*wu*], and in doing so he was endorsed by heaven and guided by spirits. Once he made an unannounced visit to the south gate of the imperial palace and saw the new graduates of the Presented Scholar examination walking out in file. He was pleased, saying: "All the heroes under heaven have entered my trap!" The Tang was able to occupy the vast central lands bordering with barbarians in four directions and stayed on the throne for three hundred years. How were all these [successes] not the result of following the way [of the examination system]?[99]

This story conveys a belief in the collective political ascendancy of examinees as the representatives of *wen*. Although the story is apocryphal in that it does not match what we know about the development of Tang civil service examinations, it indicates a valorization of both the Presented Scholar degree and its holders.[100]

This elevation of examinees, however, disguises paradoxical claims to their political potency vis-à-vis the sovereign. Heroes (*yingxiong*) formed a category of medieval character appraisal, as expounded by Liu Shao (fl. 180–240) in the *Treatise on People* (Renwu zhi): "Patterns that are exquisite and beautiful are termed *ying*, while animals that stand out among their groups are *xiong*. These terms are used to describe people with extraordinary *wen*, civil powers, or *wu*, martial powers. That is, those with outstanding intellect are referred to as *ying*, while those with exceptional courage and strength are called *xiong*."[101] According to Liu Shao, *ying* can at best serve as civil ministers or strategists and *xiong* are military generals, while *yingxiong* are those who possess the qualities of both and who are actual or potential rulers. Historical examples of heroes include Liu Bang (r. 206–194 BCE), the founder of the Han dynasty, and his opponent Xiang Yu (232–202 BCE).[102]

Wang Dingbao's story emphasizes Taizong's recognition of the Presented Scholar examinees as heroes. Resonating with post-rebellion intellectual trends that tried to revitalize *wen* as the solution to contemporary political and cultural crises, the story emboldens these examinees by conflating the multivalent meanings of *wen*: excelling in literary compositions (*wen*), these literary men (*wenren* or *wenshi*) also hold the key to cultural prosperity (*wen*) as well as political success through a civil governance (*wen*) that subsumes martial powers.[103] While these examinees are so powerful that the emperor regards them as his potential contenders, they are also willing to submit to imperial authority. By choosing to take examinations, they voluntarily enter into a trap of Taizong's design: they substitute civil competitions of paper and brush for dangerous martial conflicts; these examinations thus consume their lives and dispel their threat to the sovereign. The point is reiterated in a poetic couplet by an unnamed author cited by Wang Dingbao: "Emperor Taizong had truly far-sighted strategies; / For they made all the heads of heroes turn white [by channeling their energy into the examinations]."[104]

The story thus epitomizes the efforts of examination participants—only a small group in the late medieval literati community—to promote the significance of their voluntary life choice and to position themselves as an ultra-elite. By putting words in the mouth of Taizong, the story imbues the mundane triviality of examination participation with the grandeur and importance of contending for control of the world. Successful candidates are certified as the most outstanding men of the literati community, while defeated ones are potential heroes who have the opportunity year after year to prove themselves. Both are superior to nonparticipants, who are, by implication, unqualified to be considered (potential) heroes. This ultra-elite status mitigated late medieval examinees' clear awareness of the ideological implications of the Presented Scholar examination as an institution of domestication and enslavement. The story underscores the relationship between examinees and the emperor as a pact: if the emperor would recognize and endorse examination participants as the most important political players in the realm, then the latter would concede that they were heroes of a second order who played on the emperor's terms. The story of Taizong's alleged joy at seeing new graduates tries to cast such an idealized vision as a historical reality—the emperor had set the example of promoting examination participants, and history had proven that this approach was central to the stability and longevity of dynastic rule.

In addition to the collective meaning of examination participation, Wang Dingbao also illustrates its meaning for individuals by including many stories of personal success. For example, the future Duke Qizhang, Niu Sengru (779–847), is portrayed as a candidate newly arrived in the capital and unknown to others. He presents his scrolls to Han Yu and Huangfu Shi (777–835), both Presented

Scholar degree holders, and wins their admiration. The two visit
Niu's lodging, deliberately arriving when he is not in, and write
inscriptions on his door to show that they have been there to pay
him respect. The next day, Niu's doorway is crowded with people who come to see the inscriptions and try to meet with him: he
becomes instantly famous.[105] Such stories dramatize the ideal of
personal advancement through literary talent. This ideal must have
been inspirational to examinees, who saw themselves, according to
Wang Dingbao, as "[future] dukes and ministers in white robes"
(*baiyi gongqing*) or "[future] first-rank officials in white clothes"
(*yipin baishan*).[106] These terms convey a confidence that one could
miraculously traverse the vast social gap between a mere candidate,
who was required to wear uncolored hemp robes, to a high court
official, who was entitled to ranks and privileges.

Because of the fierce competition, however, such success was
beyond the reach of most candidates, and the disparity between success and failure became the central tension of literati sociality in the
examination community. Recounting and commenting on his predecessors' experiences, Wang Dingbao is particularly concerned about
what he calls "the way of gain and loss" (*deshi zhi dao*), especially in
terms of "the correspondence between fame and real talent" (*mingshi
xiangfu*).[107] The Tang Presented Scholar examination was fundamentally different from its Song and later imperial counterparts in that
the candidates' names were not blocked out on the test sheets, and the
chief examiner relied heavily on the input of his colleagues, friends,
and relatives in making his decisions. The main ground of competition was thus not in the examination hall but outside it. Candidates
sought to make a name for themselves through active and extensive
social networking, especially the presentation and circulation of writing samples to win patronage. Niu Sengru's success story above illustrates the importance of self-marketing (through scroll presentation)
and marketing (through patrons such as Han Yu and Huangfu Shi) in
the Tang examination community.

Wang Dingbao advocates righteous ways to make connections
and pursue success, denouncing unscrupulous zealots. Thanks to his
real talent, Niu Sengru lives up to the endorsement of his patrons,
but Wang Dingbao also offers negative examples. Citing in full the
letter that a man called Yuan Can sends to chief minister Yao Chong
to pledge his loyalty and service in exchange for Yao's support, Wang
Dingbao points out that this aspirant is "lacking in his conduct as

a Confucian scholar."[108] Wang is also critical of those who attach themselves to eunuchs and other powerful officials, shamelessly relying on their influence to pass. The advancements of such people show that the examination institution is far from meritocratic. The picture is further complicated by examples in which accidents determine the outcome. Two candidates, for instance, make a self-promotional courtesy call on the wrong person, but the accidental friendship pays off when the host is later appointed the examiner of the year.[109] The examination field is thus not always predictable. As a matter of fact, Wang Dingbao commemorates more than forty talented but unsuccessful people. He offers information on their lives and often includes samples of their writings, especially famous poetic couplets.[110]

Since such unfairness easily leads to resentment or disillusion, Wang Dingbao promotes a flexible, pragmatic philosophy for members of the examination community. He comments:

> Coda: A scholar-official who seeks to establish himself [through the Presented Scholar examination] succeeds because of his talent and fails due to his fate. The key to [dealing with] the issues of success and failure and to promoting the Way can be said to be none other than diligent self-cultivation. If he is ignorant of this and associates [examination outcomes] with personal ability or lack thereof, then he is in a precarious position like facing a cliff or walking on thin ice and becomes confused at a fork in the road. If he succeeds, he presumes it was due to his strength; if he fails, he is bitter toward others without end. People who pursue emolument—how can they not be vigilant regarding this [flaw]? In those who understand fate, this is sufficient to dispel resentment but cannot be relied upon to strive for riches and rank. If one relies on fate, his pursuit slackens, leading to the confusion of one's natural wisdom. If one uses it [as comfort], one's emotions are not obstructed, and this eliminates resentment. Therefore the reason why Confucius and Mencius invoked fate was just that they were distressed and woeful. When one conducts oneself with seriousness and follows the same path as these sages, then winning or losing, gaining a voice or not, how can one ever be made to harbor unhappiness or become too prideful? Nonetheless, what a scholar-official should never forget even upon his death is the favor and understanding [of others]. [The stories about] Bao Yi passing by mistake and about the memorial of Li Ao's [Daoist friend] can contribute only to entertaining conversations, but cannot illuminate the truth. As for those who retire after success and set their hearts on quietude and nonaction, I cannot comment.[111]

This passage is remarkable in showing Wang's strong identification with the examination institution, and his solutions to the challenges of inevitable failures and setbacks for the community of voluntary participants. On one hand, he proposes different approaches to success and failure. Attributing success to talent allows the passed candidates to affirm their faith in the meritocratic nature of the examination, while linking failure to fate helps to deflect the failed candidates' potential resentment toward and disillusion with the same institution. On the other hand, Wang argues that both perspectives are no more than pragmatic, therapeutic means and should not be taken to an extreme. A belief in one's own talent does not allow one to take rejections well. After Wei Mo, for instance, becomes established, he sends into exile the former prefectural examiner Li Hui (fl. 841–860) who failed him earlier; Li dies as a result. Likewise, a new graduate named Wang Lingran sends a letter to his former prefectural examiner Gao Changyu to boast of his success and shame the latter. Wang Dingbao sees these bitter, vengeful men as "abusive and treacherous" (lingli xianbi).[112] Meanwhile, a belief in fate is also problematic. Wang disapproves of stories like those of Bao Yi and Li Ao (774–836): Bao Yi is a candidate whom the examiner Liu Taizhen (fl. 742–780) is determined to fail due to a personal grudge but who passes because Liu cannot remember anyone else's name when asked on the spot by the chief minister to replace a name on the pass list; Li Ao enlists the help of a Daoist priest to send a memorial to the otherworldly authority to have his son-in-law pass.[113] While the first story emphasizes the futility of human manipulation because examination outcomes are predetermined by fate, the second indicates that fate itself is not immune to human manipulation. Dismissing both messages, Wang Dingbao argues that one should ideally, and paradoxically, keep trying and at the same time transcend concerns about gain and loss, success and failure.

Although Wang's strong commitment to the Presented Scholar examination can be explained by his personal success, his comments reveal another important reason: the literati fraternity of the examination community. To him, "the favor and understanding" that a scholar-official cannot forget comes from a tight-knit network that includes junior candidates (houbei), senior candidates (xianbei), successful graduates (qian jinshi), graduates of the same year (tongnian), advocates (zhiji, including patrons and friends), prefectural examiners (shiguan), and national chief examiners (zuozhu). It is well known

that the ritualized bonding among new graduates and the chief examiner lasted through the remainder of their lifetimes. The story of Niu
Sengru, discussed above, illustrates how established degree holders,
such as Han Yu and Huangfu Shi, served as advocates for their literati juniors. Wang Dingbao also recounts many stories of solidarity
and devotion among candidates. We are told, for instance, that Xiong
Zhiyi (fl. 780–808) gives Fan Ze (742 or 749–798), another candidate
whom he encounters on the road, his own horse and money so that
the latter can make it to the capital; he himself fails that year, but Fan
passes.[114] Whether or not candidates eventually pass the examinations, they develop a network of support around themselves through
social interactions that also enable them to affirm the meanings of
their shared life choice and commitment. Declining to comment on
those who become hermits, Wang Dingbao implies his disagreement
with their choice to abandon the examination community.

The network of literati fraternity in the examination community
constitutes the unofficial counterpart to the official recognition of literary talent conferred by the Presented Scholar examination. We are
told, for instance, that after thirty years of struggling to pass, candidate Gu Feixiong's (ca. 796–ca. 854) "reputation of being treated
unfairly offended people's ears," so much so that the emperor heard
about it and intervened to let him pass.[115] More often, the official
and unofficial avenues of recognition diverge rather than intersect,
as we see in Wang Dingbao's long list of talented but unsuccessful
candidates. By presenting this list and his whole collection, however,
Wang Dingbao conveys his confidence in the power of the examination community to remember and sustain its own cultural memory,
much like the communal hall of fame and infamy envisioned by Liu
Su in his *New Tales of the Great Tang*. Structurally, this examination
community also constitutes a pseudopatriarchy: if the chief examiner
is the symbolic patriarch and the supreme judge of literary excellence,
the graduates are his anointed successors, while the aspirants are
fledgling literary hopefuls awaiting recognition and admission. Precisely because of concerns about such strong literati fraternity, a Song
decree in 962 forbade new graduates from performing ceremonies of
gratitude for the examiner, rituals central to the Tang examination
culture.[116] Looking back to the Tang legacy, Wang Dingbao's vision of
literati sociality nonetheless betokened what would become the norm
in the Song and subsequent dynasties: a community of scholar-officials in fierce competition with each other for examination success, a

competition that also paradoxically unified them with common goals, values, and trajectories.

The modes of literati sociality that these four storytellers—Liu Su, Zhao Lin, Fan Shu, and Wang Dingbao—thematize in their collections are not merely idiosyncratic, but illustrate the perspectives of different groups in the late medieval literati community. Liu Su's emphasis on individuals as moral agents represents the interest of those from lesser backgrounds in downplaying the importance of pedigree and rank. By contrast, Zhao Lin's preoccupation with prestige epitomizes the preferential attitude and confidence of members of great clans who wished to maintain their privileged position in a changing sociopolitical environment. Fan Shu's focus on poetry explores how non-officeholders could constitute and assert their relevance in a broader community defined culturally rather than solely in terms of officialdom. Wang Dingbao's enthusiasm for examination participation demonstrates the efforts of members of the examination community to elevate themselves as an ultra-elite vis-à-vis other scholar-officials. Divergent beliefs about what was in store for them notwithstanding, late medieval scholar-officials achieved consensus through seeing and embracing the ongoing transformation from aristocracy to meritocracy as a positive opportunity of empowerment for their own groups and the literati community at large.

This optimism created a condition for the ultimate ascendance of examination participants, who envisioned a literati relationship with the sovereign that would appeal to imperial patrons. The different visions of literati sociality evince not only the diversity of late medieval social life but also the competition among different subgroups. In the sense that examinations became the dominant avenue of official recruitment from the Song onward, the vision of the late medieval examination community can be said to have won out. Their story of Emperor Taizong's joy at seeing Presented Scholar examinees entering his trap seems uncanny in foreshadowing the important role examinations would play in the successful centralization of the Song and subsequent dynasties. Despite their awareness of the ideological implications, late medieval examination participants enthusiastically vested their voluntary commitment with positive meanings because they were still a minority number-wise. In their strong efforts to promote themselves and their chosen way of life at this particular historical moment, they likely did not foresee that their vision of civil service examinations as the preeminent system of recruitment would become a reality for all educated men.

Meanwhile, other modes of literati sociality did not by any means become irrelevant. Quite the contrary, the bonds of morality, prestige, poetry, and exam participation were in the process of coming together to constitute the warp and weft of officialdom-centered literati life, offering the complementary avenues of mutual support and recognition essential for a strong, united community. Late medieval scholar-officials' various visions of literati sociality thus marked the formation of the core aspects of literati social identity. While this social identity denotes a communal solidarity that encompasses and subsumes individuals, late medieval storytellers also explored, particularly in stories of literati sexual bonds outside marriage, the possibilities of affirming the power of individuals to negotiate with and even subvert major power hierarchies dominating literati life.

CHAPTER 3

Sexuality

Women, Literati, and Nonmarital Bonds

While sovereignty and literati sociality define the central domains of literati life for late medieval scholar-officials, sexuality represents a vital sphere located on the periphery. Inasmuch as late medieval stories mostly concern literati romantic desires and entanglements outside of marriage, sexuality may appear to be a peripheral issue.[1] Precisely because of this liminal status, however, the stories of nonmarital bonds allowed scholar-officials to temporarily and symbolically challenge the dominant power relations in the central domains, sovereignty (embodied by the patriarchal authority) and literati sociality (personified by the social senior). Endorsing the literati right to "free" sexual conquest, and hence affirming male personal qualities such as youth and poetic talent, these challenges also serve to validate individual prerogatives to seek recognition and acceptance within the hierarchical order of the literati world. In its ability both to subvert and reaffirm power structures, sexuality demarcates a domain in which power is negotiated within the institutions of literati life.

Late medieval literati storytellers showed a new preoccupation with nonmarital bonds in the mundane world. While sexual encounters between mortal men and supernatural women remained a popular theme throughout the medieval period,[2] stories of illicit liaisons with mortal women were few in pre-Tang and pre-rebellion collections. The best-known examples are the elopement of the young widow Zhuo Wenjun with the poet Sima Xiangru (179–117 BCE) and the tryst between Jia Chong's (217–282) daughter and his handsome assistant Han Shou (d. 300?).[3] Such affairs had traditionally been condemned as immoral because they ran counter to marriage, which was arranged between two families with scant regard for the couple's personal feelings.[4] Late medieval stories on literati nonmarital bonds not only far outnumbered their earlier counterparts, but also offered new, complex plots with important thematic innovations. The storytellers' thematization of such bonds, in particular the literati hero's voluntary choice of a beautiful woman (not or not yet his wife) as his object of desire, often reciprocated by her devotion, was significant in revealing their careful explorations of literati sexual identity.

Closely related to the emergent literati "culture of romance," these stories about voluntary liaisons are often seen as quintessential examples of the "tales of the marvelous" because of their elaborate storylines, complex characterizations, and refined language.[5] Modern scholars have argued that the development of this culture emanated from the intimate associations of examination candidates and female entertainers in the pleasure quarters of urban centers such as the capital Chang'an.[6] The culture of romance inspired new poetic trends, including the genre of song lyrics (ci).[7] The façade of free choice and mutual enchantment between the literati and the courtesans, however, could hardly disguise the darker reality of sexual commerce in urban environments.[8] Nonetheless, by marking a sphere of sexual autonomy for men outside of institutional marriage, the culture of romance served literati interests by validating male "spontaneity, sensitivity, and individuality" and facilitating literati homosocial competitions and bonding.[9]

While romance helped galvanize literati sexual identity, it cannot be separated from two related themes in the spectrum of nonmarital bonds: male sexual competition and adultery. The treatments of these three themes both in tales of the marvelous and in shorter, "cruder" anecdotes reveal the real objective of literati extramarital desires and the ethical constraints placed upon them. Stories of male sexual competition and of romance spark and resolve tensions between youthful literati heroes and social authorities, the latter being represented by the social senior and the patriarchal family. In these stories, nonmarital bonds work to subvert the dominant power relations in literati life: the social senior embodies the power hierarchy of literati sociality while the patriarchal family exerts sovereign control over marriage and reproduction, perpetuating a long-standing belief in the correspondence between the relationship of father to son and of the monarch to his subject, as well as a correspondence between the family

order and that of the state. Such challenges to social authorities, however, go only so far. While literati heroes depend on (and effectively
scapegoat) knight-errant figures to defeat their social seniors in stories
of male sexual competition, narratives of adultery reveal the bottom
line of literati romance—when voluntary sexual liaisons jeopardize marriage, the foundation of patriarchy, they are condemned as
adultery.

The paradox of subversion and self-containment further manifests
in the image of the literati hero as a youthful sexual adventurer who
deviates from his proper course in life only to ultimately return to it.
In light of traditional denunciations of male infatuation with female
beauty, this persona appears to be a late medieval literati innovation.
In this regard, the story of Ouyang Zhan's (755–800) death recounted
by Meng Jian (d. 823) is telling.[10] The story describes Ouyang Zhan's
excursion to Taiyuan, where he falls in love with a courtesan whom he
must leave behind in order to assume his appointment in the capital.
The girl pines to death before he sends for her; upon receiving the sad
news and her shorn hair as a love token, he also dies of grief.[11] Meng
Jian notes that the deaths of Ouyang Zhan and his lover echo the earlier poems "Mount Hua Environs" (Huashan ji) and "The Clerk from
Lujiang" (Lujiang xiaoli), in which the death of one lover prompts the
suicide of the other.[12] In these relationships, love is reciprocated, but it
also kindles escalating, destructive passions. Such gender parity is precisely what bothers Meng Jian, as he reflects on the lesson of Ouyang
Zhan: "Generally, if one severs [the romantic tie] in time, one will not
be befuddled by female beauty. How could one then come to this?"[13]
Meng Jian's comments thus illustrate the emergence of a new literati
position that treats sexual liaisons as mere passing diversions.[14] Cor-
respondingly, it is usually a "junior," by age or social status (most protagonists are examination candidates or low-ranking officials), who
assumes the literati sexual role in stories. Stories about examinees thus
have been seen as "narratives of experience" for "para-literati," who go
through liminal states of unofficial education to complete their *rites de
passage* and become state officials.[15] The amorous diversions are not
merely part of a necessary process of social maturation, however, but
the very platforms through which literati storytellers strategically stage
and resolve the social junior's conflicts with the social senior and with
Confucian patriarchal authority.

These conflicts reveal literati ambivalences about what kind of nonmarital bonds they could and should have, and about the hierarchies

of power in the central domains of literati life. The social identities of female protagonists—including maids and household or government entertainers in stories of male sexual competition, professional courtesans and unmarried daughters in stories of romance, and wives and concubines in stories of adultery—actually demarcate different parameters of literati sexual identity. By deviating and then returning, or by subverting and then reaffirming social authorities, sexual identity effectively mitigates literati subjugation to power hierarchies without debarring them from becoming part of those establishments. In contrast to the poetic private space, which allows individuals to escape into a realm defined by what officialdom is not and modeled on the traditional ideal of reclusion,[16] sexuality constitutes an arena of power contestations. Although literati sexual adventures may be "carnivalesque" in terms of their temporary subversions of social order,[17] these sexual challenges operate within the power hierarchies of literati life rather than turning their world upside down. In other words, sexuality, as thematized by late medieval literati storytellers, distinctively negotiates dominant power relations within the structural constraints of literati life.

SEXUAL COMPETITION BETWEEN
THE SOCIAL JUNIOR AND SENIOR

Late medieval stories of sexual competitions feature a socially inferior, presumably younger literatus and an established, older counterpart, who fight for the ownership or devotion of a beautiful maid, or a household or government entertainer. Literati relationships with these women were hierarchical because such women were considered the property of their masters or the government.[18] While literati writers developed a long tradition of using the figures of women and their gendered voices as instruments for male homosocial competitions and bonding,[19] late medieval stories of sexual rivalry are preoccupied with a particular type of male tension: direct confrontations between the social junior and the senior. Specifically, these stories explore ways in which the former can turn the tables on the latter. In so doing, they affirm the social junior's right to possess the object of his passion and, moreover, by challenging the social senior, win the latter's recognition and acceptance into the hierarchy of the literati social world.

As much as late medieval literati storytellers emphasized the meritocratic nature of officialdom-centered literati life, as we have seen in chapter 2, literati sociality grew from a sociopolitical hierarchy in which the social junior depended on the senior for career advancement. We have noted how seekers of the Presented Scholar degree had to present writing samples to patrons, whose support was critical for examination success. In the Tang bureaucracy, recommendations played an important role in court appointments. Officials were subjected to an annual review by their superiors, the result of which could determine their promotion or demotion at the end of their term. Writings explicitly courting the favor of social superiors were thus commonplace, especially in a scholar-official's early career. The poet Li Bai, for instance, has been admired for his spirit of freedom and independence, as expressed in his famous lines "How can I bend down and lower my gaze to serve the high and mighty,/ making it impossible to enjoy myself?"[20] Just like any other literati hopeful, however, Li Bai had to seek out patrons. Early in his career, he sent letters to various powerful officials, praising profusely their virtue, talent, generosity, nobility, and even their physical features.[21] Such seeming inconsistencies and contradictions on the part of a writer can be disconcerting to modern readers. Arthur Waley, for example, finds Bai Juyi's letter to his patron "unpleasantly fawning and servile," although understandable given "the conventions of the time."[22]

Late medieval stories of male sexual competition provide a platform for negotiating this power relationship between the social junior and the senior. The superior position and power of the social senior of course give him great advantages over the junior. In the *Original Occasions of Poems*, Meng Qi, a Presented Scholar degree holder who later advanced to middle rank, includes stories that illustrate precisely such dynamics.[23] We are told, for instance, that official Qiao Zhizhi (d. 690) loves a maid in his household so much that he refuses to get married. After the powerful Wu Yansi snatches her away,[24] Qiao secretly sends her a poem that evokes the legend of Green Pearl (Lüzhu), who killed herself by throwing herself out of a high tower in order to remain loyal to her master, Shi Chong (249–300). Qiao's maid then commits suicide by jumping into a well; as revenge, Wu has Qiao killed.[25] While Qiao can be said to be selfish in encouraging the girl to kill herself,[26] we need to note that his poem represents the social junior's desperate but courageous attempt to fight a doomed battle against his social senior. In another story, minister Li Fengji (758–835) demands to see the beautiful household-entertainer of a certain censor and then refuses to return her. Although the censor

sends Li two poems expressing his longing for her, Li only comments
with a sly smile, saying, "Great poems!" The censor never sees the
girl again.[27] Li deliberately ignores the intended message of the poems
to focus on their aesthetic effect.[28] He can do so because he is so far
above the censor in terms of sociopolitical status. The cruel violence
of Wu Yansi and the cunning evasion of Li Fengji demonstrate the
limits of poetic efficacy and the inequalities between the social senior
and the junior in sexual competition.

Precisely because of the outrage that a predatory social senior
could inflict upon his social junior, the figure of a benign social senior
is particularly admirable. In another story from Meng Qi's collection, the prefect Rong Yu favors a government entertainer under his
jurisdiction, whose reputation for singing reaches the military governor Han Huang (727–787). As Rong Yu dares not defy Han Huang's
summoning of the girl, he composes a poem about his love for her
and asks her to sing it to Han, who promptly returns her to Rong.[29]
The story was clearly a popular one, since there were variant versions
featuring different groups of characters.[30] In Meng Qi's version, Rong
Yu's careful staging of the composition and performance of his poem
and Han Huang's equally staged reactions to it not only affirm the
efficacy of Rong's poetic competence, but also praise Han as a sympathetic, worthy character.[31] Rong's success rests upon the rhetoric
of romantic passion as a powerful moral argument.[32] Yet the effect
of such an argument depends on the willingness of the social senior
to be persuaded, for he is quite capable of robbing the junior of his
romantic prerogative.

Even more impressive than the benign social senior who backs away
from the junior's romantic interest is the generous senior who voluntarily gives his own girl to the junior. Meng Qi's collection includes
the following story:

> After Liu Yuxi finished his term as Prefect of Hezhou, he became
> the director of the Bureau of Receptions and a Jixian Academician.
> Minister of Works Li, who returned to the capital after a military
> governorship, admired Liu's [poetic] reputation and invited him to
> his house and spread a sumptuous banquet for him. In the middle of
> elated drinking, the host ordered a beautiful household-entertainer to
> sing a song urging Liu to empty his cup. Liu composed a poem on the
> spot, which was as follows:
>
> > With her beautiful hairdo and palace-style makeup,
> > Du Weiniang sings a song, [refreshing like] the spring breeze.

> Being used to seeing her, the Minister of Works is all at ease;
> But it thoroughly breaks the heart of the prefect from Jiangnan.

Li thereupon presented the girl to Liu as a gift.[33]

By emphasizing Li's immunity to the devastating effect of the girl's beauty and singing, Liu Yuxi flatters Li for his masculine self-control and his status as an affluent master. This paves the way for a magnanimous gesture, since Li is responsible for his suffering by showing him the enchanting girl. The juxtaposition of the passionate guest and the indifferent host in the poem, however, also suggests their different romantic capacities. Liu Yuxi's overwhelming reaction to the girl underscores his youthful vitality, an emotional and physical capacity for love and sex. Although Liu Yuxi politely attributes Li's indifference to familiarity, it also implies an incapacity more likely due to Li's advanced age. The story suggests that while the social senior owns the girl by dint of his wealth and influence, the junior is entitled to her by natural law. Li's presentation of the girl to Liu Yuxi affirms precisely this sexual prerogative of the junior.

The importance of poetry as a tool of negotiation for the junior indicates that sexual competition is also a veiled attempt by the junior to seek patronage. When the social senior responds sympathetically to the junior's poem, he also plays the role of a patron who appreciates poetic talent. His relinquishing of the girl is thus highly symbolic. As one of many women whom the senior owns, she represents his surplus capital in terms of power and influence, which he can afford to share with the junior by extending his patronage. In turn, by giving her away, he accumulates moral capital. For the junior, the girl as a sexual reward highlights his superiority to the senior in terms of youth, literally and symbolically. The concession of the benign or the generous senior to the romantic privilege of the junior thus shows his humility and sensitivity toward the future. Any predatory senior's arrogant treatment of the junior would only underscore his foolishness in the face of the law of nature: he will be superseded by the newcomer eventually; it is better to bond with the young. The accompanying gifts often mentioned in these stories make the concession of the girl from the senior to the junior more like marrying off a daughter; the transference of her ownership symbolizes a harmonious transmission of power across generations.

When a voluntary concession does not occur, the junior can steal the girl from the senior, with external help. This is the central theme

of "The Kunlun Servant" (Kunlun nu) from the collection *Transmission of the Marvelous* (Chuan qi) by Pei Xing (fl. 860–878), about
whom we know nothing except that he served on the staff of a military governor.[34] The story describes the visit of scholar Cui to a high-
ranking official's house. Surrounded by beautiful girls, the official
asks one wearing red silk to serve the guest. When the girl sees the
young man off, she mimes to him a riddle that he does not understand. His servant Mole solves it for him and takes him deep into
the inner chambers of the official to meet the girl on the appointed
night. Before the break of the dawn, Mole carries the couple back to
the Cui household. Two years later, however, the girl is recognized by
a servant of the official during a spring outing. After the young man
confesses his crime, the official forgives him by allowing him to keep
the girl but tries to capture Mole, who magically flies away to safety.[35]

The theft of the girl by the junior in this story makes up for the
powerlessness of his counterparts when facing predatory seniors in
the stories discussed above. Here the girl's description of the high official's affluent household as a prison and the articulation of her love
for the young man confirm the contrast in age and sexuality between
the junior and the senior, which counterbalances their disparity in
social power. By snatching the girl from the inner quarters, which
are protected by high walls, guards, and fierce watchdogs, the junior
poses an audacious, direct challenge to the power and authority of the
senior. Yet, in this subversive operation, the story carefully downplays
his role, which is strictly romantic and very limited. By expressing his
longing for the girl in a poem, he makes his desire known to his servant Mole and then turns the challenges over to him. It is Mole who
solves the girl's riddle, kills the watchdogs, and eventually carries the
couple out of the compound. When the official decides to exonerate
the young man and go after Mole, he clearly recognizes the servant as
the real threat to his power and control.

By shifting ethical responsibility to the servant Mole, the story
changes the nature of the confrontation, thereby protecting the literati hero. Mole's identity as a Kunlun servant, belonging to the dark-
skinned peoples of the Malay peninsula, underscores his ethnic
Otherness.[36] The narrative further conflates his role with the superhuman powers of knight-errantry, which Tang stories pit against the
authorities. In stories such as "The Woman in the Cart" (Chezhong
nüzi) and "General Pan" (Pan jiangjun), knights-errant often disappear at the end, embodying a social Other that threatens the political

authority yet remains beyond its reach.[37] When Mole flies away, the official is said to be so fearful of his possible return that he increases his own security forces. The story further enhances Mole's subversive power by giving him otherworldly features. The narrative concludes with the statement, "More than ten years later, someone from the Cuis saw Mole selling medicine in a marketplace of Luoyang, and he looked just like before."[38] Immunity to the passage of time and the occupation of selling medicine as a disguise are common features of an immortal. This elevation of Mole justifies his challenge to the authority of the high official because his power emanates from a higher realm than the mortal world. His assistance to the young couple thus lends moral legitimacy to their romantic pursuit, while his permanent, elusive presence essentially turns him into a guardian who can effectively keep a predatory social senior in check. By constructing this powerful subsidiary figure, the story downplays the social junior's sexual challenge to his senior and thereby facilitates the acceptance of the former by the latter.

The tension between subversion and self-containment becomes even more acute when the junior steals a palace maid from the harem of the emperor, the superior par excellence. A good example is "The Story of Wushuang" (Wushuang zhuan), attributed to Xue Tiao (ca. 830–ca. 872), a Presented Scholar degree holder who was relatively successful in his career.[39] In this story, the protagonist Wang Xianke falls in love with his maternal cousin Wushuang, who is condemned to become a palace maid because her father has surrendered to rebels. Wang befriends Officer Gu (Gu yaya), who orchestrates an intricate scheme to retrieve her. From a Daoist priest, Gu obtains a magic pill that can put a person in a deathlike state for three days. After Wushuang's former maid disguises herself as an imperial envoy to "execute" her with the pill, Gu redeems the "corpse" and brings it to Wang. Wang lives with the resurrected Wushang in hiding, but later returns to their family estate to enjoy a quiet, peaceful life.[40] Paul Rouzer rightly points out that the girl's name, Wushuang, literally "without peer," indicates her role in the story as a prize to be obtained because the hero must "infiltrate the most difficult interior space of all."[41]

The story contains its implicit threat to imperial authority carefully, however. On one hand, the emperor never figures in this story, and Wushuang is no more than a servant in the harem. On the other, the thrill of infiltration is balanced by corresponding punishments.

Although similar to Mole in that he is a facilitator of the social junior's romantic pursuit, Officer Gu is presented as a mortal knight-errant without superhuman powers. To protect the couple, he commits suicide after killing all of the minor participants in the plot to keep it secret. While his death is consistent with the stock image of a loyal retainer, it also pays for the murders he commits.[42] Moreover, he can also be said to be a prosecutor who metes out punishment for those involved in the crime, including himself, in order to exonerate the young couple. While Wushuang does pay for her escape from the harem with her (temporary) death, the only person unscathed in the story is the literati hero, who wins the girl from the most powerful superior and escapes any consequence.

These stories about sexual competition thus affirm the entitlement of the social junior to the sexual trophy and, by extension, to the power and status monopolized by the social senior. An agreeable resolution to the conflict consists of the superior's polite concession of the girl; meanwhile, stories of the senior stealing the girl from the junior are balanced by much more elaborate narratives savoring the thrill of countertheft. The construction of a subsidiary figure, the knight-errant, to bear the responsibility of countertheft indicates that challenging the social senior is not an end in itself, but a means to win acceptance in the hierarchical literati community.

ROMANCING THE COURTESAN: THE SEXUAL CHALLENGE TO PATRIARCHY

Stories of literati liaisons with professional courtesans, including the famous "The Story of Li Wa" (Li Wa zhuan) and "The Story of Huo Xiaoyu" (Huo Xiaoyu zhuan), present their relationships as romance—an idealized voluntary, seemingly equal, sexual bond rather than mere vulgar sexual transaction—and thus as the opposite of arranged marriage. In stark contrast to the passive role of girls in the stories of sexual competition discussed above, courtesans, commercial entertainers operating in the pleasure quarters of urban centers, are cast here as strong, active figures who develop romantic relationships that directly challenge patriarchal authority. By orchestrating and resolving the tensions between romance and patriarchy, these stories legitimize romantic values, particularly the prerogative of scholar-officials to enjoy temporary sexual freedom.

Although it has been widely noted that the young literati hero in these stories is caught between the conflicting demands of romantic commitments to his courtesan lover and social responsibility to his family, we must recognize the constructed nature of such conflicts. As a matter of fact, the literati's romances with courtesans complemented their family lives and official careers. In his reminiscences of the Pingkang Ward, the pleasure quarters of the capital Chang'an, Sun Qi (fl. 881–890) described in the *Records of the Northern Ward* (Beili zhi) how his distant cousin once tried to provoke her husband by hinting at her knowledge of his infatuation with a courtesan, but she was met with an ambiguous silence.[43] The account suggests that although a principal wife might dislike her husband's liaisons with courtesans, there was not much she could do about it since it was a part of male social life. Sun Qi's own special bond with Yizhi, the girl given most space in his collection, came to an end when she went so far as to request that he buy her out and take her as his concubine.[44] Sun Qi's refusal not only indicates the social stigma associated with courtesans but also that, for a scholar-official, romance and marriage could and should be kept separate.

"The Story of Li Wa" and "The Story of Huo Xiaoyu," however, transform this complementary relationship into a contradictory one in order to endow romance with the power to challenge the patriarchal family. "The Story of Li Wa" was written by Bai Xingjian (776–826), a Presented Scholar degree holder who had a respectable but much less illustrious career than his older brother Bai Juyi.[45] The story tells of a young man who falls in love with the beautiful courtesan Li Wa when he goes to the capital to take the Presented Scholar examination. After he squanders all of the money that his father gave him, he is abandoned by Li Wa and the madam, her foster mother, who move house without telling him. Forced to work for a funeral parlor, the young man wins a contest for singers of funeral music. The publicity leads to his discovery by his father, who is so outraged that he whips his son lifeless and leaves him for dead. Having miraculously survived, the young man becomes a beggar and accidentally comes to Li Wa's door. She repents and leaves her madam, devoting herself to restoring his health and social status. After he passes the examinations and starts a promising official career, his father reconciles with him and orders him to marry Li Wa, who becomes an exemplary wife and mother and is ultimately awarded the title Duchess of Qian.[46]

The story presents romance as a major threat to patriarchy by highlighting its power to seduce and destroy the cherished heir, the young man whom the father has fondly called "my family's thousand-mile colt."[47] Romance is situated in the courtesans' world, where the madam's "matriarchy" mimics and subverts the patriarchal order.[48] Modifying a passage from the Confucian classic the *Book of Rites*, Li Wa's mother tries to legitimize the young man's betrayal of his filial duties in pursuit of a life of pleasure: "Great desires exist between men and women. Even the order of parents cannot restrict them."[49] As Glen Dudbridge has put it, whereas the original passage "defines the natural appetites of man which require ritual and ethical control," the madam uses it to "urge its negation—the liberation of appetite from ethical restraint."[50] In so doing, she ushers in the traditional discourse of encountering the sensual goddess yet disguises the economic exchange as matrimonial fulfillment.[51] The madam's usurpation of patriarchal authority notwithstanding, the seductive power of romance and of the courtesan world emanates ultimately from Li Wa, whose beauty and charm prove irresistible to the young man, leading him to forsake his proper course of life.

The young man's subsequent social downfall further demonstrates the negative effects of Li Wa's sexual power. Modern scholars have noted that the downward and upward movements of the male protagonist constitute the story's most visible dynamics, a symbolic process of death and resurrection that can also be seen as a rite of passage for the young literatus.[52] Implicitly or explicitly, however, Li Wa is the driving force behind these movements. In the first half of the story, her abandonment of the young man sets him on a spiral of degeneration. As a mockery of examinations, his victory in the funerary singing contest only underscores the ironic, painful gap between where he should have been and where he actually ends up.[53] Hence, the enraged father's near-execution of him is close to the Apricot Garden, where new graduates of the Presented Scholar examination often held their celebration banquets.[54] By stripping off the son's clothes, the marker of social status in the Tang,[55] and whipping him almost to death, the father disavows him and erases his social identity. His new role as a beggar, covered in rags and subsisting on "leftover foods" (*yushi*), reinforces his status as a social outcast, a redundant nonhuman.

It is, however, Li Wa who single-handedly reverses this horrific process of dehumanization and restores the patriarchal order. She leaves the subversive matriarchy to help the young man, with a lengthy justification that acknowledges her crime of destabilizing the literati clan and shows her conversion to the orthodox patriarchal perspective.[56] By wrapping the young man with her own embroidered jacket upon their reunion, she conveys her high valuation of him and her determination to give him her best. By bathing, clothing, nourishing, and tutoring him, she demonstrates her capacity to act as a good wife and mother.[57] Enabling him to pass the examinations, secure an official post, and eventually gain acceptance by his father, Li Wa puts him back where he should have been and atones for her crime. The lower the young man sinks, the greater Li Wa's contribution becomes. His restoration also justifies her integration into the patriarchal family because it foreshadows her future performance as a wife and mother.

With the father's endorsement of Li Wa's marriage to the young man, Bai Xingjian's story achieves a reconciliation between romance and patriarchy. We are told that an unrivaled prosperity of the family ensues: not only does Li Wa prove to be an excellent housekeeper, but her sons all attain high positions and marry into top families. When her parents-in-law die, Li Wa's mourning with her husband is so moving that auspicious signs of magic fungus and white swallows appear, leading to imperial recognition. To preempt any skepticism toward such a too-good-to-be-true ending,[58] the storyteller Bai Xingjian proves the veracity of the account by describing the story's lineage of transmission, from the young man to Bai's great-uncle to himself. He also explicitly commends Li Wa: "Alas! A woman of the demimonde showed such virtuous conduct! Even exemplary women of ancient times could not surpass her."[59] Bai Xingxian further evokes his friend [Li] Gongzuo's enthusiasm for the story and admiration of Li Wa, trying to impart to his reader an exemplary reading that would look past her sordid background.

This intended reading, however, has failed to convince many later readers because of Li Wa's contradictory roles as both the destroyer and savior of the young man. Despite the lengthy justification to her mother, her transformation from a professional courtesan who does not mind deserting an impoverished customer to an altruistic figure who decides to do everything she can to rescue the young man is sudden and striking. The renowned Ming scholar Hu Yinglin's (1551–1602) comment illustrates later literati readers' discomfort with Li Wa's image: "That Li Wa later took in Li [the young man] was just enough to atone for her guilt in abandoning him. It is utterly ridiculous

for the author to praise her virtue."[60] In a similar vein, Feng Menglong (1574–1646) argues, "It was unfortunate that the young man
met Li Wa, but how fortunate it was for her to meet him again!"[61]
Attempting to smooth out her basic inconsistency and show that she
was consistently devoted, later adaptations emphasize Li Wa's innocence in the scheme of abandoning the young man and attribute the
responsibility to the wicked madam alone.[62]

Positing Li Wa as both the devil and the angel, however, is necessary for the story to make the case that it is in the best interest of
patriarchy to integrate romance. Against Li Wa's seductive charm,
the patriarchal family is defenseless, as attested by the easy loss of
its heir. This vulnerability stems from an ideological view of sex as a
matter of functionality and family duty. Sex was necessary for pro-
creation: Mencius famously designated one's failure to bear a male
heir as the greatest infiliality.[63] Furthermore, marital affections were
to be marginalized or suppressed: the *Book of Rites* states that a man
should divorce his beloved wife if his parents dislike her, but that if he
is unhappy with his wife but his parents like her, he must commit to
their marriage till the end of his life.[64] Bai Xingjian's story emphasizes
that the patriarchal, functional approach to familial and social roles
is overly rigid and limited. While the young man easily succumbs to Li
Wa's way of life, sex for the sake of pleasure, the patriarchy is unable
to rehabilitate him. Although the young man proves his talent and
potential in the singing contest, however ironic, his father sees only
disgrace, or, in the words of Kevin Tsai, "the ideological upheaval
which implies the horrifying, sterile prospect of having no proper
successor."[65] His solution is to execute his disqualified son. Li Wa,
however, proves to be the young man's *zhiyin* or *zhiji*, the one who
recognizes him and truly understands his worth.[66] In stark contrast
to the father's failure to recognize his own son while he performs in
front of him during the singing contest, Li Wa is able to identify him
solely by his cry of hunger and cold, leading to their reunion. Moreover, by transforming him from a nonhuman into officialdom's new
star, she succeeds where patriarchy has failed. By presenting Li Wa as
a threat to patriarchy and a remedy for its weakness, Bai Xingjian's
story painstakingly demonstrates that only by incorporating romance
into the patriarchal family can its patrimony be secured.

The incorporation, however, only creates an uneasy mode of coexistence as romance is subsumed in marriage. Li Wa's transformation
from a femme fatale to a paragon of female virtue is more troubling

than persuasive because it reveals a potential gap between what she is and what she does. Despite her display of virtue, she is still the same beautiful and seductive woman. As her beauty is no longer mentioned after her marriage, it is clear that romance now has a legitimate cover. If patriarchy fails to compete with romance in the first place, its control is precarious: the submerged romantic reality threatens the stability of the patriarchal surface meaning. Through this new coexistence, however, "The Story of Li Wa" finds a point of balance: domesticated romance becomes indistinguishable from romanticized marriage. In this precarious balance between the manifest and the latent, the story asserts that both the terms of romance and those of patriarchy can be fulfilled through their mutual reconciliations.

In contrast to the optimism of "The Story of Li Wa" by Bai Xingjian, "The Story of Huo Xiaoyu" by Jiang Fang (fl. 820–824) paints a picture of romance and patriarchy in stalemate. Although extant information on his life is fragmentary and inconsistent, Jiang Fang is known to have been a talented writer, was recommended for important offices by the famous poets Yuan Zhen and Li Shen, and seems to have had a fairly successful career.[67] The story he recounts describes a romantic bond between Li Yi, a talented poet and new Presented Scholar degree holder, and the beautiful courtesan Huo Xiaoyu, who claims to be originally the daughter of a prince.[68] Realizing the inevitable end of their affair given the gap between their social statuses, Xiaoyu requests a love commitment of eight years, which Li Yi promises with solemn vows. After he leaves to take up an official post, however, he discovers that his mother has arranged a marriage for him and that he will need to raise large sums of money for betrothal gifts. Busy getting ready for his wedding, he cuts off his communications with Xiaoyu, in the hope that she will give up on him. Xiaoyu pines to death, however, and turns into a vengeful ghost, who torments Li Yi by denying him any conjugal happiness.[69]

In stark contrast to "The Story of Li Wa," Jiang Fang's "Story of Huo Xiaoyu" presents romance as an insulated bubble vulnerable to the pressures of the social world. The liaison occurs during the interval of leisure after Li Yi's examination success and before his official appointment. The courtesan world constitutes an autonomous private space in which a "code of romance" takes shape, with Li Yi and Xiaoyu freely choosing each other to forge a bond between talent and beauty.[70] The bubble breaks after Li Yi assumes his proper social roles, specifically his duties to the patriarchy. Although it is his mother who actually arranges his marriage, the absence of the father makes her the sole embodiment of patriarchal authority. The inversion of value in the story is striking, for it is impossible to see Li Yi's filial piety in a positive light, and while the romantic bond in the courtesan world is a matter of free choice, marriage is presented as a mere financial transaction.[71]

The inversion is possible because the story valorizes romance through the heroine's unwavering devotion and sacrifice. The story is essentially a melodrama in which Xiaoyu fights a losing battle to retain her lover. She is an embodiment of the abandoned woman poetic persona transported to a real-life context. Unlike her poetic predecessors, who are often cast in static snapshots of hopeless longing and pathetic sorrow, Xiaoyu's adherence to her role as an abandoned woman binds her to an escalating performance of devotion. To get news of Li Yi, she uses up her savings and sells her jewelry, including the purple jade hairpin given to her by her father as a memento when she reached puberty, her most valued and symbolic possession. The dispersal of her material goods parallels the wasting away of her body, which eventually culminates in her death. Throughout her increasingly intensified process of sacrifice as an exemplary lover, she serves heroically as the sole upholder of the romantic bond and guardian of the romantic space.

For her romantic heroism, the story constructs a range of subsidiary characters to serve as the appreciative audience. This internal audience may be said to represent the external "social community of storytelling," defined by its enthusiasm for sharing stories and its network of gossip.[72] In the story, this audience enforces the "code of romance" by condemning Li Yi's betrayal and praising Xiaoyu's loyalty.[73] Moreover, they also personify all of the sympathetic perspectives on romance. The old artisan who made the hairpin illustrates a neutral, sentimental approach toward mutability: he is moved to tears by what he calls a pattern of prosperity and decline. The princess who buys the hairpin epitomizes a female audience whose members see themselves potentially in the shoes of Xiaoyu. The literati audience of "gallant or romantic scholar-officials" (*fengliu zhi shi*) are touched by the strength of Xiaoyu's passion, just as they appreciate the heroine of the long-standing poetic trope. "Knights-errant" (*haoxia zhi lun*), particularly known for their devotion and chivalry in upholding justice, are enraged by Li Yi's infidelity. A man in a yellow shirt, a knight-errant similar to Officer Gu and Mole, forces Li Yi back into the romantic space to confront Xiaoyu, along with a group of literati. The climactic scene—in which Xiaoyu reprimands a speechless Li Yi in front of the audience before she expires—is a theater of death and judgment, constituted by the good heroine, the bad hero, and the indicting audience. It is also a solemn ritual of sacrifice in which Xiaoyu's demise gives meaning and weight to the romantic ideal that she represents, for life itself, the preciousness of which is symbolized by her youth and beauty, is "a measure for value."[74]

Through her martyrdom, Xiaoyu claims for romance the moral power of a victim whose vengeance enables her to invade the familial space. Before this point, she has been confined to the private space of romance: the detail of door locking is significant both when Li Yi first enters her household and when he is forced to come back the second time. As a ghost, Xiaoyu now acquires a new mobility to take revenge on Li Yi and pose a threat to the patriarchal family:

> Li Yi was just sleeping with his wife Ms. Lu when he suddenly heard noises outside the bed curtains. Surprised, he looked and saw a man over twenty years old who looked genteel and handsome. The man took cover behind the sun drapes and kept beckoning to Ms. Lu. Alarmed, Li Yi immediately got up to chase him. He circled the drapes several times but the man suddenly disappeared. From this point on Li Yi harbored doubts and revulsion and became extremely suspicious [of his wife], [to the point that] they could not live together.[75]

In addition to assuming this phantasmal figure of a handsome young man, Xiaoyu's ghost also tosses love tokens to Li Yi's women. The tactic works: Li Yi distrusts his womenfolk; he beats them and even divorces or kills them. Li Yi is in effect tormented and destroyed by his own assumption that his women would not choose him if given choice.[76] The irony of his paranoia is seen most clearly in his treatment of a beautiful courtesan he buys from Guangling, a famous pleasure city: he confines her under a bath basin and seals it before going out and carefully examines the seals upon his return; he also tries to terrorize the girl with his stories of punishing women whom he believes have been unfaithful to him.

Through Li Yi's anxiety and fear, the story underscores the unrelenting threat of romance to subvert the patriarchy that refuses to accommodate it. In contrast to the seduction of the male heir in "The Story of Li Wa," the threat of romance here involves the seduction of domestic women. There is a paradox here: Xiaoyu's destruction demonstrates that romance is not a feasible real-life option, but her self-sacrifice testifies to the power of that ideal to inspire real-life actions. She thus embodies the vulnerability of women to romance, a seductive alternative sexual relationship. It is precisely this assumption of female vulnerability that underlies Li Yi's insecurity. Although Xiaoyu's ghostly seduction of Li Yi's women never really materializes, the danger of romance is both spectral and real because, as an ideal, its power is both symbolic and concrete.

Li Yi's anxiety and fear about the seduction of domestic women by romance dramatize not just the weakness of patriarchy but also the inherent contradictions in literati sexual identity. If "The Story of Li Wa" may be said to represent the young man's deviation from and return to the patriarchal family as a "natural" coming of age, "The Story of Huo Xiaoyu" shows how wrong the process could go. Li Yi's inability to form a romantic bond of talent and beauty with his wives and concubines as he had with Xiaoyu underscores his status as master. By turning from romance to marriage, he actually completes a transition in sexual identity from the social junior, whose youthful virility and talent win voluntary devotion from women, to the senior, who owns women because of his power and status. Whereas stories about male sexual competition project the social junior and senior as two different groups, "The Story of Huo Xiaoyu" presents them as developmental stages of male social identity. The nightmare for Li Yi is really that when he is ready to move on, his past refuses to let go of him: he is haunted by his former self in the form of a phantom Xiaoyu, revealing his inability to manage the real-life repercussions of his timely breakup. While such a repudiation of romance is what Meng Jian advises for his fellow literati in light of the death of Ouyang Zhan, the martyred Xiaoyu is a dramatic incarnation of the girl whom Sun Qi left to her own fate and probably for whom he was compelled to write his reminiscences.

This haunting also points to an impotence of even greater consequence. While Li Yi needs two sets of women for his different modes of sexual identity—passionate lovers and dutiful wives or concubines—and needs to keep these two sets separate, he cannot fully control the boundary between them. Xiaoyu comes to him voluntarily through romance, and his wives and concubines involuntarily through arranged marriage or purchase, yet they are well capable of crossing this boundary. Xiaoyu's spirit invades his domestic sphere and his wives and concubines can turn into romantic lovers if seduced by a social junior, with whom Li Yi is by definition unable to compete sexually. But what if such a nightmare about wives and concubines comes true?

ADULTERY: THE ETHICAL LIMIT TO ROMANCE

When wives and concubines become lovers, they also become adulteresses who undermine their husband's authority and the institution of marriage. Late medieval literati storytellers' dark representations of the adulterous wife mark the ethical boundary of their romantic challenge to patriarchy. Usually from a lesser background, a concubine is "surplus" in a marriage, purchasable and transferable between men; thus the adulterous concubine presents an ambivalent case that allows for both sympathy and condemnation. These stories about adultery also consistently show literati anxieties about the dangerous power of female sexuality.

Adultery was traditionally designated as an ethical transgression, particularly on the part of women. Referred to as "lewdness" (*yin*), "illicit sex" (*jian*), or other variant terms, adultery was one of the "seven warrants of expulsion" (*qiqu* or *qichu*) by which a woman could be divorced, as stated in the Confucian texts the *Book of Rites Collated by the Elder Dai* (Da Dai Li ji) and *Analects of the Confucian School* (Kongzi jiayu).[77] Tang law singled out adultery and "nasty diseases" (*eji*) as the most serious warrants among the seven. Women who met the other five criteria for severance, "bearing no children" (*wuzi*), "being unwilling to serve their parents-in-law" (*bu shi jiugu*), "gossiping and sowing discord" (*koushe*), "stealing" (*daoqie*), and "being jealous" (*duji*), could be exempt from divorce if some other conditions were met, such as having mourned properly for her deceased parents-in-law. By contrast, no exceptions could be made for adulterous women or those with nasty diseases.[78] Moreover, although both the adulterer and the adulteress could be sentenced to forced labor, the latter had to serve two years, half a year longer than her lover.[79] These ethical and legal prescriptions aimed to defend the husband's exclusive sexual right to his wives and concubines, and to maintain the order of the patriarchal family.

Although as a voluntary nonmarital bond adultery is not different in nature from the literatus-courtesan romance discussed above, late medieval literati storytellers' negative portrayals and strong condemnations of the adulterous wife show their refusal to endorse nonmarital bonds that destabilized marriage, the foundation of patriarchy. "The Story of Hejian" by Liu Zongyuan (773–819) demonizes the transgressive wife by elaborating on her sexual compulsion. A Presented Scholar degree holder, Liu Zongyuan was an accomplished mid-Tang prose writer, best known, along with his friend Han Yu, for leading the Archaic Prose movement.[80] In the story, Liu features an adulteress who is so abominable that he is too embarrassed to mention her name, only her native place, Hejian (in modern Hebei). Originally a virtuous woman devoted to her husband and her mother-in-law, Hejian arouses the jealousy of her dissolute female relatives, who are determined to corrupt her. They invite her to visit Buddhist temples where they would secretly meet and have sex with men. Hejian runs away the first time, but she gives in the second time and becomes so attached to her newfound lover that she refuses to go home. When she does, she can no longer stand her husband. Pretending illness, she asks him to perform night sacrificial ceremonies prohibited by the court and then informs against him. After having her husband killed, she leads a life of dissipation with her lover until he is sexually exhausted. To get a continuous supply of sex partners, she opens a tavern, where she peeks at her customers and invites them upstairs to have intercourse with her. She eventually dies of "marrow exhaustion" after more than a decade of unabated sexual indulgence.[81]

For many readers, this story is so disturbing that it is difficult to believe that Liu Zongyuan actually wrote it. For those who accept Liu's authorship, allegorical reading offers a good way out of their discomfort. The Song scholar Hu Yin (1098–1156), for instance, proposes that Hejian is a figure for Emperor Xianzong, who aborted the Yongzhen Reform started by his father and punished reformers, including Liu Zongyuan.[82] As a matter of fact, even Liu Zongyuan himself was uncomfortable, and he was the first to attempt to allegorize the story. He sees Hejian's corruptibility as an analogy for the vulnerability of ethical relations, pointing out the parallel between her role as wife and daughter-in-law and that of a scholar-official as friend and subject. Hejian's weakness lies in her forced virtue: by staying away from any man other than her husband, even her own father-in-law, she only creates an artificial vacuum.[83] To Liu, the pure wife turned licentious woman is a figure for the scholar-official, who despite his commitment to moral ideals, cannot resist the temptations of self-interest and ends up betraying his friends and lords. Although male sociability seems a major culprit here, just as Hejian's relatives are responsible for her debauchment, Liu takes the individual to task for failing to withstand the real test.

The discomfort of both readers and the storyteller actually emanates from the story's representation of the dark forces of female sexuality. "The Story of Hejian" is in effect a grim inversion of the happy ending of "The Story of Li Wa." As noted above, the integration of Li Wa into the patriarchal system submerges her previous identity as femme fatale under her new identity as an exemplary wife and mother. This precarious balance between feminine virtue and sexuality is destroyed in the case of Hejian: a taste of pleasure awakens her sexual appetite, the root of her downfall as a devoted wife and daughter-in-law. To wonder why she and her husband do not enjoy any sexual pleasure is beside the point. The contrast between marriage as duty and adultery as pleasure for Hejian represents the conflict between the patriarchal view of sex for reproduction and the individualistic pursuit of sex for its own sake, echoing the distinction between the patriarchal world and the courtesan world in "The Story of Li Wa." Whereas Bai Xingjian's "Story of Li Wa" tries to legitimize the male right to sexual pleasure and freedom by integrating romance into patriarchy, Liu Zongyuan's "Story of Hejian," through its horrifying lesson, reveals deep anxieties about the female pursuit of such pleasure.

Hejian shows how patriarchal prescriptions of female virtue and identity could lose their binding power. Hejian's sexual appetite prompts her to get rid of her husband, the symbol of the patriarchal institution that confines her, and transforms her into a depraved creature, a slave to her own insatiable sexual desire. In line with the traditional Chinese medical view of excessive sex dissipating essential life forces, Hejian the sexual vampire depletes her lovers' energy as well as her own. It is significant that she dies of a natural cause, "marrow exhaustion," rather than by social punishment, for her death signifies the dead end of the female pursuit of hedonistic sex. Nevertheless, the fact that Hejian can only be destroyed through the operation of natural laws also reveals the ultimate inability of patriarchy to tame this dangerous power of female sexuality: the abyss of her animalistic desires belongs to the part of nature that cannot be fully domesticated by the patriarchal order. The story is deeply unsettling because it is a cautionary tale that betrays the very limit of its own didacticism.

While Liu Zongyuan's "Story of Hejian" is pessimistic about the power of patriarchy to rein in the desires of an adulterous wife, "The

Story of Feng Yan" (Feng Yan zhuan) by Shen Yazhi (781–832) is optimistic about the efficacy of male solidarity and violence against such
a transgressive woman. A Presented Scholar degree holder and well-
known poet of his time, Shen Yazhi met with little luck in his official
career and traveled extensively to seek employment and forge connections. He wrote this story probably around 819.[84] The story tells
of Feng Yan, a knight-errant who kills a villain in a local dispute and
hides in the army of a military governor, Jia Dan (730–805). One day
Feng sees a beautiful woman standing in a doorway, looking at him
from behind her sleeve; he makes contact with her and manages to see
her while her husband Zhang Ying, a military officer, is away. This
voluntary liaison, however, leads to a horrific ending: Feng kills the
woman, believing that she is trying to have him kill her drunken husband. When the husband is taken to be the wife's killer and is about
to be executed, Feng turns himself in. Jia Dan petitions the emperor
and volunteers to give up his office in exchange for Feng's pardon.
The emperor is moved and grants amnesty to all convicts who have
been sentenced to death in the area.[85]

Feng Yan's murder of his lover results from an ambiguous, silent
contest of will and power between the two for control of their relationship. The contest occurs in the presence of the husband, scarcely
conscious due to his intoxication:

> It happened that [the husband] Zhang Ying joined his friends for a
> drinking party. Feng Yan took advantage of this interval and slept
> [with the wife] in the bedroom again, with the door closed. When
> Zhang returned, the wife opened the door to let him in and used her
> gown to conceal Feng. Feng crouched low to hide behind her and then
> moved to hide behind the door. He [inadvertently] dropped his head-
> scarf below the pillow next to [Zhang's] sword. [As] Zhang [fell into]
> a drunken sleep, Feng pointed to the headscarf, gesturing for the wife
> to fetch it for him. She picked up the sword instead and handed it to
> him. Fixing his gaze [on the sword], Feng [suddenly] slit the wife's
> throat. He then put on his headscarf and left.[86]

The interpretive uncertainties of silence leave open the possibility
that the wife might have simply misunderstood Feng. But by killing her, he rules out the possibility of her innocence and convicts
her of attempting to murder her husband. Underlying the tension
between these divergent interpretations is an intense struggle between the male and the female perspectives on this extramarital affair. Although Feng seems to enjoy his liaison with Zhang's wife,

he does not intend to challenge her husband. The fact that he visits her when her husband is absent indicates that he does not want to compete directly with the husband but simply alternate with him. His hiding from the husband when the latter returns further confirms his avoidance of any confrontation. To him, the affair thus means sexual enjoyment rather than commitment. By giving Feng the sword, however, the wife forces him to confront the love triangle that makes him her husband's competitor. Whether or not she indeed misunderstands Feng's hand signal for the headscarf as being for the sword, her gesture imposes on Feng the image that she desires, a devoted lover who can and is willing to free her from an abusive husband. Her act also reveals her confidence in the sexual bond she has established with him and, by extension, in her sexual power, especially when all this takes place immediately after they have had intimate relations.

With actions taking the place of words, (mis)interpretation has dire consequences in that each "articulation" is given the power to violently counter its earlier counterpart. Just as the wife's wishful reading of Feng Yan's hand gesture erases his original "innocent" message about his headscarf, her message is erased in turn by Feng's murder of her. Feng's deliberation, "fixing his gaze [on the sword]," reveals a process of weighing choices: he could have put down the sword and walked away, but he chooses to kill her. By capitalizing on her sexuality to control their relationship, and by trying to turn him into an instrument of her wish to escape her marriage, she has turned his enjoyable liaison into a nightmare. Feng Yan asserts a countercontrol by killing her, which not only offers him a convenient exit from the liaison but also justifies his violence by proclaiming her an evil woman. Her guilt is twofold: by her intent to pit her lover against her husband, as perceived by Feng, she becomes a dangerous figure who threatens the interests of both.

The story celebrates a male victory: the indictment and execution of the wife make it possible to reunite the male community. Feng Yan's endorsement by secular authorities, represented by the military governor and the emperor, is a commendation of him as a defender of patriarchy. Feng Yan saves the husband twice: first from the evil clutches of his wife and then from the wrongful charge of murder. It is no mere coincidence that the husband is named Ying, literally "baby, child, kid." His infantilization throughout the story is a strong parallel to the innocence and powerlessness of Hejian's husband. If "The

Story of Hejian" finds patriarchy inadequate to curtail the dangerous power of female sexuality, "The Story of Feng Yan" enlists the
help of a violent knight-errant to protect patriarchy and eliminate the
threat, in stark contrast to the knights-errant seen above, who serve
as guardians of romance. The irony that the wife dies at the hand of
her own lover is important, for her death creates fraternity between
her husband and her lover. Although Feng Yan's relationship with
her husband at the beginning resembles the competition between the
social junior and senior, the rivalry is transformed into a unified front
against the manipulative wife in the end. The celebrated righteousness
of Feng Yan lies in the fact that he essentially executes her on behalf
of her husband.

Fraternity not only binds the internal characters in the story,
from the emperor down to the pardoned criminals, but also extends
to the storytellers and readers. Shen Yazhi comments at the end of
the story: "Alas! The licentious heart [of a woman] is worse than
flood or fire—how can one not fear it! But Feng Yan killed the
wicked [wife] and absolved the innocent [husband]. He was truly
a valiant man of ancient times."[87] Shen Yazhi compares himself to
the famous historian Sima Qian, whose "Biographies of Knights-
Errant" (Youxia liezhuan) established the historiographic conventions of representing these figures. By ensuring that Feng Yan's good
name and the wife's infamy pass down in history through his writing, Shen joins the unified male front. This male solidarity is sustained by a shared fear of the wife, who embodies a categorical
threat in her anonymity. This male bonding continues in later poetic
retellings of the story, including the "Ballad of Feng Yan" (Feng Yan
ge) by Sikong Tu (837–908) and the "Seven Rounds of the Water
Tune" (Shuidiao qibian) by Zeng Bu (1036–1107).[88] Sikong Tu's ballad, for instance, fills in the gap of Feng Yan's silent deliberation by
spelling out his reasoning: "Since she is able to betray him [i.e., her
husband], she will also betray me. / By whose hand will she do it [to
me]?"[89] Sikong Tu makes explicit the male identification that underlies this fraternization: all men are in the same boat, as no one is safe
in the face of female sexual manipulation. Sikong Tu also links himself to Shen Yazhi: "Because I was moved by the writer Shen Yazhi,/
I composed a long verse to expound clearly on his message."[90] The
literati fraternity is thus bound not just by a common fear of the
power of female sexuality but also by collective, continuous efforts
to exorcise the threat, literally and textually.

While late medieval literati storytellers were unanimous in denouncing the adulterous wife and defending the foundation of patriarchy, they were divided in their approaches to the adulterous concubine. For some, she represents no less serious a threat than the adulterous wife. Lu Hongzhi (d. 850), a Presented Scholar degree holder who later became a military governor, relates a story about Meng Sixian, a concubine of general Wang Zhi. Meng jumps over walls to see her lover until she is expelled by her husband; later, having nowhere to turn after the death of her lover, she returns to her ex-husband, who breaks her legs and tortures her to death.[91] The symbolic meaning of her punishment is clear: as the means for her to escape from her rightful place in the domestic space in pursuit of sexual pleasure and freedom, her legs become the very locus of her pain and suffering and ultimately bring about her demise. The story, however, neutralizes the husband's cruelty by making her death a karmic retribution for the jealous murder of her lover's maid. This adulterous concubine is presented as a selfish, jealous, and cruel woman who deserves her violent end.

Thanks to a concubine's "surplus" status in marriage, she also represents an ambiguous possibility for romance within the domestic sphere. In his collection *Minor Documents by [a Man from] Sanshui* (Sanshui xiaodu), for example, Huangfu Mei (fl. 874–910) includes a story that explores such ambivalences. Huangfu Mei was a low-level official and grandson of the chief minister Bai Minzhong (792–861), cousin of the famous writers Bai Juyi and Bai Xingjian.[92] Entitled "Bu Feiyan," the story describes the liaison between Bu, the favorite concubine of a clerk named Wu Gongye, and her neighbor Zhao Xiang, a handsome young literatus. After stealing a glimpse of Bu Feiyan through the cracks of the wall, Zhao becomes crazy about her and bribes the gatekeeper's wife to send her poems and letters. Revealing that she has stolen glances of him too, and is unhappy with her less refined husband, she matches his writing with her own. After extended written communication, she invites him to cross the wall, and they meet whenever her husband goes on night duty. However, a maid mistreated by Bu Feiyan divulges her secret to the husband. The husband catches them in a tryst: Zhao Xiang manages to run away, but Bu Feiyan is badly beaten by her husband and dies.[93]

Huangfu Mei's story tries to aestheticize the romantic bond without denying its transgressive nature as adultery. The stream of poems and letters that the lovers exchange underscores their mutual appreciation of literary talent, echoing the earlier tradition of poetic "rituals of seduction."[94] The rituals here are enacted through their intertextual performances, evoking earlier romantic legends and clichéd images of passion and longing. Moreover, the couple fetishizes the material medium of their poetic exchange: each composition is written on special, exquisite stationery, including Xue Tao paper, Golden Phoenix paper, Jade Leaves paper and Green Moss paper. This aestheticization diverts attention away from the ethical tension as the husband temporarily disappears from the scenes of sexual seduction and consummation. Nevertheless, the tension has to be confronted. With the husband's discovery of the affair and the escape of Zhao Xiang, Bu Feiyan alone has to pay the price. The story underscores her willing acceptance of her husband's punishment and her continuing devotion to her lover, as she states, "Since in life I was able to be intimate with [Zhao Xiang], in death what rancor can I have?"[95]

Huangfu Mei's story foregrounds competing perspectives on Bu Feiyan as a devoted romantic heroine and an unfaithful concubine. The poetic lines by scholar Cui, a friend of the husband, represent a sympathetic reading: "It is just like the scattering of people who passed flowers in drinking games. / The most luxuriant branch is left on an empty couch."[96] Cui emphasizes the tragic nature of Bu Feiyan's death in terms of the destruction of a young and beautiful life, and avoids any moral judgment of her. By contrast, another friend of the husband, scholar Li, adopts a critical position: "If her beautiful and fragrant soul indeed had an afterlife, / she would have felt ashamed to meet the girl who threw herself down from the tower."[97] Li thus contrasts Bu Feiyan with the famous Green Pearl mentioned above, who died for her master, and condemns Bu's infidelity. Interestingly, the story allows Bu Feiyan's ghost to come back, not to take revenge on her cruel husband or her selfish lover but to control the interpretation of her own story. She appears in dreams to thank Cui and scold Li; Li dies a few days later because she demands to have a face-to-face confrontation with him in the underworld. While the phantom of Huo Xiaoyu invades the domestic space to seduce domestic women, the ghost of Bu Feiyan embodies the courage and power of such a fallen woman. Apart from audaciously pursuing her passions, she musters and even coerces sympathy for her romantic transgression.

But the storyteller Huangfu Mei has the last word, counterbalancing Bu Feiyan's control by arguing that she deserves punishment as well as sympathy. He comments, "Although the crime of Feiyan cannot be excused, the perceptible [sincerity] of her heart also makes one feel sad."[98] To him, the romantic bond between talent and beauty is inevitable because talent and beauty naturally attract each other. This bond occurs, however, at the expense of morality. In his words, "Thus a scholar-official who is proud of his talent has insufficient virtue, and a woman who is complacent about her beauty develops liaisons."[99] If romance is inevitable, so is its punishment. The tension is resolved by the devoted heroine: through her voluntary transgression of ethical rules and her subsequent redemption through the sacrifice of her own life, she fulfills the demands of both romance and patriarchy and, in so doing, relieves her lover of any real social consequences. The hero Zhao Xiang changes his name and gets back on track with an official career.

In seeing Bu Feiyan's infidelity as an unforgivable betrayal, Huangfu Mei is like Liu Zongyuan, Shen Yazhi, and Lu Hongzhi before him. Adultery must be condemned because it threatens both male solidarity and the patriarchal family. The consensus of these storytellers in defending the sexual right of the husband to his wives and concubines also makes clear what the bottom line is for literati endorsements of romance: a voluntary sexual liaison should not jeopardize the institution of marriage or the male position as domestic master of female sexuality. The youthful persona of the literatus lover thus has a temporal limit: he will eventually marry and become a husband himself. That is, the right of the husband represents a more fundamental aspect of male sexual identity than extramarital liaisons.

A DAUGHTER'S ROMANTIC DEVIATION: THE PARADOX OF SUBVERSION AND SUBMISSION

While late medieval literati storytellers affirm romance in stories of literati bonds with courtesans but defend patriarchy in those of adultery, a problematic balance is achieved in the famous love story of a literatus and an unmarried daughter, "The Story of Yingying." If the sexual right to wives and concubines belongs exclusively to the husband, ownership is still uncertain in the case of an unmarried daughter, guarded by the parents and other senior members of the family who will make marriage arrangements for her. Through the romantic deviation of a daughter and her literatus lover and their ultimate separation and return to their normal tracks in life, "The Story of Yingying" explores the radical possibilities of affirming both romantic and patriarchal values. Condoning romance as an illicit liaison and a controversial subject, the story paradoxically makes possible both the subversion of and submission to patriarchal authority.[100]

"The Story of Yingying" has traditionally been attributed to the poet Yuan Zhen and read as an autobiographical account, although its authorship is still open to debate.[101] Whatever the case, the story provides a verisimilar account of the liaison between the lovely Cui Yingying, a girl from a good family, and the scholar Zhang, a handsome examination candidate known for his self-restraint. Zhang helps to protect Yingying's family from marauding soldiers when the family stays at a Buddhist temple on their way to the capital. To express her gratitude, the widowed mother invites Zhang to dinner and asks her children to meet him. Despite her unwillingness, Yingying is forced to come out, and her beauty stuns Zhang. He then tries to seduce her with poems and receives a favorable reply. After he climbs the wall to get to her chamber, she appears in formal clothing and gives him a severe scolding. A few days later, however, she voluntarily comes to spend the night with him. After some intermittent secret meetings, he finally leaves for the capital to take his examination. He sends a letter and gifts to her and receives a moving reply, which he shows to his friends and which prompts their poetic responses. But Zhang decides to end the relationship, and each ends up marrying someone else. He tries to see her again, but she refuses and sends him two poems instead. They then each go their separate ways. The storyteller claims that he often tells this story to his friends as a lesson.[102]

In contrast to "The Story of Li Wa" and "The Story of Huo Xiaoyu," which highlight the threats of romance to patriarchy in order to justify the integration of the former into the latter, "The Story of Yingying" refuses to reconcile the two. An unmarried daughter's romantic deviation represents an audacious challenge to patriarchal authority and is condemned as immoral in orthodox Confucian texts. Mencius, for instance, states, "If, without waiting for the order of their parents and the words of matchmakers, [young people] bore holes to peek at each other and climb walls to be together, they will be despised by their own parents and compatriots."[103] This illicit relationship could become socially accepted only through patriarchal endorsement. In the earlier stories of the elopement of Zhuo Wenjun with the poet Sima Xiangru and the rendezvous between Jia Chong's daughter and his assistant, the heroine's father eventually approves their relationship and accepts them into the family. The liaison of

Yingying and Zhang, another voluntary bond of beauty and talent, ultimately fails on its own, without evolving into marriage. By resisting the normalization and domestication of romance, "The Story of Yingying" represents a radical departure from earlier narratives on the love affairs of daughters.

The authenticity of the liaison, in particular that of Yingying, is essential to the condoning of romance as an immoral but independent existence in "The Story of Yingying." Although late medieval literati storytellers usually claim their trustworthiness in writing down incidents that had actually occurred, "The Story of Yingying" is particularly concerned about authentication. The story presents, for instance, a convincing "reality" of the social milieu in which Zhang and the storyteller's literati friends, all historical personages, including Yuan Zhen, Yang Juyuan (ca. 755–ca. 833), and Li Shen, accept and respond to the love affair as a real incident. Moreover, the story offers Yingying's "self-representations" as evidence for her existence. Although Zhang is said to have seduced Yingying with poems, they are not included; by contrast, Yingying's writings through different stages of the love affair are provided. With its pleasant images of the moon, the breeze, and gently swaying flowers, her first poem in response to Zhang's poems of seduction vividly portrays the state of mind of an innocent girl who has not yet experienced love and is full of positive expectations for this first rendezvous. Yingying's letter to Zhang after his final departure conveys her sadness and longing over his absence, her hope for his continuing devotion, and her anxiety that he will abandon her. In the words of Stephen Owen, the letter is "a beautiful example of Tang eloquence, in which feeling, rhetoric, and gracious deference are held in a delicate balance."[104] In addition, Yingying's last two poems to Zhang after their breakup describe her complex emotions and her resolution to put her romantic escapade behind her. Her writings thus chronicle a young woman's touching emotional journey. The effect of authenticity is so compelling that the long-standing interpretation has conflated the "I" narrator, the hero Zhang, the internal character Yuan Zhen, and the historical poet Yuan Zhen, treating the story as Yuan's autobiographical account of his affair with Yingying.

The authenticated female subjectivity in the story, however, is also conventional. In her last two poems, Yingying adopts the persona of the abandoned woman found in earlier poetry.[105] In addition, her other voices—as an innocent girl anticipating love and a pathetic

young woman worrying about her insecure status—are also traditional feminine personae established in the male literary tradition.
Although Owen is right in stating that "Yingying is a young woman
performing an image of romantic passion,"[106] it is in fact the *male*
expectation of female passion that she tries to fulfill. Her voices attain
coherence and authenticity because of the conventional constructions
of female subjectivity, while her perceived authenticity in turn inte-
grates and substantiates earlier poetic imaginings of romantic heroines by male writers.

By authenticating Yingying, however, the story presents her as
Zhang's real, willing accomplice in their romantic escapade and
hence foregrounds romance as an immoral yet irresistible tempta-
tion for young people. Zhang and Yingying exemplify the gender-
specific struggles of coming to terms with the immorality of romance.
Although Zhang has a reputation for being self-restrained and, as a
savior of her family, is in a good position to ask for her hand in marriage, he justifies his choice of romance by citing the intensity of his
passion: because Yingying's beauty completely overwhelms him, his
life is jeopardized by his strong desire; he thus cannot wait out the
time-consuming process of marriage arrangements. Displacing his
interest in romantic fulfillment with that of saving his own life, he
evades the moral stigma of romance with a shift of focus to its life-
saving power.

Such ethical evasion is impossible for Yingying. To be involved in
romance, she has to break away from propriety; the two cannot coexist, and yet, paradoxically, they must. Without romantic passions,
the virtuous Yingying would not enter into the liaison, and romance
would not be possible. Without virtue, the romantic Yingying would
be indistinguishable from a licentious woman. The tension between
romance and propriety is so strong that the shift in Yingying's persona causes her to appear to become a completely different person,
as she first berates and rejects Zhang and then voluntarily goes to see
him, staying silent throughout their first sexual consummation. The
absence of Yingying's self-justification for her choice of romance is no
coincidence: it is in fact impossible to justify. Her predicament shows
that the ideological conflict between romantic and patriarchal values
in the case of an unmarried daughter is specifically a contest for control of the heroine's sexual body. An earlier narrative, "The Story of
a Detached Soul" (Lihun ji) by Chen Xuanyou (fl. 766–780), offers a
fanciful resolution. In this story, the girl's soul elopes with her beloved

while her body remains sick at home; the soul, with full corporeality, produces two sons, and upon its return reunites with the body.[107] Yingying's dilemma, however, originates from the painful reality that she has only one body—a body that both romance and propriety want to claim.

The different pressures of romance and social propriety on Zhang and Yingying further reveal a conflict of male and female interests regarding the prospect of their relationship. Yingying's plight is not resolved by her decision to embrace romance, but is rather intensified by it. Her letter to Zhang after he leaves for the capital conveys a female perspective on the liaison:

> You charmed me, like that gentleman [i.e., Sima Xiangru] playing the zither [for Zhuo Wenjun]. I did not refuse you, like the girl who threw her shuttle [at her seducer]. When I presented my pillow and mat [to share with you], your devotion was strong and your feeling deep. Out of my naïve love, I thought I had found my eternal commitment. How could I have foreseen that after I had met with you, I could not make you settle your love on me? Now that I bear the shame of offering myself to you [in private], I can no longer openly serve you as a wife. I harbor eternal regret until I die, sighing without anything else to say. If, being a benevolent person, you deign to have any regard for [me in my] obscurity, even on the day of my death, [my love] will be as in that year of my life [when we met]. But if, as an intelligent scholar, you take our love lightly, leaving aside the insignificant for the important because you think a previous liaison is shameful, that an oath of love can be violated, my sincere heart will never die even after my bones have dissolved and my form has vanished. Riding on the winds and dews, my spirit will still follow the dust of your graceful movements. My sincerity, whether in life or death, is exhausted with these words. Weeping as I compose this letter, I cannot fully express my feelings.[108]

This letter indicates that Yingying is in effect trapped by romance. Although she has the power to decide whether to begin the liaison, Zhang has the final say on whether to end it. Since her voluntary choice of romance is at the same time her willing deviation from propriety, a decent return to propriety becomes difficult, if not impossible. To be a good wife is to observe the rules of propriety, but she has shown that she is capable of transgressing them. Only if Zhang were to agree to initiate the proper procedures of a marriage arrangement through a matchmaker could Yingying achieve a smooth transition from romantic heroine to wife. The sophisticated rhetoric of her letter subtly begs Zhang to marry her, a painstaking yet futile effort that points to the tragic fact of her powerlessness as a romantic heroine.

By contrast, Zhang is not interested in turning romance into marriage. The incompatibility between romance and propriety enables Zhang to conveniently evade one or the other, first for his entry into the liaison and later for his exit from it. He labels her a manipulative "creature of bewitching beauty," like other notorious femmes fatales in history. He thus justifies his decision to abandon Yingying in terms of his moral courage to escape the evil influence of her beauty and to return from his deviation, claiming a lesson of male moral maturation.[109] Meanwhile, with her letter as trophy and evidence, Zhang divulges his affair with Yingying to his friends, an act consistent with his refusal to marry her. To him, romance is only an erotic experience, about which he can brag and which does not necessitate any long-term commitment. By introducing Yingying to the world as his lover rather than his wife, Zhang decisively keeps romance intact by, paradoxically, terminating it and thus preventing it from evolving into marriage. Although Zhang makes the same decision as Li Yi, he is luckier than Li because Yingying does not turn into another Huo Xiaoyu, but swallows her regret and marries someone else.

Through a verisimilar account of the formation and dissolution of the couple's liaison, the story creates a radical disconnection between their subversion of and resubmission to patriarchal authority. Both Zhang and Yingying flout the constraints of patriarchy to pursue their romantic passions. Due to their irreconcilable gendered interests, however, their bold, joint romantic escapade falls apart and they return to their own proper social roles. Yingying's rejection of Zhang's request to see her again after their breakup indicates that as a wife, she now belongs to her husband and is no longer accessible for romance. If the conventional stories of the daughter in love make the subversion of and submission to patriarchy a linear development that subsumes and dissolves the dangerous power of romance, "The Story of Yingying" disrupts such a smooth process to retain the ambiguities of subversion and submission. On one hand, romance takes shape because of the couple's willing transgression of patriarchal values; it also fails because the lovers' internalized patriarchal values tear them apart (Yingying wants to become a legitimate wife, but Zhang wants a virtuous one). On the other hand, although the failure of romance may signal a victory for patriarchy, the return of the mavericks also destabilizes its very foundation: the faithful wife has a prehistory as a romantic heroine, of which her husband is oblivious. Through the inevitabilities of this "authentic" liaison, the story also demonstrates that despite its immoral nature, romance attains its own legitimacy, a right that originates not from patriarchal endorsement but from the mere facts of life.

This factuality of romance makes it possible to further embolden it as a legitimate story subject while upholding patriarchal values. The story achieves such paradoxical maneuvers through its detailed description of the reception of the love story within the contemporary literati community. The poetic responses of Zhang's literati friends exemplify an amoral, aesthetic approach. Yang Juyuan's quatrain, "Poem on Miss Cui" (Cui niang shi), envisions Zhang alone in a poetic scene reading Yingying's letter and displaying his strong emotional reactions to it. The fact that Yang uses the letter only as a love token indicates that, rather than confronting its underlying tensions, he is interested in creating a poetically sentimental surface of romance. Likewise, Yuan Zhen's long poem, a continuation of Zhang's "Poem on Encountering a Perfected One" (Huizhen shi), projects the couple's meeting in the conventional mode of a mortal man encountering an immortal lady. Yuan first introduces the heroine as seen from afar, and then shows the details of her clothing, her coiffure, and her shoes, before providing a glimpse of her beautiful face. She is brought even closer when she overcomes her reservations and moves into the bed:

> Being shy, she knitted her painted eyebrows slightly;
> Because of warmth, her lip rouge melted even more.
> Her clear breath was as fragrant as orchid flowers;
> Her skin was smooth and her fair muscles plump.
> Languid, she would scarcely move her wrists;
> Full of coyness, she tended to draw herself close.
> Her sweat flowed, like drops of pearls;
> Her hair was in disorder, lush and black.[110]

After elaborating on the climactic sexual intercourse, the poem describes the sad separation that follows in moving terms. The poem avoids addressing its moral implications, and centers instead on the sentimental and amorous aspects of the sexual encounter. Thus Yang's and Yuan's poems both position the love affair not in the moral dimension but in the poetic tradition of love, sex, and feelings.

At the same time, "The Story of Yingying" also presents a didactic approach that treats Zhang and Yingying's affair as a moral lesson. The storyteller states:

Many contemporaries of Zhang praised him as someone good at cor-
recting his mistakes. I have often told this story during gatherings
with my friends. This is so that those who know the story will not
make the same mistake, or if they have, will not become confused. In
the ninth month of a certain year during the Zhenyuan reign [785–
805], minister Li Shen stayed at my house in the Jing'an Ward [of the
capital]. Our conversations led me to recount this story. Astonished,
he proclaimed it extraordinary and then composed "The Ballad of
Yingying" to commemorate the heroine. Ms. Cui's personal name
was Yingying, which he used as the title of his ballad.[111]

While the opinions of Zhang's contemporaries and the storyteller
echo Meng Jian's advice on a timely breakup, the emphasis here is
on the immoral nature of romance. This moralistic injunction to repudiate or avoid romance altogether represents the literati commitment to patriarchal values.

By including both the aesthetic and the didactic approach, "The
Story of Yingying" tries to achieve an ambiguous balance between
endorsing romance as a positive story subject and condemning it as
an immoral act. To endorse romance would be to encourage transgressive acts, but a negative projection of romance would also make
its appreciation problematic, if not impossible. The presumed authenticity of Yingying and her illicit affair provide an ultimate rhetorical
refuge. On one hand, poets are so amazed by this liaison that they
write poems about it. On the other hand, by stating that he passes
on this "real-life" love story as a moral lesson, the storyteller emphasizes that telling this subversive story will help prevent similar subversions in the future. Nonetheless, he shows no sense of irony when
he tells us that his narration of the love story only prompts his friend
Li Shen to produce an enthusiastic poetic rendition, "The Ballad of
Yingying," which, though not included, must have been similar to the
poems by Yang Juyuan and Yuan Zhen. Ending the story with this
revelation destabilizes the storyteller's self-projection as a moralist,
calling attention to the potential hypocrisy of his proclaimed didactic
agenda.

This hypocrisy is confirmed by the gender asymmetry underlying the didactic and aesthetic approaches. The moral lesson that the
storyteller champions is meant for scholar-officials who could find
themselves in Zhang's position. Meanwhile, the story avoids any
explicit moral judgment on Yingying and remains sympathetic to her
throughout. That is, the story is more interested in her as a romantic
heroine than as a negative example of womanhood. While poets in

the story offer morally neutral renditions that aestheticize Yingying and her romantic escapade, "The Story of Yingying" itself chronicles her moving, realistic struggles to meet the incompatible demands of romance and social propriety. Both the aesthetic poems by the internal audience and the verisimilar oral and prose accounts of the storyteller in effect commemorate her romantic heroism, not in terms of martyrdom, as in the cases of Huo Xiaoyu or Bu Feiyan, but in terms of her knowing embrace of romance and willing acceptance of the consequences.

"The Story of Yingying" thus delineates acceptable modes of representing romance as a morally problematic story subject. While the didactic approach in the verisimilar mode of retelling is a morally correct stance, the aesthetic approach in the poetic mode is a morally detached position. They constitute complementary ways of legitimating textual representations of romantic transgressions that directly challenge patriarchal authority. Moreover, the story also naturalizes these modes by presenting them as the consequences of the power of romance to set in motion an unstoppable chain of discourse development. Zhang's disclosure of his liaison prompts his friends to write poems, which the storyteller includes in his detailed account, and the storyteller's own narration further inspires his friend's poetic production. Through this endless lineage of discourse proliferation, "The Story of Yingying" demonstrates that the aesthetic and didactic modes are mutually constitutive and that literati storytelling can achieve the paradoxical goal of affirming both romantic and patriarchal values within carefully circumscribed limits.

Moreover, the story also shows how, in this irrepressible discourse proliferation, Yingying becomes an iconic lover for the literati community at large. This "real" girl who cannot resist the seduction of romance and embraces it audaciously enables literati storytellers and audiences to reimagine her romantic adventure and to participate in it vicariously. Yuan Zhen's "Poem on Encountering a Perfected One," for instance, is a continuation of Zhang's original poem. Here it does not seem to matter that an outsider who had no actual experience with Yingying can take on Zhang's perspective and write about it. In reenacting Zhang's sexual experiences, Yuan's poem gradually exposes Yingying's eroticized body, the sensual details of which invite the reader's caressing gazes and even touches. This beautiful body that Yuan carefully unveils in his poem is no longer that of an elusive unworldly goddess as in the poetic convention, but that of the "authentic" Yingying. The vicarious nature of enjoyment, however, also indicates how the literati discourse on romance tests the limit of patriarchal control but never really exceeds it.

Our examination of romance and the related themes of male sexual competition and adultery expands our understanding of late medieval love stories and the construction of literati sexual identity therein. While romance can be said to denote an autonomous, private space in terms of an intimate sexual relationship, or a social space in terms of its facilitation of literati competition and bonding, nonmarital bonds in general represent a platform for negotiating the fundamental power relations in the central domains of literati life. This important aspect explains the peculiar ways in which these stories present and resolve the social tensions surrounding the sexual relationship. These tensions do not emanate simply from a conflict between the young couple's pursuit of freedom for love and the feudal society that denied it, as conventionally believed, but, more precisely, from a basic paradox of subversion and submission underlying the relationship of the literatus with social authorities.

This paradox accounts for late medieval literati storytellers' contradictory maneuvers in delineating the nature and parameters of literati sexual identity. On one hand, nonmarital bonds are used to challenge the authority of the social senior and the patriarchal family. On the other, such subversion is balanced with self-containment, revealing that the sexual challenge is not meant to really overthrow these power hierarchies. The construction of literati sexual identity thus entails combining and sequencing these opposing tendencies: the subordinate may deviate from and resist his superior, but he will eventually return and submit in order to keep open the possibilities of moving up the ladder (to become the social senior and the patriarch). If literati sociality and sovereignty define the normative order of literati life, nonmarital bonds allow scholar-officials both to take issue with and become part of that order. It is in this sense that literati sexual identity constituted a crucial dimension of late medieval scholar-officials' myth of empowerment. Meanwhile, the paradox also betrayed deep literati ambivalences toward the powers and limits of this sexual identity.

The late medieval constructions of literati sexual identity also define a new mode of literati relationship with women vis-à-vis social authorities. By affirming male sexual competition and romance, storytellers portray women as allies to the literatus as sexual adventurer in his temporary "rebellion" against social authorities. This representation departs from the poetic convention in which literati poets identified with or employed a feminine position in defining their relationship with the superior; it also differs from the traditional moralistic perspective that viewed beautiful women as competitors of courtiers for the lord's favor.[112] Although the active roles of women as literati allies in late medieval stories seem to confirm historians' belief in the higher social status of Tang women in general compared to their later counterparts,[113] we need to note the constructed nature and inherent contradictions of these female images. In their strong subjectivities, romance heroines, including Li Wa, Huo Xiaoyu, and Cui Yingying, bear the tension between romantic and patriarchal values, facilitating the literati heroes' deviation and return. As a result, the male figures appear much more ineffectual or passive, so much so that they become the prototype for the later "fragile scholar."[114] Meanwhile, the denunciations of adulterous wives and concubines also demonstrate literati storytellers' anxieties about the sexual power of women to threaten the foundations of patriarchy. By contrast, stories of male sexual competition carefully control female characters, in effect reducing them to trophies for literati heroes. These different images of women reveal the literati ambivalence toward female sexuality, the power of which could be enlisted to serve the purposes of men but which always threatened to escape their control.

Although late medieval stories of literati nonmarital bonds sometimes invoke supernatural elements (such as the ghosts of Huo Xiaoyu and Bu Feiyan), the vicissitudes of sexual identity empower scholar-officials within the decidedly earthly, social world. In stories about literati experiences of the supernatural, late medieval literati storytellers also try to explore more fantastic means of dealing with the institutional constraints of literati life.

CHAPTER 4

Cosmic Mobility

The Possibility and Impossibility
of Moving Beyond

While stories of literati nonmarital bonds demarcate a periphery outside the central domains of literati life, narratives of cosmic mobility relativize these domains by situating them in the expansive dimension of the cosmos. Late medieval literati storytellers present officialdom, the embodiment of the normative pattern of literati life, as the reference point of this cosmos. On one hand, such constructions naturalize officialdom as the inescapable destiny of scholar-officials by justifying their centrality in a bureaucratically defined cosmos. On the other hand, storytellers also explore ways for scholar-officials to move beyond officialdom. As a vast physical and conceptual space, the cosmos thus allows these storytellers to define a literati cosmic identity, situating the privileged places, movements, and powers of scholar-officials in a greater scheme that enables them to rationalize or transcend the structural constraints of literati life.

Late medieval stories about literati cosmic mobility were in line with the traditional *zhiguai* in terms of subject. These "records of the strange" are usually reportage-style accounts that describe human observations of and interactions with supernatural beings and forces, although modern scholars have classified some longer, more complex stories as "tales of the marvelous." Early medieval anomaly accounts that mark the formation of the *zhiguai* genre are extremely heterogeneous, expressing the worldviews of esoteric masters, Daoist practitioners and exponents, Buddhist monks and laypersons, Confucian historians, bibliographers, academicians, and so on.[1] These stories feature characters from all walks of life and have often been seen as indices of popular religious beliefs and folk customs. While scholar-officials appear quite frequently as major or secondary figures in these accounts, their experiences of the supernatural constituted but one segment of the wide spectrum of the strange in the cosmos that early medieval writers tried to capture in their collections. In the most famous compilation from the period, *In Search of Spirits* (Soushen ji) by Gan Bao (fl. 317–336), for instance, accounts featuring scholar-officials make up roughly one third of the extant 498 entries.[2]

By comparison, late medieval literati storytellers seem to be much more interested in accounts of scholar-officials' encounters with the supernatural.[3] This tendency is already visible in pre-rebellion *zhiguai* collections. Although a comprehensive counting is not feasible, since many collections have been lost or have survived only in portions, a cursory look into a few extant examples can still be instructive. In the *Records of Miraculous Retribution* (Mingbao ji) by Tang Lin (600–659), for instance, about 60 percent of his entries feature scholar-officials.[4] Moreover, judging from extant entries, most pre-rebellion collections seem to be inclined toward Buddhist- or Daoist-related themes, indicating the particular compilers' religious agendas or personal interests. Tang Lin, for one, was a pious lay Buddhist. By contrast, post-rebellion literati storytellers were more concerned with supernatural phenomena in general but scholar-officials' experiences in particular. In Niu Sengru's *Collection of the Mysterious and the Strange* (Xuanguai lu), 80 percent of his accounts center on scholar-officials, while the *Sequel to the Collection of the Mysterious and the Strange* (Xu Xuanguai lu) by Li Fuyan (fl. 830–847) includes only one entry without literati figures.[5] Although late medieval literati storytellers carry on the earlier diverse themes on the supernatural, their thematic innovations and their preoccupations with the experiences of scholar-officials also indicate their efforts to explore the powers and positions of literati in the cosmos, or to delineate a literati cosmic identity.

The following analysis focuses on four groups of narratives to illustrate the tensions and ambiguities in these identity constructions, which grapple in particular with literati cosmic mobility vis-à-vis officialdom, the embodiment of the structural constraints of literati life. Stories about predetermined fate rationalize officialdom as the collective destiny of scholar-officials, promoting a faith in certainty and passivity to alleviate the pressures of fierce competition on individuals. By contrast, stories of the underworld bureaucracy represent a belief that scholar-officials can have active roles in exploiting the bureaucratic power of officialdom, which extends into the realm of the afterlife. Despite their contrary perspectives, these two groups of stories endow the structural constraint of literati life with positive meaning and promote attitudes of acceptance.

Meanwhile, literati storytellers also explore the fantastic possibility of moving beyond the limitation of officialdom. Stories about becoming immortals affirm fantasies of literati physical mobility in the cosmos and advance optimistic visions of leaving the world behind for better alternatives. By contrast, accounts of literati experiences of officialdom in dreams advocate an epistemic mobility, turning the relativity of dreaming and waking into new ways of subverting the control of literati life by officialdom. Late medieval literati storytellers' visions of cosmic mobility are thus filled with contradictions, demonstrating the deep divides among late medieval scholar-officials as well as their persistent efforts to come to terms with the inescapable, normative pattern of literati life. Contradictions notwithstanding, and despite their wish-fulfilling nature, these visions also affirm the privileged status of scholar-officials in the cosmos and offer a wide range of solutions for them to further expand the reach of their actions.

EMBEDDED IN LIFE: A PREDETERMINED FATE

In late medieval stories, the concept of a predetermined fate—referred to in terms of *ming, dingming,* or *qianding*—naturalized the hold of officialdom on the lives of individuals. Given that the livelihood of late medieval scholar-officials depended on bureaucratic service, predetermined fate made it possible to rationalize the embedded status of scholar-officials in officialdom. Fate attributed to officialdom a supernatural authority and empowered individuals by justifying their sense of diminished personal agency and control over their own lives in the competitive literati community. The overall framework of fatalism in life, the limited scope of individual agency in officialdom, and the guaranteed success in marriage gave positive spins to this powerlessness through a reassurance that every scholar-official has his place and that literati life unfolds according to a divine design, so there is no need to fight it, or fight other scholar-officials, to get ahead.

From as early as the era of oracle-bone inscriptions, *ming* was a complex and variegated concept, the semantic nuances of which have been well analyzed by modern scholars.[6] Despite historical shifts in the meanings of *ming*, a fundamental tension between beliefs in its predetermined nature and in its malleability persisted. For instance, users of the almanac handbook *Daybook* (Ri shu, 216 BCE), likely common people, believed that their life course was preordained at the moment of birth, yet they tried to negotiate a better *ming* by using the text's instructions to guide their daily actions.[7] By the early medieval period, the idea of manipulating *ming* had become the focal point of many esoteric Daoist doctrines and practices. Clearly, many people were convinced that they could achieve longevity and even avoid death by performing good deeds, by using talismans and rituals to deceive the register-keeping spirits, or by creating refined embryonic versions of themselves.[8]

When late medieval literati storytellers evoked the idea of *ming*, however, they were preoccupied with how predetermined fate manifested in officialdom-centered literati life. While stories about fate can be seen in many collections, there were at least five devoted exclusively to the theme: the *Discourses on Predetermined Fate* (Dingming lun) by Zhao Ziqin, *Records of Predeterminations* (Qianding lu) by Zhong Lu, *Records of Predetermined Fate* (Dingming lu) by Lü Daosheng, the *Sequel to the Records of Predetermined Fate* (Xu Dingming lu) by Wen She, and the anonymous *Records of Reflections on Predetermined Fate* (Gan dingming lu). We know very little about these compilers. Zhao Ziqin served as Director of the Palace Library during the Tianbao reign (742–756). Zhong Lu compiled his collection during the Dahe reign (827–835), when he served as Editor in the Palace Library at the beginning of his career. He is often taken to be the same person as Zhong Lu, who passed the Presented Scholar examination in 828. Lü Daosheng was a contemporary of Zhong Lu, while Wen She was active at court during roughly the same period and is sometimes referred to as Wen Hui. The unknown author of the *Records of Reflections on Predetermined Fate* is believed to have lived in the post-Tang era.[9] Despite the scarcity of information on these storytellers, their collections demonstrate a continuing interest in stories about fate in the late medieval literati community.

These stories usually describe how fate unfolds in the lives of past scholar-officials in relation to predictions regarding their respective lifespans, career advancement, and marriages, the most important aspects of literati life in the matrix of officialdom. The perspective of fate represents a faith in certainty and a philosophy of passivity,

much needed in a highly uncertain, competitive social world. Zhong
Lu states in the preface to his *Records of Predeterminations* that he
"only hopes that scholar-officials with thorough understandings will
know that [predetermined fate] is not spurious and that folks bus-
tling around and competing with each other [for personal advance-
ment] will also use it to caution themselves."[10] Striving for success
was, however, precisely the living reality of late medieval scholar-officials. As we have noted in chapter 2, the Presented Scholar examination had a success rate of only 2 to 5 percent. Although most people
earned their eligibility through other avenues, the great disproportion
between available positions and eligible appointees made competition
unprecedentedly fierce in the second half of the dynasty. Since evalua-
tions and recommendations by superiors and supporters were crucial
for official appointments at court or to the staffs of military governors, forging and sustaining advantageous social connections was
imperative. Expressions of individuals' sense of vulnerability and lack
of control in the treacherous sociopolitical world were commonplace.

Accounts of inexorable fate thus allay anxieties about such uncertainties by offering a comforting vision that things will work out
the way they are supposed to. Zhong Lu's collection, for instance,
includes a story of Li Kui (711–784), in which a scholar and fortune-
teller named Wang not only predicts Li's imminent appointments but
also gives him a sealed envelope for later verification. Sure enough,
Li's first appointment fits Wang's description; soon after, his memorials on behalf of the head of his clan catch the attention of the emperor,
who promotes him to the rank of censor after testing him with three
topics of poetic composition. Li opens Wang's envelope as instructed
and discovers his three compositions inside, with the exact erasures
and modifications that he had made during his earlier impromptu
performance.[11] The story calls into question the hallmark of individual creativity, poetic talent, by depriving the poet of his agency: even
his drafting process is preordained. This theme is reiterated in other
stories, which describe how even the food one eats, something that is
subject to personal whims and circumstantial variations, is beyond
one's control.[12] In the words of Zhong Lu, "Even the slightest gain or
loss, going or stopping, drinking or eating—there is nothing that is
not predetermined."[13]

Fatalism alleviates one's sense of vulnerability not just through
a guarantee of patterns and outcomes but also through the introduction of higher authorities. Late medieval stories about fate and

scholar-officials do not address the question of how individuals' fates are determined, emphasizing instead the role of supernatural authorities as the true force behind official promotions and demotions. These higher authorities consist of heavenly and infernal bureaucracies, referred to in terms of "heaven" (tian), "celestial bureaucracy" (tiancao), "underworld offices" (difu), "bureaus of darkness" (mingsi), and so on. These supernatural bureaus conduct government surveillance on mortals and enforce what is in store for them in their ledgers of fate. Another story from Zhong Lu's collection describes how a skeptic is convinced of the working of these authorities:

> During the Kaiyuan reign [713–742], Ma Youqin, a clerk in the Ministry of Personnel, became eligible for reappointment after the end of his waiting period. Pei Guangting, then director of the Ministry, asked him what he desired in light of his former status as a ministry employee. Ma did not answer. Pei repeated his question and Ma said, "I already know [what] my new post [will be] and thus dare not put forward any request to you." Pei said, "That should be decided by me. How can you know [in advance]?" Ma did not respond, nor did he show any fear. Angrily, Pei said, "Since you already know, can you tell me?" Ma said, "I can write it down but cannot say it." Pei then ordered him to record it and concealed the paper in person between pillars and beams, expecting to open it [for verification] after the formal announcements of appointments. Later on, Lord Laozi manifested himself on Mount Li and the royal chariot of [the Illustrious Emperor] visited the locale. The emperor then ordered that the name of Encountering Prosperity County (Huichang xian) be changed to Clear Providence County (Zhaoying xian). There had never been any county named Clear Providence; therefore, thinking Ma had no way of knowing of it, Pei appointed him Office Manager of that county. On the day in which appointments were announced, Pei retrieved the paper he had hidden earlier and it turned out to be just as Ma had said, [for it recorded Ma's exact post in the renamed county].[14]

The story mocks Pei Guangting's (676–733) sense of power and control, revealing that he is as powerless as the clerk whose career path he appears to direct. The clerk Ma Youqin belongs to a special category of people featured in these stories that includes fortune-tellers, hermits, Buddhist monks, Daoist priests, and other mysterious figures who have access to information on the fate of individuals. His refusal to take advantage of Pei's offer of special consideration exemplifies the proper attitude to fate, namely, awaiting and accepting what is to come. In related twists on the theme, we also learn that when people in authority abuse their power to pursue

personal grudges, they end up unknowingly advancing their enemies' careers.[15] These stories drive home the point that an official's
confidence in his own authority is no more than self-delusion. The
conception of officialdom as a mere instrument of supernatural authorities thus subverts the social senior's domination of his junior
counterpart and, more generally, officialdom's seemingly incontro-
vertible control over its members.

Furthermore, thanks to its power to change individuals' existing
positions in the sociopolitical hierarchies, fate can offer poetic justice
for underdogs in officialdom and bring humiliation to dignitaries. In
one story from Lü Daosheng's *Records of Predetermined Fate*, Yuan
Jiazuo, an outstanding local official who wishes to expedite his reappointment, approaches two chief ministers and is scolded by them
for his eagerness. Greatly embarrassed, Yuan leaves and encounters
two men in yellow robes, presumably underworld clerks, who laugh
and tell him that he will soon be the judge presiding over the trial of
those two chief ministers.[16] The story emphasizes the reversibility of
the hierarchy between the superior and the subordinate, a change that
enables Yuan to get back at those high officials who treated him arro-
gantly and condescendingly. In another example, Cheng Xingchen
(634–726), who is teased and insulted by his colleagues for becoming only a county sheriff at the age of sixty, goes on to enjoy a long
and successful career that none of his tormentors can match.[17] The
story thus ridicules snobs who judge people according to their current
low stations. Nevertheless, even if one attains the two most desirable
goals for a scholar-official, longevity and the highest official positions, one is not necessarily immune to the irony of fate. In a story
about the chief minister Cui Yuanzong (fl. 690–705), for instance, a
fortune-teller predicts that he will be exiled but eventually return to
the same position and that he will live to the age of ninety-nine but
starve to death. It turns out that since he outlives other members of
his family and is too old to discipline his servants and maids, they fail
to take care of him.[18] These ironies of fate thus put a meaningful gloss
on the unpredictability of officialdom in particular and literati life in
general, conveying a sense of justice, vindication, or poignancy.

Paradoxically, however, fate as the driving force behind the vicissitudes of officialdom also legitimates it and in effect becomes the very
embodiment of its authority. Fatalism actually makes it possible to
rationalize social disparities. In another story from Zhong Lu's collection, a county sheriff named Liu Miaozhi is feasting his visiting cousin

Lu Kang (fl. 756–766) and two colleagues, Yang Yu and Zhang Yĭng, when a hermit insists on joining them and offers to predict their fates after the meal. According to the hermit, Yang Yu should avoid eating any donkey meat, and Zhang Yĭng should try to get along with his colleagues; Liu Miaozhi is expected to serve two terms as county magistrate and die twenty-five years later; only Lu Kang will become successful in the following year's examination and attain more than ten official posts. All of the hermit's predictions subsequently come true: Yang later dies from eating donkey meat and Zhang is killed by a colleague-turned-enemy, while the careers of Liu and Lu turn out exactly as foretold.[19] The story emphasizes how the four young men feasting together are originally at the same starting point, but their lives take drastically different courses. Although the differences in their fates seem unfair, they are as indisputable as they are arbitrary. In another telling story, when the chief minister Yao Chong is shocked to learn that Pei Guangting is destined to become a chief minister, he argues that Pei does not have the necessary talent (cai); the fortune-teller declares authoritatively that "talent and fate are definitely different."[20] In other words, everyone is equal in front of fate, which asserts its absolute power by making any personal qualities or efforts irrelevant.

This arbitrariness of fate thus effectively dissociates social disparities from the imperfections and injustices of official institutions, validating the status quo. In a story about the chief minister Li Fan (754–811), for example, we are told that the underworld bureaucracy covers the future chief ministers with invisible gauze cages in order to protect them from any harm.[21] In another account, the seemingly good-for-nothing Wei Gao (745–805) is despised by his father-in-law, chief minister Zhang Yanshang (727–787). A female shaman points out, however, that Wei is constantly accompanied by more than a hundred underworld clerks, an invisible entourage much larger than Zhang's own, which indicates Wei's future prominence.[22] Emphasizing the divine protection of future high officials, these stories show how fate naturalizes the institutional reality of officialdom by reauthorizing its power hierarchy. Thus, at the heart of fatalism there is a call for full submission to the authority of officialdom qua fate. This is consistent with Wang Dingbao's promotion of fate as a fundamental mechanism for the examination community to dissolve their resentments in the face of inevitable setbacks, as discussed in chapter 2.

Late medieval literati's advocacy of fatalism, however, does not mean a complete renunciation of individual agency, for they also subscribed to the ideal of individuals improving their lots and those of their family members. The underworld clerks who come to enforce death decrees and arrest souls can be persuaded or bribed to help the condemned.[23] In addition, a foreknowledge of fate could be used to guide personal actions, especially in trying times. This is illustrated in the case of chief minister Wei Yuanzhong, who attempts suicide several times through years of turmoil but gives up because he recalls his fortune-teller's prediction of his future prominence.[24] Likewise, warnings of future harm enable people to avoid or reduce it by taking appropriate measures. In a story about the chief minister Li Bi (722–789), a fortune-teller reveals to the official Dou Tingzhi that his family will be executed unless he can befriend the then-obscure Li. Dou does this, and, as it turns out, when Dou is later implicated in the rebellion of Zhu Ci (742–784), Li, now a chief minister, intervenes on his behalf.[25] The fortune-tellers themselves also try to take advantage of their privileged knowledge of the future by entrusting their sons to the would-be dignitaries that they recognize and advise.[26] Although these stories contradict those of fatalism, they provide a different, complementary reassurance: while it is futile to fight the institution of officialdom qua fate, it is possible to make the best out of it within limits, through knowing the right information and the right person. In this regard, stories of individual agency help to prevent the pessimistic extreme of nihilism and strengthen the legitimation of officialdom by fate.

Since such stories may risk fostering overconfidence about knowing or even tampering with the future, late medieval literati storytellers also include accounts that assert the limits of individual agency. In a story about Li Jiongxiu (d. 712), Director of the Ministry of War, for instance, he is not worried about his illness because he believes that he is destined to reach the high position of Director of the Chancellery; he soon dies and is posthumously awarded that title.[27] Li's self-assurance is mocked because fate is inherently uncertain, always awaits verification, and hence demands awe and humility. In another story, an old fortune-teller gives the future chief minister Zhang Jiazhen two scrolls listing his official posts. Sure enough, Zhang's career unfolds consistently with the listing on the first scroll. Later, when he becomes ill, he does not anticipate the end of his life because there is another scroll still unopened and he thinks there are more posts to come. He dies shortly after he opens this second scroll, which turns out to be filled only with the character *kong* (empty).[28] Although it is not clear whether the old man means well when he gives Zhang an extra scroll, it is after all fate's joke on Zhang. We are also told, for example, that having learned of an imminent disaster associated with *ma*, the prefect Huan Chenfan (fl. 713–715) carefully avoids horses (*ma*) but later suffers at the hands of a bad acupuncturist named Ma.[29] The ironic twists in these stories thus highlight the limited capacity of human beings to circumvent the operation of inscrutable fate.

In endorsing fatalism, however, such ironic stories inadvertently highlight the vulnerability of scholar-officials, a vulnerability that literati storytellers remedy by displacing it onto women. Stories about fate in marriage offer a more optimistic picture of literati life. While these stories also rationalize the imposition of fate, specifically the arranged marriage, on individuals, they dramatize the futility of personal efforts in more light-hearted ways. In the story of Zheng Tao's beautiful wife, for example, a female shaman foretells the physical appearance of the beauty's future husband on the eve of her wedding, a description that does not match her betrothed, the scholar Lu. In the middle of the ceremony, however, Lu suddenly turns and flees because he sees that the bride has "two red eyes as big as wine cups, with inches-long teeth coming out the two corners of her mouth."[30] Lu's friend Zheng Tao, whose appearance conforms to the shaman's description, then marries the girl. Here the original bridegroom's terrifying vision is attributed to the working of fate, which seems to have played a joke on the characters involved. In the well-known story "The Inn of Betrothal" (Dinghun dian), the protagonist Wei Gu willfully fights his fate by trying to murder a poor, ugly toddler who is destined to be his wife. Fourteen years later, after he is happily married to a beautiful wife, he finds out that she was indeed that little girl, as evidenced by the scar in between her eyebrows from the wound he inflicted.[31] Although Wei Gu's attempted murder may be horrifying to modern sensibilities, the action is meant to be laughable in its desperation and futility.

In these stories about preordained marriage, the disparity between the ages of the couple is significant because it marks the inequality between them. Wei Gu is at least twenty years older than his wife. In another story, Cui Yuanzong marries his nineteen-year-old bride after he turns fifty-eight.[32] These enormous age differences epitomize the arbitrary nature of fate, but they also reveal the gender-specific implications of acquiescing to the imposition of marriage arrangements. Male protagonists get married late in life but still enjoy an advantageous, ideal union with a young, beautiful girl from a respectable family. For these girls, however, marrying a much older man truly represents the unfairness of fate, to which they must submit. While these stories of preordained marriage justify and even romanticize the institution of arranged marriage, they do so from a male perspective, which in turn reveals that these young women are the principal victims of an arbitrary and even violent institution. The response of Wei Gu's bride after learning of his earlier attempted murder makes her an exemplary wife: she is neither scared nor resentful, but amazed and becomes even more devoted than before to her husband and would-be murderer. The happy endings of these stories thus reiterate the gender hierarchy in an arranged marriage.

Predetermined fate thus naturalizes officialdom as an inescapable reality for scholar-officials by mitigating their sense of powerlessness and endowing their embedded status with positive meaning. Whereas stories about the disparities in officialdom reveal strong anxieties about the uncertainties of the political realm for literati, those of marriage offer reassurance of their advantageous, favorable position in the marital domain. This further confirms what we have seen in chapter 3, that literati storytellers endorse literati romance only so far, but not to the point of endangering mastery over their wives and concubines. With the emphases on gender hierarchy and limited agency in the larger framework of officialdom qua fate, late medieval storytellers effectively transform the structural constraint of officialdom into something positive, a collective destiny that is endorsed by supernatural authorities and that scholar-officials, the privileged ones at least, can accept and have faith in.

NEGOTIATING DEATH: THE UNDERWORLD BUREAUCRACY

While fate predetermines a scholar-official's officialdom-centered life, death does not really bring it to an end, but leads him into the underworld, where another bureaucracy reigns. Late medieval stories about literati experiences of the Bureau of Darkness are preoccupied with how scholar-officials can collaborate with one another, thereby exploiting officialdom. Although these stories advocate an activism vis-à-vis officialdom that is in stark contrast to the fatalism discussed above, this activist perspective still reinforces the structural constraints of literati life, for officialdom simply extends into the afterlife. In fact, activism represents an opposite but complementary angle from which late medieval literati storytellers further rationalize officialdom. If, by reauthorizing officialdom, fatalism helps scholar-officials dissolve internal tensions in the community due to fierce competition and social disparity, activism allows them to assert their class solidarity.

The idea of an afterlife that was governed by a bureaucratic system had already been firmly established by the second century BCE.[33] A dualistic view of the soul—in which the lighter, upward-moving *hun* of a human being persists, while the heavier earth-bound *po* gradually decays after death—had become dominant, and the departed *hun* souls were subjected to an underworld administration conceived in the image of the Han imperial government. Reinforced by the new influence of Buddhism, which offered a systematic imagining of post-mortem judgment and punishment, ancestors were no longer seen as powerful gods that could confer or withhold blessings, as in the Shang (ca. 16th–11th century BCE) and Zhou (ca. 11th century–256 BCE) eras, but pathetic spirits under the jurisdiction of infernal deities such as the Yellow Emperor and the Lord of Mount Tai (Taishan fujun). Buddhist and Daoist liturgical developments and popular religious movements catered to this bureaucratic model by providing methods of delivery from and even avoidance of this morbid afterlife.[34] By the tenth century, belief in a purgatory ruled by ten kings had become widespread. Of both indigenous and foreign origins, these kings were said to review the detailed records of the deceased's life and then mete out punishment accordingly before decreeing the deceased's ultimate path of rebirth. To offer relief to the spirit of the deceased, family members prepared sutras, food, paper money, and other offerings, and performed mortuary rites at specific intervals timed to fit the scheduled tribunals of the Ten Kings.[35]

Stories about encounters with the underworld bureaucracy, however, are often "return-from-death" narratives featuring individuals who are actually able to escape the terrifying purgatorial process, albeit temporarily, and come back to life. To explain why early medieval anomaly accounts seem more concerned with ghosts than with ancestors, Robert Campany points out that "the ancestral cult was part of the normal, assumed background of life against which strange events stood out; it became an instance of the 'strange' only when relations between ancestors and their descendants took an unusual turn."[36] The same may also be said of return-from-death stories. They are noteworthy because they describe the extraordinary experiences of individuals reversing what seems to be an inexorable journey down the path of death. The early medieval return-from-death accounts emerged at a time when the bureaucratic model of the underworld was taking shape. They established a range of conventions in presenting death as "a bureaucratic event," in terms of the arrest, questioning, and dismissal of individuals' souls by infernal bureaucrats.[37]

By comparison, late medieval return-from-death stories show not only the imprints of earlier conventions in terms of narrative structure and basic elements, but also distinctive literati interests and innovations. While such stories are scattered across different collections, the *Extensive Records of the Extraordinary* (Guangyi ji) by Dai Fu (fl. 757–771) includes the largest number of them and will therefore serve as our primary example for analysis, supplemented with other sources when necessary.[38] Dai Fu passed the Presented Scholar examination in 757 and served only in provincial posts. The collection has a preface by Dai's more famous classmate, the poet Gu Kuang (ca. 727– ca. 816). Although not extant in its entirety, the collection still boasts more than three hundred entries, dispersed in later encyclopedias and other compilations.[39] The return-from-death stories in Dai Fu's extant corpus all feature local scholar-officials at or below the middle ranks, an indication of his story sources and his career associations.[40]

Dai Fu's entries demonstrate important thematic developments in late medieval return-from-death accounts. In one story, for example, the protagonist Fei Ziyu, Adjutant of Qianwei Prefecture, who is keenly aware of the motif in which people are sent back from death because of mistaken identities and other bureaucratic glitches, tells King Yama that he is the Adjutant of Jiazhou Prefecture instead. The perceptive King Yama scorns his deceit but eventually lets him go because of the intervention of Dizang Bodhisattva (Dizang pusa or Kṣitigarbha), whose assistance Fei requests upon his arrival, a convention in the cult of the Ten Kings that he apparently puts to good use.[41] Fei's use of his knowledge is not meant to parody earlier conventions; it signifies his status as a bureaucratic insider who understands how the system works. This illustrates a feature shared by late medieval return-from-death stories: they are less concerned about the nature of the underworld bureaucracy than about how scholar-officials could navigate and even take advantage of it.

Scholar-officials are well positioned to take advantage of the Bureau of Darkness because of similarities and continuities with its counterpart in the world of light. The worlds of men and of spirits were both believed to be governed by the same kind of centralized, bureaucratic power.[42] Moreover, both bureaucracies drew from the same pool of scholar-officials, the only eligible candidates.[43] Late medieval stories emphasize in particular the friendship of scholar-officials across the divide of life and death. In another story from Dai Fu's collection, for example, the mountain-dwelling scholar-official Chang Yi befriends the ghost of Zhu Jun, whose tomb is nearby and who serves as an underworld functionary. When Chang becomes ill, Zhu explains that it is because a leading infernal bureaucrat wants to appoint Chang to his staff. As a result of the encouragement of his friend, Chang is pleased with the prospect of death, and, after refusing medicine for several days, passes away.[44] Death thus enables the hermit-like Chang to enter officialdom and enjoy the company of his friend indefinitely in the afterlife.

Such friendship easily translates into more practical benefits of power and status. In earlier stories, a scholar-official might recommend to an underworld deity that another person fill an office that he himself has been summoned for; such a recommendation would be self-serving and even vicious, as the scholar-official saves himself at the cost of a colleague's life. Although a living man's reluctance to accept an underworld appointment is still a common theme, late medieval stories emphasize the advantages of such a post, presenting a more positive image of peer recommendation. The story of Du You's (735–812) recommendation of his former colleague Ma Zong (d. 823) is a good example. Clearly a popular one, the story has multiple versions. The version in the *Records of Collecting the Extraordinary* (Jiyi ji) by Xue Yongruo (fl. 806–827) is short: Ma wakes up from a dream and recounts how he saw the deceased Du, who now serves in the powerful underworld position equivalent to a secretariat directorship, and who has nominated Ma as his replacement. After Ma's repeated objections, Du allows him to return to the waking (living) world with a prediction of their future reunion in twenty years, but Ma actually dies two years later.[45] Although missing an ending, a later and longer version identifies the position as a military one, campaign commander (*dutong*), and portrays a lengthy exchange of Du's entreaties and Ma's rejections.[46] Despite Ma's resistance in these versions, in another narrative, the protagonist Cui Shao dies and is taken to the underworld; the presiding official turns out to be none other than Ma, now happy in his powerful position as Du's replacement.[47] These stories picture the underworld bureaucracy as a mirror image of its earthly counterpart, defined by a system of rotations between offices that builds and reinforces fraternal bonds between scholar-officials.

The similarity and continuity between the two bureaucratic systems not only ensure the privileged status of scholar-officials in both life and death, but also allow them to collaborate with and benefit one another. Such collaborations and mutual benefits bring outright corruption, marking an important shift away from earlier return-from-death accounts. In earlier narratives, the reasons for a person's release from the infernal regions can be diverse, including bureaucratic mistakes, a presiding official's leniency, ties of kinship or friendship, or interventions by religious specialists.[48] In addition, ghost functionaries sent to arrest a person's soul may be moved to change their minds by his or his family members' virtue, but they must either find a substitute victim or incur punishment themselves.[49] These stories show an interest in discovering the range of acceptable loopholes underlying the framework of a just underworld bureaucracy. New to late medieval stories is a clear endorsement of literati manipulation of the underworld bureaucracy to ensure their class solidarity. The following entry in Dai Fu's collection is representative:

During the Kaiyuan reign [713–742], the vice magistrate of Liuhe County died suddenly but returned to life after a few days. According to him, just after he died, he was brought to the presence of [the underworld] administrative assistant, who turned out to be [former] Magistrate Liu of Liuhe County. They were both happy and sad to see each other again. When Liu inquired about his family, the vice magistrate said, "Your home is rather close to here. Have you not returned yet?" Liu said, "The paths of darkness and light are different. How can I get to return?" The vice magistrate said, "Your son has passed the Presented Scholar examination early on, and the family has had very few untoward happenings. Your wife, however, has become older and suffers slightly from rheumatism." Liu said, "Your allotted time is not up yet. Some sheep [here] have brought a lawsuit against you, and so you have been arrested. You should try to defend yourself and I shall quickly repatriate you." After a short while, dark clouds came from the east, carrying a big boat. After the boat landed with a loud noise, four sheep heads appeared. Liu asked the vice magistrate, "Why did you wrongly execute these creatures?" The vice magistrate replied, "They were designated as food for the prefect, and [thus their deaths] were not my fault." Two of the sheep heads became silent. Liu scolded them, saying, "You were supposed to give your lives for the prefect. How can you accuse the vice magistrate?" The boat then flew away, as the sheep shouted boldly, "The administrative assistant is biased. We shall see the sovereign to dispute his verdict." Liu said to the vice magistrate: "The sovereign is the Heavenly Emperor. How can these creatures get to see him! It is like commoners trying to meet with the Son of Heaven on earth. Isn't it just as hard? But you should [commission Buddhist works] to earn merit on their behalf sooner or later." After these words, he sent the vice magistrate back.[50]

The story shows how literati solidarity is achieved at the cost of non-scholar-officials. By giving his former colleague information on the reason for his arrest, the underworld administrative assistant Liu enables the vice magistrate to improve his response to his accusers; Liu also quickly rules in his colleague's favor without giving the sheep plaintiffs any opportunity for further dispute. His comparison of the four sheep to commoners in the world of the living makes it clear that these animals represent socially disadvantaged figures. First, they are slaughtered in life; then, although the underworld bureaucracy seems to offer them a chance to redress their grievances, their litigation against their killer is easily foiled because the underworld legal staff belongs to the same camp as their enemy. Despite compensation in the form of Buddhist merit to appease them, these sheep cannot change their status as prey, the epitome of powerless objects of oppression. The remoteness of the Heavenly Emperor underscores scholar-officials' monopoly on the actual operation of the underworld bureaucracy. While the dismissal of an animal litigation can be taken as an apt metaphor for power abuses by bureaucrats, the story also makes it clear that partiality and injustice are requirements for the class solidarity of scholar-officials, marking the insiders from those excluded and dominated.

This literati solidarity also proves profitable for scholar-officials across the divide of life and death, further reinforcing their bond. On his way out, the vice magistrate encounters a young girl who should be sent back to life but has been detained by a lascivious gatekeeper; the girl promises the vice magistrate money and concubinage in exchange for help. The vice magistrate then turns back to speak to his friend Liu, who demands his cut in the payment: 20 percent to be given to his surviving son, and another 20 percent to be used to produce Buddhist merit for himself. Although the vice magistrate ultimately does not get the girl as his concubine, he accepts monetary compensation from her family and delivers the promised amount to Liu's living kin. Such frequent references to money—real cash or paper—are an important feature of late medieval return-from-death stories, indicating a "commercialization of purgatory" in popular religious imaginations.[51] In exchange for favor and assistance, ghost functionaries who arrest and escort souls, as well as higher-level underworld officials, routinely ask for payment in the form of paper money, Buddhist merit, food and drink, and so forth.

More than merely indicators of corruption, these demands of the underworld staff embody an activism vis-à-vis officialdom, predicated on literati solidarity. Literati relationships across the divide of life and death are actually defined by a mutual dependence. Living persons are at the mercy of the underworld staff, which exercises jurisdictional power over their lives. At the same time, the dead rely on the living to make the afterlife "comfortable." Dai Fu's entries describe the underworld staff eating human noses and fingers, drinking special tea of the dark world, or simply suffering hunger for lack of human sustenance. Another story recounts how an administrative assistant to King Yama is burned to ashes and then resurrected, a daily punishment from which he hopes to escape by obtaining Buddhist merit made on his behalf.[52] Although underworld officials and clerks are usually presented as the privileged in the infernal regions, as opposed to the inmates, these details highlight the unpleasant aspects of their afterlife, which can be relieved or overcome only with the help of the living. Officialdom and the divide between life and death create a necessary structure for effective literati collaborations: the underworld scholar-official intervenes for the living counterpart and saves his life; in return, the latter provides paper money and other offerings to the former or brings a message or cash to the former's surviving family. Although supposedly no living person can escape the surveillance of underworld officials and clerks, the same staff are often said to be paradoxically unaware of the well-being of their own surviving families. The purely bureaucratic identity of underworld scholar-officials represents the impersonal nature of bureaucratic power. Only through reestablishing personal connections with former colleagues, relatives, or fellow scholar-officials in the world of the living can the underworld staff translate such power into tangible benefits for themselves, their relatives, and their social group.

Late medieval return-from-death stories thus affirm literati sociality, especially the social senior-junior relationship. As we have noted in chapter 3, the senior-junior relationship constituted a central tension in the literati community. In stark contrast to stories of male sexual competition, late medieval return-from-death stories present an amicable image of the senior-junior relationship. The underworld scholar-official plays the role of the social senior because he has the power to determine the life or death of his mortal, junior counterpart. His ignorance of his surviving family symbolically represents human weakness that cannot be remedied by bureaucratic power; however powerful the social senior is, he has descendants whose well-being is beyond his control and will be in the hands of the upcoming social junior. The positive cycle of mutual benefits in these stories underscores the advantages of a cordial relationship between senior and junior, though often at the cost of those outside the literati community.

Moreover, stories featuring a chance encounter between an underworld scholar-official and a mortal counterpart promote the moral obligation of the social senior in particular to use his power and influence to help the junior. Dai Fu's collection, for example, includes three stories about an examination or reappointment candidate who encounters respectively an envoy of the god of Mount Hua, the god's son, and the deity Grand Unity (Taiyi shen) inspecting the Mount Hua area.[53] These stories were part of Mount Hua lore, indicating an active local religious culture in which the god of Mount Hua was seen as both the overlord of the region and subordinate to a larger divine bureaucracy.[54] At the same time, these stories also highlight the natural process of bonding between scholar-officials across different realms: despite being complete strangers at the beginning, the candidate and the traveler he encounters on the road are naturally drawn to each other and become friends. This friendship turns out to be beneficial to the candidate: the deity Grand Unity and the envoy of the god of Mount Hua release the soul of the candidate's wife and allow her to come back to life, while the son of the god of Mount Hua modifies the register of the candidate's fate in order to fulfill his fervent wish of passing the examination that very year. Although the social senior in these stories does not appear to derive any personal benefit, his altruism toward the social junior foregrounds literati solidarity, for he is in effect helping his alter ego and his surrogate family in the world of the living. This point is further borne out by a later story in which the protagonist scholar Cui, on his way to assume his new post as local inspector of Tongzhou, meets a traveling companion who turns out to be the underworld appointee to the same position; Cui manages to have his underworld "double" release his wife's soul.[55]

The underworld bureaucracy, furthermore, reinforces literati solidarity by affirming a belief in a bureaucratized cosmos that expands the avenues of career advancement for scholar-officials. Although the story of Du You's recommendation of Ma Zong as his successor does not explain what would become of Du after the latter took his place, the likely future for an underworld official is rebirth or ascendance to the celestial bureaucracy. A story in Dai Fu's collection, for instance, describes how two ghost officers—one formerly a clerk in the Ministry of Revenue, the other in the Metropolitan Prefecture—request that the county sheriff whom they escort back to the realm of the living copy Buddhist sutras and sponsor vegetarian feasts and rituals on their behalf so they can be reborn as humans.[56] Apart from the option of rebirth that loops back to the world of the living, Duan Chengshi, in his collection *Miscellaneous Morsels from the South Side of Mount You*, presents a belief in upward movement: virtuous people in life become underworld officials, whose extended service will allow them to be promoted to the status of low-ranking immortals in the divine bureaucracy.[57] The underworld is thus a transitory stage in a broader, cosmic bureaucratic order, which offers a promising, open-ended ladder of advancement for scholar-officials. Late medieval literati storytellers thus effectively dissolve the negative implication of officialdom as the structural constraint that traps individuals: this constraint is turned into a fundamental condition of the cosmos that actually guarantees the privileged status and collective prosperity of scholar-officials within it.

PHYSICAL MOBILITY: FANTASTIC POSSIBILITIES OF TRANSCENDENCE

In contrast to stories about fate and the underworld bureaucracy, which emphasize the ineluctable hold of officialdom on scholar-officials, accounts about leaving the world (*chushi*) endorse the ideal of transcendence, that is, physically moving beyond such a structural constraint. While pursuit of such transcendence often takes the form of the traditional quest for becoming an immortal, late medieval literati storytellers use this fantastic alternative to delineate possibilities particularly for scholar-officials. These possibilities are linked specifically to the different social positions of literati vis-à-vis officialdom: hesitator, winner, loser, or sojourner. In affirming the accessibility of transcendence to all scholar-officials, however, storytellers also paradoxically reiterate the very power structure of officialdom. Transcendence thus does not negate but is inseparable from what it transcends, for the latter shapes how the former is imagined.

The life of an immortal is clearly much more attractive to a scholar-official than that of a recluse, defined solely by his repudiation of officialdom and often associated with material hardship. Although medieval Daoist schools such as the Highest Clarity (Shangqing) promoted a vision of a bureaucratized celestial pantheon, the long-standing cult of immortality encompassed a wide range of discursive ideas and beliefs. Whether or not immortals were tied to the Heavenly Bureau, they were believed to enjoy supernormal powers, sensual pleasures, and freedom from the constraints of family, temporal authority, and the underworld bureaucracy, among other fantastic features. They inhabited mysterious islands off the east coast, sacred peaks in the central ranges, and Mount Kunlun in the west, or simply lived in the heavens. One could achieve the status of an immortal through ascetic practices such as making and taking elixirs, ingesting magic herbs and minerals, sexual discipline, controlled breathing, and corpse liberation through an apparent death.[58]

Scholar-officials were not only drawn to the ideal of immortality as practitioners of such ascetic arts, they were also major producers of discourses about immortality. Medieval literati developed the poetic subgenre of "wandering in transcendence" (youxian shi), featuring imagery of otherworldly realms and the spiritual journeys to reach them.[59] They also sustained in writing a lineage of stories about immortals and immortality-seekers. Tang literati interest in the cult of immortality has been attributed in part to the ascendance of religious Daoism, which received official patronage from the Tang royal house.[60] Moreover, modern critics have also been apt to point out that immortality offered promises of freedom, happiness, transcendence, and other wishes that scholar-officials could not find in their lives.[61]

While such observations are right in a general sense, a closer look at late medieval stories sheds light on conflicting positions among literati regarding the cult of immortality. Although surviving only in fragments, the Records of Exposing the Dubious (Bianyi zhi) by Lu Changyuan (d. 799) illustrates a skeptical approach. Having begun his career on the staff of a military governor, Lu rose steadily through the ranks before being killed by soldiers dissatisfied with his strict control.[62] Apparently a skeptic, Lu sought to debunk the myth of transcendence with various stories in his collection. For instance, a Daoist priest with over three decades of self-cultivation is devoured by a tiger because, instead of running away, he resorts to meditation to protect himself; another practitioner tries to use incantations to stop fires but ends up with his house burned to the ground. Elsewhere, a scholar spots anachronisms in statements made by a man who claims to have lived for hundreds of years, while a governor executes an unfilial son who declared that his father had transformed into a white crane and flown away, but who has in fact dumped the old man's corpse into a river.[63] Through these examples, Lu asserts that the obsession with the quest for immortality is nothing but self-delusion and deception: supernatural attainments are vulnerable to encounters with hard reality, and manipulations of innocent, credulous people can be exposed and punished.

By contrast, other literati storytellers affirm the pursuit of immortality as a real alternative to an official career. In his collection *Transmission of the Marvelous*, for instance, Pei Xing includes a story in which an examination candidate named Zhao He delivers the physical remains of a female ghost to her hometown for proper burial and takes a message to the residents of Wuyuan on behalf of another ghost, that of the former prefect, Li Wenyue (d. 834), whose leadership had saved the city from the invasion of Tibetans in 805.[64] To the disappointment of Zhao He, however, the current prefect and residents of the city do not believe his story and refuse to honor Li Wenyue's request for a commemorative stele. Although Li later takes revenge by causing famines, the incident shows Zhao the futility of court service, so he enters Mount Shaoshi to pursue transcendence, using as his guide the Daoist esoteric texts that the grateful female ghost has given him.[65] The forgetfulness and ingratitude of the Wuyuan officials and residents counter the long-standing ideal of earning an undying name through devotion to the people and the state.[66] If the ghost of Li Wenyue shows one's sociopolitical dependence, while the female ghost illustrates one's reliance on family, the quest for immortality constitutes an ultimate path of self-salvation. Through the protagonist's final decision to pursue immortality, the story embraces the alluring promise of transcendence.

The tension between the skeptical and the faithful positions plays out fully in stories of two friends, one of whom chooses the path to officialdom, the other to immortality. These stories are included in the *Extensive Records of the Extraordinary* by Dai Fu, in the *Collection of the Mysterious and the Strange* by Niu Sengru, in *The Lost History* by Lu Zhao, and in the *Supplements to the Tradition of Immortals* (Xianzhuan shiyi) by Du Guangting (850–933). Like Dai Fu, both Niu Sengru and Lu Zhao were Presented Scholar degree holders, but they had more successful careers than Dai; by contrast, Du Guangting was a famous Daoist priest, who had good relations with the court of the Tang and with subsequent regimes.[67] Although the versions they offer vary in detail, each of these storytellers describes an encounter that occurs years after the two protagonists have parted ways. The official takes pity on his poor, decrepit friend, who invites the former to visit him. To the official's surprise, the friend lives in a magnificent mansion and treats him to wondrous food and music, showing off a life of sensual pleasures and magical powers. In both Dai Fu's and Niu Sengru's renditions, the official realizes that one female musician looks like his wife and, after returning home, confirms that she indeed was made to attend the banquet in a dream.[68] In these two stories, the wife's relegation to the status of an entertainer is meant to humiliate the official.[69] In Lu Zhao's and Du Guangting's versions, however, the immortal friend demonstrates superiority by granting the wish of the official to have his favorite girl from the banquet.[70] While these narratives affirm the pursuit of immortality as a superior option to an official career, the two protagonists actually represent the split persona of the scholar-official. He embodies a hesitator who has to make a choice between two incompatible alternatives.

The hesitator represents a scholar-official at the beginning of his career unsure of his prospects in officialdom. If that future is assured, he no longer wavers in his final decision. The following story about the early life of Qi Ying (747–795) from Lu Zhao's *The Lost History* is a telling example:

When [the future] chief minister Qi Ying was a candidate for the Presented Scholar examination, he went to the Ministry of Rites to get some information and stopped in the south office of the Ministry. It was raining and he had not had lunch. Hesitating about where to go, he walked back and forth along a wall. An old man in a white robe, holding a cane and followed by two servant boys, made a bow with his hands clasped and said to Qi Ying, "The sun is already high and you probably have not had your lunch. My residence is not far from here. Can you stop by?" Qi Ying was embarrassed and grateful. After they went out the door of the south office, the old man said, "I will go first and leave a servant as your guide." He jumped on the back of a white donkey and [left as quickly] as if he were flying. Qi Ying was guided to the north of West Market and entered a new house in

a quiet ward; the layout inside the door was neat and clean. After a
long while, the old man came out, followed by over ten maids, each
holding something in her hands. He seated Qi Ying in the main hall,
[the furnishing of which] was splendid and luxurious. After a long
while, a banquet was spread in a tower and the food and wine were
sumptuous and extraordinary. Presently, someone announced the
delivery of a hundred strings of cash. The old man said, "This is my
income from a tavern. I make an urn of wine with a pill." Qi Ying
requested to leave at nightfall. The old man said, "You have a rare
physiognomy. Do you want to be a chief minister? Or do you want to
ascend to heaven in broad daylight?" Qi Ying thought for a long time
and said, "Chief minister." Smiling, the old man said, "You will pass
the Presented Scholar examination next year and certainly obtain
that position [later]." He gave Qi Ying several dozen bolts of silk as
gifts, saying, "Be careful not to tell anyone. Come for a visit whenever you have time." Qi Ying prostrated himself to thank him. After
that he visited the old man a couple of times and was always given
monetary assistance. When the spring arrived, Qi Ying indeed passed
the Presented Scholar examination. Graduates of the same year saw
that he had neat carriages and clothing. They questioned him when
he got drunk and he unwittingly told them everything. With more
than twenty of his classmates, he set up a time for them to call on the
old man together. When the old man heard about it, he was regret-
ful. He declined to see them on the grounds of a disabling illness but
sent each of them a bolt of silk. He summoned Qi Ying in alone to
reproach him, saying, "How could you so readily divulge [the secret]?
Formerly, you could have also become an immortal, but now this has
become unlikely." Qi Ying apologized profusely and accepted the
blame before going out of the old man's door. When he came again
after a period of ten days, the house had been sold and no one knew
where the old man had gone.[71]

Qi Ying is not the only figure who chooses official success over immortality. Lu Zhao also includes similar stories about Li Linfu,
Wang Qi (760–847), and Lu Qi (?–ca. 785), all powerful chief ministers of the past. The ending may not be surprising given that these
stories try retrospectively to explain the career trajectory of those
historical personages. Yet it is striking that these narratives do not
elaborate on why the position of chief minister, the highest civil office with term limits, is more appealing than becoming an immortal,
the most desirable and constant life imaginable. The protagonist's
intuitive or deliberate choice, however, makes it clear that for the
scholar-official who is assured of his success in the competitive literati community, even an alternative life as fantastic as that of an immortal becomes less attractive. In other words, the winner does not

need to transcend officialdom. By featuring a mysterious figure, an old man, a Daoist priest, or a goddess who reveals to the young man his future eminence, these stories provide supernatural endorsements of officialdom's winners, echoing, as we have seen above, the invisible protection of future chief ministers by the underworld.

Despite his eschewal of immortality, the winner can still access wondrous powers by developing a positive relationship with Daoist adepts. Lu Zhao's *The Lost History*, for instance, includes an entry on chief minister Liu Yan's (716?–780) friendship with a gardener, Wang the Eighteenth. Wang saves Liu from a fatal illness with three pills and later comes to reclaim them before Liu's designated lifespan comes to an end.[72] In addition to curing disease, other examples of supernatural assistance include financial aid, the rescue of family members from disasters, forewarnings of imminent danger or changes, and refuge during times of chaos. On one hand, the official symbolically forsakes his secular power, demonstrating his insight and humility by recognizing and paying proper respect to an adept disguised as a socially marginal person such as an old man, a gardener, a servant, a night-soil collector, a poor man, or an idiot. By lowering himself to associate with the socially inferior, the official also creates a debt of gratitude that requires the adept to repay him with magic feats. On the other hand, the friendship emphasizes mutual recognition and alliance between successful people of the human world and the world beyond. The winner in officialdom, as the story of Qi Ying and other similar narratives remind us, could have become an immortal after all.

The winner's choice of officialdom does not necessarily mean that the life of an immortal is no longer available to him. Although in the story of Qi Ying, he loses this opportunity because of his indiscretion, other stories affirm the posthumous immortal destiny of the winner. In Lu Zhao's entry on Li Linfu, for instance, a Daoist priest advises Li to refrain from killing too many people in his future position as chief minister and promises his attainment of immortality in three hundred years. Despite Li's failure to heed the advice, the Daoist gives him a tour of the underworld office where Li is expected to preside after death, and predicts his ultimate ascendance six hundred years later.[73] Although this story implies criticism of Li Linfu's abuse of power as chief minister, by indicating that he is bound for an extended underworld appointment and ultimately an immortal life, it marks a significant departure from many other post-rebellion stories condemning

him as an evil minister responsible for the failures of the Illustrious
Emperor and the outbreak of the An Lushan Rebellion.[74] Rather than
a political explanation of historical cause and effect, Lu Zhao's story
evinces a reverence for Li Linfu's long stay in power. Li's ability to be
the Illustrious Emperor's trusted minister for two decades must have
seemed miraculous to post-rebellion scholar-officials accustomed to
political instability and frequent changes in personnel.

In stories featuring a loser in officialdom, however, immortality is presented as the better option, for it provides opportunities
to achieve what he cannot in this world. In the well-known stories
"Liu Yi," attributed to Li Chaowei, and "Pei Hang," from Pei Xing's
Transmission of the Marvelous, both of the title characters are failed
examination candidates. Liu Yi helps a young woman mistreated by
her husband deliver a letter to her father, the dragon king of Lake
Dongting. He later reaps the rewards of wealth, marriage with the
dragon princess, and longevity.[75] By contrast, Pei Hang falls in love
with a beautiful girl he encounters on the road, and in order to marry
her, he abandons his examination quest and spends all that he has
to find a jade mortar and pestle for her grandmother. After fulfilling his promise of pounding the old lady's elixir for a hundred days,
he is welcomed into the immortal family.[76] In contrast to the famous
early medieval story of Liu Chen and Ruan Zhao's lucky encounter
with and marriage to two fairies,[77] these stories emphasize the protagonists' virtue: Liu Yi's righteous chivalry and Pei Hang's steadfast
loyalty. Whereas the winner earns immortality through political success, the loser does so through moral qualities. Moreover, the marriages of Liu Yi and Pei Hang both resemble unions with noble Tang
families. The dragon king is not very different from a human prince,
and in the eyes of Pei Hang, when his bride's house is decorated for
their wedding, it is "even more like that of a royal relative."[78] For a
Tang scholar-official, marriage into a great clan or a family of powerful officials provided a shortcut to success because the influence of
the bride's family could greatly advance his official career. For Liu Yi
and Pei Hang, however, marriage becomes both a means and an end,
for it recasts success in terms of fulfilling familial happiness outside
of and free from a bureaucratic career.

This is consistent with other stories that give the loser of officialdom a marginal place at most in the celestial bureaucracy. The story
of a failed examinee, Bai Youqiu, from the *Erudite Collection of the
Extraordinary* (Boyi zhi) by Gushenzi, is a good example. Gushenzi is

believed to be the pseudonym of Zheng Huangu (fl. 817–842), a Presented Scholar degree holder from one of the great clans.[79] The story recounts Bai Youqiu's adventure on a sea journey after his repeated failures in examinations. Coming upon an island with imposing palaces, Bai learns that it is the spring resort of the gods of the five sacred peaks. After serving as a messenger for the gods, he is offered the position of sweeper on the island, which he declines.[80] Although he claims nostalgia for home, his decision likely has more to do with the menial nature of the position, for this servant-like status ironically echoes his failure and marginality in the mortal world.

Thus, while late medieval literati storytellers envision immortality as being available to both winners and losers alike, they also reproduce the hierarchy of officialdom in the world beyond. As a matter of fact, the emergence of the notion of "banished immortals" (*zhexian*)—sent down to the mortal world for their transgressions and bound to return at the end of their punitive terms—illustrates how the status quo in officialdom is revalidated and naturalized. Late medieval stories identify political, cultural, and literary icons as banished immortals, including the high officials Li Su (773–821) and Jia Dan, and the famous poets Li Bai, Li Shen, and Bai Juyi.[81] The divine origin of these figures explains their accomplishments and fame in life, while the transcendental afterlife becomes their rightful reward.

Unsurprisingly, the realms of immortals become an anachronistic world in effect, crowded with past luminaries who retain their former identities. The *Records of Compiling the Extraordinary* (Zuanyi ji) by the little-known Li Mei, for instance, includes a story that tries to picture such a world.[82] In this story, two young men unsuccessful in the mortal world are invited to serve as ritual masters at a wedding of two immortals on Mount Song. They witness the interactions of the guests: the Queen Mother of the West and Emperor Mu of the Zhou toast each other, singing songs that reminisce about their earlier encounter, as described in *The Story of Son of Heaven Mu* (Mu tianzi zhuan); Emperor Wu of the Han and the Illustrious Emperor of the Tang discuss their handling of memorials as bureaucrats at the court of the Supreme Sovereign (*shangdi*); the Daoist adept Ye Jingneng kneels down to offer the Illustrious Emperor a drink, with a song recalling the monarch's tragic fall from power as a result of the rebellions.[83] The story's foregrounding of historical sovereigns and its affirmation of political hierarchy (for example, Ye Jingneng is presented as a subject of the Illustrious Emperor) reveal a conservative stance. Meanwhile, the intertextual references also indicate that the mortal identities of these immortals, along with their corresponding former power relations, are necessary for maintaining their individuality. Although the two young men are supposed to serve as wedding ritual masters, this duty is no more than a pretext to give them glimpses of the world beyond; throughout the story, they mainly function as witnesses to the interactions among those immortals. Their role as mere mortal observers also signifies the inevitable marginality of losers in a bureaucratized world of immortals.

As a way out of the dilemma, late medieval literati storytellers also turn the loser into a sojourner, for whom the mobility between different worlds and states of being is more important than the destination. The story of Bai Youqiu ends with his travel and sojourn in the five sacred peaks, as he attempts to regain entry into the realms of immortals, because a taste of immortality makes him completely lose interest in officialdom. While the open ending of this story suggests ambivalence about the uncertainty of the sojourner's future, another story from Niu Sengru's *Collection of the Mysterious and the Strange* celebrates his mobility. In this complex narrative, a scholar-official named Xue Juncao meets two young lads coming out of his own ear. One of them invites Xue to enter the Kingdom of Enclosed Mystery through his ear. After Xue jumps in the lad's ear, he discovers a land of beauty and pleasure, presided over by a Daoist patriarch. He later becomes homesick and is expelled, falling out of the lad's ear back to his old home. He then passes away. In his next life, he encounters the lad again, who not only enlightens him with the story of his previous life but also gives him a silk talisman that enables him to live one thousand years. Now an old man, he relates his experiences to a Presented Scholar degree holder he encounters on the road and shows off his record of historical events that he has witnessed and that are unavailable in official histories.[84] The protagonist finds immortality wanting because of its inherent paradox, not because of his marginal status like Bai Youqiu. Serving as an official in the Kingdom of Enclosed Mystery, with few duties and all of his desires instantly known and met by his attendants, Xue becomes homesick and composes a poem with the lines "I ascend heights to gaze afar forlornly; / This place is truly beautiful, but it is not my hometown."[85] Transcendence is inherently paradoxical in that its fulfillment risks turning us into alien beings, resulting in the loss of our humanity.[86] The story shows another paradox at work: as the perfect alternative to the mortal world, transcendence presumably leaves no desire unfulfilled, but it cannot merge with its antithesis as the protagonist wishes. In his second life, he finally reaches an ideal, intermediate state as a long-living historical witness both outside and above history, without being either bound by or fully detached from the temporal world of officialdom.

This state indicates that for the late medieval scholar-official, leaving the world is not an end in itself but a fantastic means of achieving flexible mobility and control over his destiny. Although late medieval stories envision different endings, they assume that the path of transcendence is open to literati heroes, who receive favorable treatment and assistance from transcendent figures. The image of the sojourner, along with those of the hesitator, winner, and loser, thus reiterate the privileges and mobility of scholar-officials in the cosmos.

EPISTEMIC MOBILITY: DREAMING AND AWAKENING

While stories about leaving the world affirm the physical mobility of scholar-officials in the cosmos, those about dreams (meng) advocate an epistemic mobility. To create new ways of understanding the meaning of officialdom, these stories frame the protagonist's experience of his official career within a transient dream. Capitalizing on the fluidity of boundaries between dreaming and waking, late medieval literati storytellers promote temporal, spatial, and historical perspectives on literati life, which symbolically subvert the institutional hold of officialdom on individuals through value inversion or displacement.

Dreams figured prominently across traditional Chinese culture, from the level of personal life to that of statecraft. This preoccupation can be traced to the earliest oracle-bone inscriptions.[87] Apart from physiological and psychological explanations, dreams were considered an important medium of communication between humans and supernatural forces, the message of which had to be properly deciphered. The meanings of dreams in early periods centered on war, the deaths or births of important figures, affairs of government, leadership succession, and illness.[88] Because the interpretation of such dreams was fraught with tension and ambiguity, "the readability of dreams," in Wai-yee Li's term, was a field of contestation for different ideologies.[89] The extant fragments of dream interpretation handbooks such as the Book on Dreams (Meng shu) illustrate the methods and importance of such decoding in later popular culture.[90] Meanwhile, metaphorical readings of dreams shaped early philosophical and religious discourses. Daoist texts such as *Zhuangzi* (ca. fourth century BCE) and *Liezi* (ca. third–fourth century CE) famously dwell on the transition and reversibility between dreaming and waking states to question received categories of self, knowledge, and experience.[91] In Buddhism the fleeting nature of both dreams and awakening became a powerful analogy for the impermanence of the human world.[92] The multifarious meanings of dreams gave rise to a rich and complex tradition of dream literature and culture.[93]

Apart from reiterating earlier themes,[94] late medieval stories about dreams also offer ingenious adaptations, the most influential of which is the displacement of the protagonist's official career into the dream world. "The World Inside a Pillow" (Zhenzhong ji) by Shen Jiji is one such story. The story tells of a young scholar named Lu, who, on his way to work in his field, encounters an old Daoist priest named Lü at an inn. Hearing the young man lament his inability to lead a more successful life, the old man takes out a blue porcelain pillow and asks him to rest on it. Falling asleep instantly, the young man embarks on a dream in which, despite some ups and downs, he fulfills his ambitions and enjoys a prosperous career at the court of the Illustrious Emperor. After he dies at the end of his life in the dream, he wakes up and is astonished to discover that what he has experienced was merely a dream, so short that the innkeeper has not yet finished cooking the millet.[95]

Modern critics have often interpreted the young man's awakening as his disillusionment with officialdom, which conveys the author Shen Jiji's own pessimism or nihilism.[96] Shen Jiji was recognized by chief minister Yang Yan (727–821) and promoted to the position of court historian. After no more than two years, however, Yang fell from power and was executed. Shen was implicated and demoted to a remote area in the south, and soon after being recalled to the capital, he died. Critics assume that, while drawing from his historical knowledge of the Illustrious Emperor's court, he wrote "The World Inside a Pillow" because of his personal experiences of failure and suffering.[97]

The belief in the story's negative message, reinforced by an autobiographical reading, stems from the story's effective manipulation of temporality. The dream constitutes what Carrie Reed has called "stretched time," in which the young man experiences a fifty-year career.[98] This long span of time in the dream amounts to, however, only a fleeting moment in the waking world, shorter than the time

required to make a meal. This revelation turns the dream into a miniature version of one's whole life at an accelerated pace. The image
of the pillow is central here. With its two openings, one at each
end, marking the young man's entry into and exit from the dream
world, and, by extension, life itself, the pillow epitomizes the temporal embeddedness of human existence. The accelerated pace of time
defamiliarizes it and reveals its ephemeral nature. Any complacency
one has over the passage of time is shattered, deflating one's sense of
power and control, destabilizing the meaning of human endeavors,
and thereby provoking one's own sense of existential crisis.

Yet the lesson that the young man learns is not simply disillusionment with officialdom but more importantly, a temporal perspective
that allows him to reflect on his desire for officialdom. The story
focuses on his growth as an exemplary student and reader not only
before the dream but within and after it as well. Before the dream, he
sees officialdom through rose-colored glasses because of his discon-
tent with his life as a farmer; it is the only path to happiness that he
can envision. Only after he enters officialdom in the dream does he
discover the missing parts of his picture. When his outstanding performance provokes the jealousy of his colleagues and his life is endan-
gered, he regrets his fateful choice to embark on an official career. His
nostalgia for his old life as a farmer shows his realization that official
success is indeed a luxury beyond the basic needs of life and is inex-
orably wedded to greater dangers. His regrets, however, disappear
once his status becomes secure again. Toward the end of his career,
the memorial he submits to the emperor offers a review of his official
life, revealing that he is no more than a humble and loyal servant at
the mercy of the royal will, a fact underscored by his repeated failure
to get permission to retire.

Only when he finally wakes up after his "death" and contemplates
his "previous life" with an "after-life" perspective does he recognize
the full meaning of his dream. He says to the old man, "As to the
ways of favor and humiliation, the fortunes of distress and success,
the principles of gain and loss, and the feelings about life and death, I
have known them all. This is how you have averted my desires. How
dare I not accept your lesson?"[99] The lesson that the young man takes
away is the dialectical nature of life, framed by the ultimate limit
imposed by time, or death.[100] In the dream, the young man enjoys the
most successful career by Tang standards: with a wife from one of
the great clans and a coveted Presented Scholar degree, he moves on

to become an effective military general and civil administrator, eventually obtaining the top office of chief minister and a ducal enfeoffment.[101] Yet even such a life mixes success with disappointment, joy with anguish, triumph with setback. Learning this, he can largely dispense with his gnawing desire for an official career, for it is desire that haunts him, rather than any real necessity. His material needs are actually quite simple; desires, however, torment him with the prospect that he could be happier with more, or with the curse that he cannot be happy unless he attains what he desires. In this respect, it is significant that the story actually ends with Lu's departure without his making any explicit life choice: since he has learned his lesson, it does not matter what he finally chooses to become. Although the presence of the old man, who is said to possess the arts of the immortals, represents the easy solution of transcendence, the story clearly resists that possibility.[102]

While "The World Inside a Pillow" offers a temporal mode of reflection, "The Story of the Governor of the Southern Branch" (Nanke taishou zhuan) by Li Gongzuo (fl. 797–818) provides a spatial one. Li Gongzuo was a low-ranking official and an avid storyteller who wrote several famous stories. Modern scholars also believe that he was the friend who encouraged Bai Xingjian to write "The Story of Li Wa."[103] "The Story of the Governor of the Southern Branch" tells of a rich military officer named Chunyu Fen, who, in a dreamy drunken stupor, visits a kingdom where he marries the king's daughter. Chunyu also governs Southern Branch Prefecture for more than twenty years with the help of his two friends. After the death of the princess, however, the king distrusts him and sends him home. Waking up, he realizes that he has just had a brief dream, before his drinking companions are even done with washing their feet. Retracing his dream journey, he discovers that the country he visited was in fact an ant kingdom under the locust tree near his house, and the prefecture he governed was an ant nest on a southern branch of the tree. In response, he gives up drinking in pursuit of immortality, but passes away three years later, just as predicted by the ant king.[104]

The similarities of this story to "The World Inside a Pillow" are strong, leading many to argue that it has similar messages about the transience of life and disillusionment with officialdom.[105] Chunyu's dream is fundamentally different from the young Lu's, however, in the sense that it is his disembodied soul that visits the ant kingdom.[106] In fact, he verifies his dream experience by digging open the anthills:

There was a hole where roots [of the locust tree] were open and visible, so big that a couch could fit in it. There was piled dirt, which looked like inner and outer city walls, terraces, and palaces. Several bushels of ants had inobtrusively gathered therein. At the center was a small terrace with a color like cinnabar, where two big ants stayed. They were about three inches long, with white wings and red heads. They were attended by dozens of big ants on their left and right, and other ants dared not get close. They were the ant king [and queen]. [This hole] was the capital of the Kingdom of Locust Peace. [Chunyu and his friends] traced [the ants] to another nest, which was located at a southern branch about thirteen yards from the roots. Winding around in the center were also earthen city walls and tiny towers, and there was another swarm of ants living there. This was the Southern Branch Prefecture that Chunyu had governed. . . . Recalling his previous experiences, Chunyu sighed with deep emotion. He thoroughly perused those traces, all of which matched his dream.[107]

By having the protagonist peruse the ant nest and reflect on his dream experience therein, the story foregrounds spatiality as a new perspective on officialdom, predicated upon paradoxical relations between the ant kingdom and the human world. The ants are at once less than human, just like humans, and more than human. Digging open the ant kingdom creates the effect of alienation because of the otherness of ants: the display of their lowly animal form makes it comical, absurd, and even repulsive to be associated with them, let alone pursuing official success among them.

Meanwhile, the ant kingdom as a miniature of human society also encourages identification with these insects, doubling the repulsion back onto humans. Just like the Tang empire, this microcosm has a king, a court, and an administrative system, populated with officials, clerks, Buddhists, Daoists, local elders, musicians, carriage drivers, military guards, and commoners. While the artificial temporality of the dream world results from the manipulation of the old man in "The World Inside a Pillow," the quickened temporal pace of the ant world is natural, proportional to its much smaller spatial scale. It takes Chunyu and his ant wife several days to travel from the capital to Southern Branch Prefecture. But it may take only a couple of seconds for the awakened Chunyu. Identification with the microcosmic ant kingdom effectively trivializes official glory, as stated in the coda by a certain Li Zhao: "[People] with the highest ranks and positions, / [And those] holding sway over the capital and the state. / A wise man sees them / as no more than swarming ants."[108] The wise man embodies a spatial perspective of self-reflection, the "zooming out" to attain a "loftier" point of view. When Chunyu is inside the ant world, his vision is actually "horizontal," which produces his sense of its immensity as well as his own privileged position. Only after he can behold the entirety of the ant world can he perceive the presumptuousness and absurdity of his earlier sense of power and pride. The "lofty" perspective is superior to the "horizontal" point of view because it is the detached mode of the former that reveals the true identity of the ant kingdom. This spatial mode vividly literalizes self-reflection, which is precisely seeing oneself as an Other from a superior epistemic point of view.

Moreover, the superiority of the ants to men in terms of their numinous powers also expands the visual field of the "lofty" perspective. The ants can foretell the future, such as the digging open of the anthills and the time of Chunyu's death. They also have contact with other realms beyond the human world, including the world of the dead. Chunyu's marriage with the (ant) princess is arranged by his deceased father and the king; when he sends a letter to his father, he receives his handwritten reply in several days, a lapse of time that implies the distance in between.[109] These different worlds indicate that humanity does not occupy the full space of the cosmos, as the storyteller Li Gongzuo comments: "Alas! Even the numinous mystery of ants cannot be fully fathomed. How much more the transformations of bigger creatures hiding in mountains and crouching in woods?"[110] The infinity of spaces occupied by numinous Others underscores the spatial limitations of human existence. It is when seen in this vast cosmic dimension that men are no different from "swarming ants."

The spatial perspective not only dissolves any sense of haughtiness resulting from one's fame and position, but also offers a way to mitigate the tyranny of time as the terminator of human life. Chunyu's futile attempt to transcend time is after all an overreaction to, or a misreading of, his own dream, because life actually does not end with death.[111] Death means a transition from the world of the living to that of the dead, both of which coexist with many other worlds in the cosmos. If "The World Inside a Pillow" evokes the absolute power of time as the fundamental condition of human existence, "The Story of the Governor of the Southern Branch" shows the contingency of time in relation to space—spatiality is actually as essential as temporality, if not more so.

In contrast to these two stories, which are unsettling because of their deflation of the rosy aura of officialdom, the "Record of a Dream of Qin" (Qin meng ji) by Shen Yazhi offers a reassuring alternative.

Unlike the third-person narrative "The Story of Feng Yan" discussed earlier, this story describes how Shen Yazhi himself stops at a hostel outside Chang'an and has a daydream of serving at the court of Duke Mu of Qin (Qin Mugong, r. 659–621 BCE). He gives advice on policies to the duke and leads successful military campaigns. As a reward, he is given the widowed princess Nongyu in marriage, whose death later prompts the duke to send him off. He wakes up and tells his friend, who cites documentary evidence for the proximity of the hostel to the duke's tomb. Shen verifies this by consulting geographic records.[112] Dated to a point near the end of Shen's life, the story has been seen as an expression of Shen's artistic creativity as well as his attachment to his deceased favorite concubine.[113]

Regardless of Shen's personal investment, the story is striking for the absence of any existential crisis for the hero upon awakening, in contrast to its predecessors "The World Inside a Pillow" and "The Story of the Governor of the Southern Branch." The different ending here is consistent with the story's use of the dream frame to create a historical perspective that embraces the temporally and spatially embedded conditions of human existence. Although Shen's dream may have been triggered by staying close to the duke's tomb (unknowingly, so he claims), it is different from a ghost encounter in which spirits of the past appear in the present to interact with living people. Here the protagonist is literally drawn into the world of the past, where he fulfills his ambitions of career advancement and marriage. Whereas the dreams in "The World Inside a Pillow" and "The Story of the Governor of the Southern Branch" are seamless extensions of the heroes' waking realities and previews of their potential futures, Shen's dream is safely contained in the past, to which he is a visitor. His advice to the duke to become a leader of feudal lords like Duke Huan of Qi (Qi Huangong, r. 685–643 BCE) and others indicates the historical knowledge and political awareness appropriate for an educated man of the Spring and Autumn period. His poetic compositions in regulated verse and rhapsody, in response to the death of his wife and his own departure from Qin, however, clearly show his Tang sensibility.

While the earlier dream stories interpret human embeddedness in time and space as a limit to our perspectives, the "Record of a Dream of Qin" presents it as a source of power. The power lies in one's role as an agent of the present whose connections and engagements with the past broaden his horizons. Shen's dream represents an intimate mode of engaging the past: historical distance seemingly disappears and he becomes an actor in the reenacted past. This past consists of both history and legend: Shen exerts himself well in Qin's ambitions to subdue its neighboring rival Jin and the western non-Chinese tribes, as documented in Sima Qian's *Records of the Grand Historian* (Shi ji), and he is wedded to Princess Nongyu, who in the *Tradition of Immortals* (Liexian zhuan) is said to have become an immortal along with her husband by flying off on the backs of phoenixes summoned by their playing of flutes.[114] The wish-fulfilling nature of Shen's dream is clear, given that he had served only on the staffs of military governors and as a low court official throughout his life. In the dream, he not only achieves literati ambitions as the ruler's civil advisor, military assistant, and even son-in-law, but also experiences the loss of his status, which he turns into literary success by composing moving poems that win the praise of the duke and others.

At the same time, Shen's response upon waking represents a more rational, detached mode of engaging the past. By discussing with his friend and checking relevant historical records, Shen not only proves the veracity of his dream but also turns the past into an object of scholarly inquiry. His efforts to explain his dream and rationalize the gap between dream and reality indicate his control of the interpretation of the past in general. The intimate and detached modes thus affirm his full power as a historical subject, who can project himself onto the past and fashion an alternative reality even if he is powerless in the present.

This historical perspective thus both contradicts and complements the temporal and spatial ones. In contrast to the earlier two dream stories, which diminish and even subvert officialdom's allure and control through value inversion, the wish fulfillment in the "Record of a Dream of Qin" in effect reaffirms the values of officialdom through displacement. Meanwhile, the historical perspective actually offers an additional mode of epistemic mobility. While the temporal and spatial perspectives enable a symbolic repudiation of officialdom, the historical perspective provides an escapist approach. This escapism, however, also calls attention to its common ground with symbolic repudiation: regardless of its efficacy, epistemic mobility after all does not entail any real change of reality but a better acquiescence to it.

Late medieval literati storytellers' conceptions of cosmic mobility are full of contradictions, revealing a great ambivalence among scholar-officials toward officialdom as the epitome of the structural constraints of literati life. Stories about predetermined fate and the underworld bureaucracy portray a bureaucratized cosmos in which the constraint of officialdom can be accepted as a positive attribute and even an advantage. At the same time, stories about transcendence and dreams assert the possibilities of overcoming the institutional hold of officialdom on individuals. These seemingly contradictory messages do not really negate each other. Physical and epistemic mobility do not actually allow the full repudiation of officialdom, whereas the bureaucratic order of the cosmos expands the space of literati mobility.

Since officialdom constituted both the structure and the constraint of literati life, freedom beyond this constraint was appealing, but repudiation of the structure was not really feasible. Yet the ideal had to be kept alive. The tendencies to acquiesce to or move beyond officialdom represent not just contradictory impulses but indispensable options. They justify the privileged position of scholar-officials in the cosmos, affirming their ability to make choices. In fact, late medieval stories about literati cosmic identity lay out a spectrum of options for dealing with officialdom, from the acceptance of it as a collective destiny, to the exploitation of its bureaucratic power, to the physical transcendence of its limitations, and to the symbolic subversion of its control. These options empower scholar-officials, allowing them to choose their modes of engagement with officialdom while extending their spheres of action into the unlimited expanse of the cosmos.

Nonetheless, late medieval literati storytellers were also aware of the wish-fulfilling nature of their visions of literati cosmic mobility. The life of the sojourner casts doubt upon the ideal of transcendence, while the historical perspective of dream displacement calls attention to the painful fact that the manipulation of perspective does not change reality. Late medieval scholar-officials did not, however, question the bureaucratic order of the cosmos that governed life and death, for that very order ultimately defined who they were and held them together as a community.

Conclusion

*The Power and Legacies of Late Medieval
Literati Storytelling*

Through storytelling, late medieval Chinese scholar-officials constructed a multifaceted collective identity in response to the challenges of the newly intensified officialdom-centered literati life. These identity constructions illuminate the intertwining of literary and social dimensions in stories, which has rich implications for our understanding of both literary and social history. Late medieval literati storytelling not only facilitated the communal adjustments of contemporary scholar-officials to the momentous transformations of the Tang-Song Transition, but also created lasting literary and cultural legacies for the literati communities of the following millennium.

Because late medieval literati storytelling gave literary expression to social concerns of the time through thematizations, it provides a distinctive vantage point on historical aspects of the reconfiguration of the Chinese elite. While the breakdown of the medieval aristocracy has been the focal point of scholarly attention, late medieval scholar-officials' identity constructions through storytelling shed light on the simultaneous building of a new consensus about the meaning of officialdom-centered literati life. The four most prominent story themes, namely, sovereignty, literati sociality, sexuality, and cosmic mobility, indicate the careful delineation of literati powers and positions in the fundamental domains of literati life. These different facets of literati identity complement each other in articulating a myth of empowerment. Sovereignty and literati sociality affirm the collective ascendancy of scholar-officials in the sociopolitical spheres; insofar as these central domains of literati life can be restrictive for individuals, sexuality allows measured challenges to the dominant power relations, while cosmic mobility maps out strategies for coming to terms with the structural constraints. As we have seen throughout this book, however, the myth of empowerment was also fraught with tensions and contradictions because of the divergent perspectives of late medieval literati storytellers.

These tensions and contradictions evince the vitality and diversity of the late medieval literati community; they also indicate that the formation of consensus about the new literati identity consisted not in a unified understanding but in the dialogic contestations that created a communal discourse and its underlying common grounds. Although late medieval scholar-officials might have differed in their ideas about the modes of engagement with the sovereign and the types of communal bonds, they accepted the centrality of the sociopolitical domains in literati life. Likewise, while literati storytellers offered conflicting visions regarding the possibilities of challenging the dominant power relations and the structural constraints of literati life, they shared a preoccupation with sexuality and cosmic mobility as the essential means of negotiation. Their explorations of the political, social, sexual, and cosmic dimensions of literati identity created a common field of dialogue and contestation. This interactive field brought late medieval scholar-officials together as a group, as they struggled to define the boundaries of their collective existence and self-image in post-rebellion society. Their divergent articulations bespoke a general recognition of the fundamental shift in literati life and a shared interest in exploring its implications.

The apparent contradictions in the visions of late medieval scholar-officials, however, also reveal their deep ambivalence about the myth of empowerment. This ambivalence centered on the imbricated positive and negative implications of the officialdom-centered literati life for individuals and the community. Post-rebellion instabilities enabled late medieval scholar-officials to claim superiority as an expanding elite community by asserting themselves as the solution to contemporary political, social, and cultural crises. Meanwhile, they were also experiencing intensified competition among themselves, or stronger pressures on the normative pattern of literati life, as a result of the expansion of their community. Stories about sovereignty and literati sociality promoted positive meanings by affirming the collective ascendancy of scholar-officials, whereas narratives about sexuality and cosmic mobility resolved negative implications by offering ways for individuals to deal with those pressures. In other words, late medieval scholar-officials were keenly aware of the advantages and pitfalls of the officialdom-centered literati life and tried to reconcile its conflicting meanings.

In advocating that scholar-officials welcome the positive benefits and dodge the negative implications that came with the package, the myth of empowerment also betrays its wishful nature and its therapeutic function. Solutions to the negative implications were actually limited: literati's sexual challenges to social authorities were carefully contained, whereas their physical and epistemic mobility could not really allow them to move beyond a bureaucratized cosmos. Despite these limitations, the myth offered a reassuring picture that everyone had a place and that any detrimental effects could be brought under control. In so doing, the myth alleviated and even disguised the embedded status of late medieval scholar-officials in the historical process of transition and transformation. Since the officialdom-centered literati life was becoming an inescapable living reality for late medieval scholar-officials, it was all the more important for them to sustain a belief in their power and control. Through their storytelling, these literati defined themselves as active agents who could celebrate, rationalize, challenge, or transcend their embeddedness, rather than as passive victims of historical vicissitudes.

To call late medieval scholar-officials self-deluding is beside the point, for it is the fundamental power of storytelling to play "make believe." Literati storytelling created a sense of reality that late medieval scholar-officials could live with, allowing them to grapple and come to terms with the conditions of their existence. The contradictions and ambivalences that we have seen throughout this book, however, also indicate that late medieval scholar-officials were able not only to construct a myth of their empowerment but also to see through their own constructions. By accommodating disparities and developing common ground through storytelling, late medieval scholar-officials rallied themselves around the myth of their empowerment in the officialdom-centered literati life, thereby paving the way for the advent of an examination society in the Song and later. The myth was thus both cause and effect: it was a response to the changing conditions of literati life, and at the same time was instrumental in bringing about communal adjustment to the reconfiguration of the Chinese elite.

The identity constructions in late medieval literati storytelling contribute to a more nuanced understanding of the contemporaneous literati community. While Presented Scholar candidates and degree holders have been considered the most visible figures in the examination community in particular and the literati community in general,[1] the dynamics of late medieval literati storytelling shed light on the social milieu of which they were an integral part. As we have seen through Wang Dingbao's *Collected Words*, Presented Scholar examinees and degree holders, still a minority in terms of numbers, tried to define themselves as an ultra-elite vis-à-vis other scholar-officials. Meanwhile, they also actively participated in the broader communal discourses as storytellers. Although authorship information may not always be reliable or even available, Presented Scholar degree holders constituted roughly one third of late medieval literati storytellers as known from the extant single stories and story collections in bibliographies. In particular, they were associated with about two thirds of stories on literati nonmarital bonds. This may not be surprising, given what we know about the intimate connections between the examination culture and the courtesan culture on one hand and, on the other, that Presented Scholar degree holders were among the most productive writers of their time. The analysis of their points of view, along with those of others, however, makes it clear that their voices, though prominent, were part of a wide spectrum of vibrant articulations among late medieval scholar-officials. While this diversity of the late medieval literati world may seem like an obvious point, it is important for putting in perspective the unique place of the examination community in an era before civil service examinations became so predominant that the literati community turned in effect into an examination community.[2]

Meanwhile, the case of late medieval literati storytelling also sheds light on other aspects of medieval intellectual and social history. Literati storytellers' careful delineation of complementary platforms of actions for scholar-officials coincided with the emergence of the Archaic Prose movement and other intellectual trends that valorized *wen*,[3] showing the extent of literati efforts to assert their power in post-rebellion society. Moreover, the communal identity that late medieval scholar-officials constructed through storytelling also complements what we have known about elite social behaviors and family strategies,[4] providing a more comprehensive picture of literati responses to the breakdown of the medieval aristocracy. Stories thus have much to contribute to social and intellectual history, although they are usually excluded for being less reliable than typical historical data such as family genealogies, official biographies, treatises, and letters. The historical value of stories lies not in their descriptions of specific past incidents and figures, however, but in their thematizations of collective desires and anxieties, which offer insights into the subjective experiences and ways of thinking of the storytelling community at large.

The inextricability between the literary and social dimensions of stories also expands our understanding of literary history. Although the debate between fiction and nonfiction in the field of medieval Chinese literature is invigorating, it cannot be fully resolved because there is not sufficient information to determine whether writers were faithful recorders of accounts about past figures and incidents, as they claimed to be, or whether they were disingenuous fiction writers who tried to boost the veracity of their writings. In fact, the authorial role of the literati storyteller was defined precisely by such a fundamental ambiguity, which makes literati storytelling fit squarely neither into the folktale nor the fiction model. While we cannot deny the pretensions of literati storytellers to historical authenticity, it is necessary to examine the cultural investments and social functions of such pretensions insofar as the role of literati storyteller served as a crucial conduit for scholar-officials to actively participate in and contribute to communal discourses of their time. The extant stories, products of both communal and individual forces that cannot be fully disentangled, become our entry points to the lively discourses that shaped the very social meanings of these literary productions for contemporary literati storytellers and audiences.

The extensive, dialogic relations among late medieval stories elucidate not only the complex dynamic of the literati storytelling culture but also its linkages to the poetic culture of the time. Fan Shu's story collection *Master Cloud Creek's Discussions with Friends*, for instance, envisioned a cultural community of poets and poetic aficionados worshipping poetic art, which dovetailed with mid- and late-Tang poets' obsession with poetic craftsmanship.[5] While constructing a male *fengliu* (gallant, romantic) persona and articulating male romantic desires were new poetic trends in the mid- and late Tang, these innovations were conveniently couched in the poetic language of love, sex, and feeling, and detached from social contexts.[6] Stories about literati nonmarital bonds explored precisely the moral implications and parameters of this male sexual subjectivity, revealing the social stakes of poetic innovations. Likewise, the new poetic trope of private space within officialdom was not just an ingenious deviation from the conventional hermit ideal,[7] but very much a part of post-rebellion literati efforts to come to terms with the structural constraint of officialdom, as illustrated in stories about cosmic mobility. Although some literati storytellers belonged to the same circle of family and friends, such as Bai Juyi, Bai Xingjian, Chen Hong, and Yuan Zhen,[8] the majority likely did not, and many were less well-known, even obscure, figures. Their thematizations or participations in the communal discourse of their time thus bring to light an important mode of medieval elite social and literary connections, apart from the personal or intertextual relationships among poets of various poetic circles or traditions.[9]

Moreover, the case of late medieval literati storytelling also broadens our perspectives on the intimate relationship between elite and popular culture. The shared thematizations between elite narratives and Dunhuang transformation texts about the power of the sovereign, for instance, indicate the continuum between literati and popular storytelling. More studies are needed to fully understand the complex relations between these traditions. Given that many stories taken as sources for studying popular religions were gathered and recorded by literati writers, the filtering of such stories by scholar-officials and their relationship with popular religions are also issues of fundamental importance that deserve more in-depth research.

Late medieval literati storytelling also established enduring legacies for scholar-officials of the following millennium. After the mid-tenth century, the sociohistorical conditions of literati culture had shifted significantly, with the growth of commercialization and urbanization, the spread of printing, the expansion of the elite social base, and the establishment of civil service examinations as the primary means of official recruitment. Nonetheless, the themes that we have examined in this book remain prominent in literati writings. This continuity indicates the fundamental importance of the political, social, sexual, and cosmic dimensions of literati identity. In this sense, late medieval scholar-officials pioneered composite strategies for identity construction that allowed their successors to reconcile the fundamental tensions in their lives, foreshadowed by increased literati competition and dependency on officialdom during the late medieval period.

Late medieval scholar-officials also created influential story subjects and prototypes for later writers. From the Song onward, various forms of popular, professional storytelling and performances became widespread, while the written language started to bifurcate into the classical and the vernacular. In addition to compiling classical-language collections of stories by and for the elite in the tradition of literati storytelling, scholar-officials were instrumental in the development of literary forms accessible to people on a wider social spectrum, including vernacular short stories, vernacular novels, and drama. Their indebtedness to late medieval literati storytelling is conspicuous in that they relied on many late medieval stories as the foundation of their literary productions. As a matter of fact, more than one hundred Tang stories were adapted by later writers, often multiple times.[10] Many of the stories examined in this book are among them.

These adaptations of late medieval stories went beyond genre boundaries. The love story of the Illustrious Emperor and Precious Consort Yang is representative. While Bai Juyi's "Ballad of Eternal Sorrow" became canonical and continued to be extensively read and recited, the love story itself was expanded and transformed in diverse ways. The *Unofficial Biography of Precious Consort Yang* (Yang Guifei waizhuan) by Yue Shi (930–1007) combined Chen Hong's prose narrative with other related anecdotes to produce a composite account of her life and afterlife. The anonymous Song composition "Biography of Consort Mei"(Meifei zhuan) invented a beautiful and virtuous heroine to be Precious Consort Yang's rival, developing a sexual triangle and turning the story into a political fable. Although extant only in fragments, the *Surviving Tales from the Tianbao Era: A Zhugongdiao* (Tianbao yishi zhugongdiao), attributed to Wang Bocheng (fl. 13th century), illustrates outright eroticization of the story in popular performances. Moreover, dramatic renditions explored in particular the emotional depths of the characters, trying to affirm the couple's love without giving up political didacticism, as we can see in extant plays such as *The Illustrious Emperor of the Tang [Listening to] the Autumn-Night Rain on Pawlonia Leaves* (Tang Minghuang qiuye wutong yu) by Bai Pu (b. 1226), *Dance of a Startled Goose* (Jinghong ji) attributed to Wu Shimei (fl. 1573), and *Palace of Eternal Life* (Changsheng dian) by Hong Sheng (1645–1704). The vernacular novel *Romance of the Sui and the Tang* (Sui Tang yanyi) by Chu Renhuo (fl. 1675–1695) turned the Illustrious Emperor and Precious Consort Yang into the reincarnations of the last Sui emperor and his favorite concubine, creating a framing device to connect a wide range of episodes about the two dynasties. The cross-genre disseminations and transformations of late medieval stories thus demonstrate their lasting influence on elite culture in particular and traditional Chinese culture in general.

By offering influential story subjects and prototypes, late medieval literati storytelling in fact opened up sites of discursive production and proliferation. As mentioned in chapter 1, the Song literati were horrified by their Tang predecessors' portrayals of the Illustrious Emperor as a lover, because in their own times such "disrespect" toward a monarch of the reigning dynasty would have had serious political consequences for oneself and one's family. Nonetheless, they continued to retell the stories of the Illustrious Emperor and Precious Consort Yang, for these stories about figures of a previous dynasty provided a politically safe ground on which they could explore their ideas of sovereignty and their relationship to the ruler.

Likewise, "The Story of Yingying" underwent many transformations. The most famous example was Wang Shifu's (1260–1316) drama *The Story of the Western Wing* (Xixiang ji), which is still being performed in China today.[11] Replacing scholar Zhang's abandonment of Yingying in the original story with a happy ending in idyllic marriage, Wang's dramatic rendition downplays the radical challenge of romance to the patriarchal family; but his play fails to fully resolve the conflict between romance and patriarchy and the radical implications of the premarital liaison of Zhang and Yingying. The play further engendered a large number of adaptations that continued to grapple with this problem.[12] The profound ambivalence inherent in romance, first explored by late medieval scholar-officials, underlay the flourishing of the cult of *qing* (love, desires, sentiments) in late imperial philosophical, literary, and theatrical discourses. By affirming the spontaneity and authenticity of individuals' emotions in general, the cult of *qing* not only served as a major field for the contestation of Confucian orthodoxy, but also underpinned twentieth-century discussions of modern love.[13] As the fountainhead of later literati discourses, late medieval literati storytelling laid an important foundation for the subsequent development of literati culture.

Even more profoundly, late medieval scholar-officials established the precedent of using storytelling as the communal forum of the elite, a tradition carried on from the Song throughout the late imperial period. Later scholar-officials continued to enjoy amateur storytelling among themselves as conversational entertainment, and their compilations of miscellanies flourished with the expansion of the elite social base and the spread of printing. More than 1,400 titles were produced from the mid-tenth century to the early twentieth century.[14] Although the contents of these miscellanies were diverse and not necessarily limited to stories, the gathering of stories continued to be a central aim of the compilers. An avid lifelong story collector, Hong Mai (1123–1202), for instance, accumulated accounts from thousands of informants as well as from written sources over six decades, resulting in a staggering 420-fascicle corpus entitled *Records of the Listener* (Yijian zhi).[15] Likewise, the renowned scholar-official Ji Yun (1724–1805) gathered and published five collections in ten years, the best known of which is the *Random Jottings from the Cottage of Close Scrutiny* (Yuewei caotang biji).[16] Along with *Liao Studio's Records of the Strange* (Liaozhai zhiyi) by Pu Songling (1640–1715) and *What the Master Would Not Discuss* (Zi bu yu) by Yuan Mei (1716–1797), these well-known works represent a very small portion of extant collections that has rightfully attracted persistent critical attention.[17] The number of texts that have not been sufficiently studied, however, can literally fill a small library.

This untapped treasure trove promises to offer new insights into traditional Chinese literature and culture. While late medieval scholar-officials played a formative role in the development of the tradition of literati storytelling, the specific contours of that tradition after the mid-tenth century remain murky, since a large number of later collections have not been studied. Such studies are much needed, for they also serve, rather than contradict, modern scholars' meaningful efforts to trace the origins and evolution of Chinese fiction: contextualized analyses of literati storytelling will contribute to a more nuanced understanding of both its crucial differences from and its fundamental continuities with fiction writing. Moreover, because literati storytelling was inextricably linked to shifting sociohistorical conditions, stories produced and circulated by later scholar-officials can allow us to attain a cultural-historical understanding of how they perceived and defined their worlds, offering invaluable insights into literati communities of different historical periods.

That traditional Chinese literati storytelling does not fit squarely into the model of folktale or fiction also underlines its significance for the evolving paradigms of research on story cultures worldwide. These paradigms have been built on a series of binaries, such as the oral and the written, the popular and the elite, and the collective and the individual. Modern scholars have argued that a neat polarization between orality and literacy, as found in the Parry-Lord studies, cannot fully account for the rich dynamics of popular storytelling traditions around the world.[18] The rise of Chinese vernacular novels in the Ming dynasty (1368–1644), for instance, suggests a notion of the "Chinese-type" of popular orality, characterized by the cumulative process of oral performances and "textualizations" by literati transcription and composition of story cycles.[19] The development of Chinese vernacular novels thus complicates the conventional binaries by showing the important roles of writing and literati interventions in popular storytelling. Likewise, the case of literati storytelling reveals these hybrid features on the elite end. On one hand, the overlap between literati collections of miscellanies and Dunhuang transformation texts indicates powerful interconnections between elite and popular storytelling. On the other hand, in addition to the active roles of individual writers, literati storytelling also demonstrates the communal dimension of elite literary production. With a long history lasting more than a millennium, traditional Chinese literati storytelling thus constitutes an important form of narrative production that can enrich our empirical and theoretical understanding of the complex, universal phenomena of storytelling around the world.

CHINESE CHARACTER GLOSSARY

An Lushan 安祿山

Bai Juyi 白居易
Bai Minzhong 白敏中
Bai Pu 白樸
Bai Xingjian 白行簡
Bai Youqiu 白幽求
baixing 百姓
baiyi gongqing 白衣公卿
Bao Si 褒姒
Bao Yi 包誼
"Bei zheng" 北征
Beili zhi 北里誌
Benshi shi 本事詩
bianwen 變文
Bianyi zhi 辨疑志
Boyi zhi 博異志
Bu Feiyan 步飛煙/非煙
bu shi jiugu 不事舅姑
Bukong (Amoghavajra) 不空

cai 才
Cao Shu 曹叔
Chang Yi 常夷
"Changhen ge" 長恨歌
"Changhen ge zhuan" 長恨歌傳
changke 常科
Changsheng dian 長生殿
chaolie 朝列

chaoting 朝庭
chaoye 朝野
Chaoye qianzai 朝野僉載
Che Ruoshui 車若水
Chen Hong 陳鴻
Chen Hongzu 陳鴻祖
Chen Xuanyou 陳玄祐
Cheng Xingchen 程行諶
chengjie 懲戒
"Chezhong nüzi" 車中女子
chifa 持法
Chu Renhuo 褚人獲
Chu Suiliang 褚遂良
Chuan qi 傳奇
chuanqi 傳奇
Chunyu Fen 淳于棻
chushi 出世
ci 詞
Ci Liu shi jiuwen 次柳氏舊聞
Confucius 孔子
Cui (sheng) 崔生
Cui Shao 崔紹
Cui Yingying 崔鶯鶯/鸎鸎
Cui Yuanzong 崔元綜
"Cui niang shi" 崔娘詩

Da Dai Li ji 大戴禮記
Da Ji 妲己
Da Tang xinyu 大唐新語

Dai Fu 戴孚
Daizong （唐）代宗
"Dao Fan Shu chushi" 悼范攄處士
daoqie 盜竊
deshi zhi dao 得失之道
Dezong （唐）德宗
difu 地府
"Dinghun dian" 定婚店
dingming 定命
Dingming lu 定命錄
Dingming lun 定命論
Dizang pusa (Kṣitigarbha) 地藏
    菩薩
"Dongcheng laofu zhuan" 東城
    老父傳
Dou Tingzhi 竇庭芝
Du Cong 杜琮
Du Fu 杜甫
Du Guangting 杜光庭
Du Mu 杜牧
Du You 杜佑
Du Yuanying 杜元穎
Duan Chengshi 段成式
duji 妒忌
dutong 都統

eji 惡疾

Fan Shu 范攄
Fan Ze 樊澤
Fei Ziyu 費子玉
feng 封
Feng (sheng) 馮生
Feng Menglong 馮夢龍
Feng Yan 馮燕
"Feng Yan ge" 馮燕歌
"Feng Yan zhuan" 馮燕傳
Feng Yuanchang 馮元常
fengliu 風流
fengliu zhi shi 風流之士

Fuchai 夫差
fushi 賦詩

Gan Bao 干寶
Gan dingming lu 感定命錄
Ganlu zhi bian 甘露之變
Gao Changyu 高昌宇
Gao Lishi 高力士
Gao Yanxiu 高彥休
Gaozong （唐）高宗
ge 歌
gong 宮
gongju 貢舉
gongqing zidi 公卿子弟
Gu Feixiong 顧非熊
Gu Kuang 顧況
Gu yaya 古押衙
Guangyi ji 廣異記
guanzhe 觀者
guijian 規諫
Guo Ba 郭霸
"Guo Huaqing gong" 過華清宮
Guo Ningsu 郭凝素
Guo Ziyi 郭子儀
Guoshi bu （唐）國史補
Gushenzi 谷神子
guwen 古文

hainei 海內
Han Huang 韓滉
Han Shou 韓壽
Han Wudi 漢武帝
Han yu 漢語
Han Yu 韓愈
Hanlin gongfeng 翰林供奉
Hanlin xueshi 翰林學士
hanshi 寒士
haoxia zhi lun 豪俠之倫
He Xun 何遜
Hejian 河間

"Hejian zhuan" 河間傳
Heshang gong 河上公
Hong Mai 洪邁
Hong Sheng 洪昇
houbei 後輩
Hu Yin 胡寅
Hu Yinglin 胡應麟
Hu Zheng 胡證
huaigu 懷古
Huan Chenfan 桓臣範
Huangfu Mei 皇甫枚
Huangfu Shi 皇甫湜
Huaqing gong 華清宮
"Huashan ji" 華山畿
"Huizhen shi" 會眞詩
hun 魂
Huo Guang 霍光
Huo Xiaoyu 霍小玉
"Huo Xiaoyu zhuan" 霍小玉傳

Ji Yun 紀昀
Jia Chang 賈昌
Jia Chong 賈充
Jia Dan 賈耽
jian 姦
Jiang Fang 蔣防
jiao 角
jieyi 節義
jijian 極諫
Jingangzhi (Vajrabodhi) 金剛智
Jinghong ji 驚鴻記
Jingzong （唐）敬宗
jinshi 進士
Jinyang men 津陽門
"Jinyang men shi" 津陽門詩
Jiyi ji 集異記
junzi 君子

Kaiyuan Tianbao yishi 開元天寶
  遺事

kong 空
Kongzi jiayu 孔子家語
koushe 口舌
kuangzan 匡贊
"Kunlun nu" 崑崙奴
kuren 酷忍

Lai Junchen 來俊臣
Laozi 老子
Li (sheng) 李生
Li Ao 李翱
Li Bai 李白
Li Bi 李泌
Li Chaowei 李朝威
Li Deyu 李德裕
Li Fan 李藩
Li Fengji 李逢吉
Li Fuyan 李復言
Li Gongzuo 李公佐
Li Hui 李回
Li Huizheng 李彙征
Li ji 禮記
Li Jifu 李吉甫
Li Jingliang 李景亮
Li Jiongxiu 李迥秀
Li Kui 李揆
Li Linfu 李林甫
Li Mei 李玫
Li Qi 李錡
Li She 李涉
Li Shen 李紳
Li Shizhi 李適之
Li Su 李愬
Li Wa 李娃
"Li Wa zhuan" 李娃傳
Li Wenyue 李文悅
Li Xianyong 李咸用
Li Yi 李益
Li Yue 李約
"Li Zhangwu zhuan" 李章武傳

Li Zhao 李肇
Lianchang gong 連昌宮
"Lianchang gong ci" 連昌宮詞
Liang Wudi 梁武帝
Liaozhai zhiyi 聊齋誌異
Liexian zhuan 列仙傳
Liezi 列子
"Lihun ji" 離魂記
Lingche 靈澈
lingli xianbi 陵轢險詖
Liu Bang 劉邦
Liu Binke jiahua lu 劉賓客嘉話錄
Liu Changqing 劉長卿
Liu Chen 劉晨
Liu Dan 柳澹
Liu Fang 柳芳
Liu Ji 劉泊
Liu Ling 劉伶
Liu Mian 柳冕
Liu Miaozhi 劉邈之
Liu Pi 劉闢
Liu Qichu 劉栖楚
Liu Shao 劉邵
Liu Su 劉肅 (fl. 806–820)
Liu Su 劉餗 (fl. 728–742)
Liu Taizhen 劉太真
Liu Xiyi 劉希夷
Liu Xuanzuo 劉玄佐
Liu Yan 劉晏
Liu Yi 柳毅
Liu Yiqing 劉義慶
Liu Yuxi 劉禹錫
Liu Zongyuan 柳宗元
Lu (sheng) 盧生
Lu Changyuan 陸長源
Lu Hong 盧鴻
Lu Hongzhi 盧弘止
Lu Kang 陸康
Lu Lun 盧綸
Lu Qi 盧杞

Lu Yu 陸羽
Lu Zhao 盧肇
Lü (weng) 呂翁
Lü Daosheng 呂道生
"Lujiang xiaoli" 廬江小吏
lunzhe 論者
Luo Gongyuan 羅公遠
Lüzhu 綠珠

ma 馬
Ma Youqin 馬遊秦
Ma Zong 馬總
manzuo 滿坐
"Meifei zhuan" 梅妃傳
Mencius 孟子
meng 夢
Meng Jian 孟簡
Meng Qi 孟棨/啓
Meng shu 夢書
Meng Sixian 孟思賢
ming 命
Ming Chongyan 明崇儼
Mingbao ji 冥報記
Minghuang （唐)明皇
Minghuang zalu 明皇雜錄
mingjing 明經
mingju 名句
mingshi 名詩
mingshi xiangfu 名實相符
mingsi 冥司
Mole 磨勒
Mu tianzi zhuan 穆天子傳
Muzong （唐)穆宗

"Nanke taishou zhuan" 南柯太守傳
neixiang 內相
Niu Sengru 牛僧孺
Nongyu 弄玉

Ouyang Zhan 歐陽詹

Pan Haoli 潘好禮
Pei Du 裴度
Pei Guangting 裴光庭
Pei Hang 裴航
Pei Wu 裴武
Pei Xing 裴鉶
Pei Yan 裴炎
po 魄
Pu Songling 蒲松齡

Qi Huangong 齊桓公
Qi Ying 齊映
qian jinshi 前進士
qianding 前定
Qianding lu 前定錄
Qiao Zhizhi 喬知之
qichu 七出
"Qin meng ji" 秦夢記
Qin Mugong 秦穆公
Qin Shihuang 秦始皇
qing 情
Qingjiang 清江
qinglian 清廉
qiqu 七去
Qu Yuan 屈原
quanxuan 銓選
Que shi 闕史
qungong 群公

ren 人
"Ren shi zhuan" 任氏傳
renli 人吏
Renwu zhi 人物志
Ri shu 日書
Rong Yu 戎昱
rongshu 容恕
Ruan Zhao 阮肇
Ruizong （唐）睿宗

Sanshui xiaodu 三水小牘

shan 禪
shang 商
shangdi 上帝
Shangqing 上清
Shanwuwei (Śubhākarasiṃha) 善
　無畏
Shen (shi) 慎氏
Shen Jiji 沈旣濟
Shen Tianshi 申天師
Shen Yazhi 沈亞之
shi 士
Shi Chong 石崇
Shi ji 史記
Shi jing 詩經
shi yan zhi 詩言志
shiguan 試官
shilin zhi rong 士林之榮
shiren 時人
Shishuo xinyu 世說新語
shiyi 時議
"Shuidiao qibian" 水調七遍
Shuren 蜀人
Sikong Tu 司空圖
Sima Qian 司馬遷
Sima Xiangru 司馬相如
Song Jing 宋璟
Song Shenxi 宋申錫
Song Yong 宋雍
Song Zhiwen 宋之問
Soushen ji 搜神記
Su Ting 蘇頲
Su Weidao 蘇味道
Sui Tang jiahua 隋唐嘉話
Sui Tang yanyi 隋唐演義
Sun Qi 孫棨
Suzong （唐）肅宗

Taishan fujun 泰山/太山府君
Taiyi shen 太乙神
Taizong （唐）太宗

Tan Zhu 譚銖
Tang Lin 唐臨
*Tang Minghuang qiuye wutong
yu* 唐明皇秋夜梧桐雨
Tang Te 唐特
Tao Yuanming 陶淵明
tian 天
Tianbao yishi zhugongdiao 天寶
遺事諸宮調
tiancao 天曹
tianxia 天下
tianxia mingshi 天下名士
tonglie 同列
tongnian 同年

Wang Bocheng 王伯成
Wang Dingbao 王定保
Wang Lingran 王泠然
Wang Qi 王起
Wang Renyu 王仁裕
Wang Shifu 王實甫
Wang Wei 王維
Wang Xianke 王仙客
Wang Xuan 王軒
Wang Zhi 王制
Wei Dan 韋丹
Wei Gao 韋皋
Wei Gu 韋固
Wei hou 韋后
Wei Kang 韋抗
Wei Mo 魏蟊
Wei Siming 韋思明
Wei Xuan 韋絢
Wei Yuanzhong 魏元忠
Wei Zheng 魏徵
wen 文
Wen Hui 溫會
Wen She 溫畬
wenren 文人
wenshi 文士

wenyan xiaoshuo 文言小說
wenzhe 聞者
Wenzong （唐）文宗
wu 武
Wu Gongye 武公業
Wu Jing 吳兢
Wu Rong 吳融
Wu Shimei 吳世美
Wu Yansi 武延嗣
Wu Zetian 武則天
wuli 無禮
Wushuang 無雙
"Wushuang zhuan" 無雙傳
wuxing 五行
Wuyun xi ren 五雲谿人
wuzi 無子
Wuzong （唐）武宗

Xi Shi 西施
xian 仙
xianbei 先輩
Xiang Yu 項羽
Xianzhuan shiyi 仙傳拾遺
Xianzong （唐）憲宗
Xiao Song 蕭嵩
Xiao Yingshi 蕭穎士
xiaoshuo 小說
xiaoxing 孝行
xiexue 諧謔
xin yuefu 新樂府
Xiong Zhiyi 熊執易
Xixiang ji 西廂記
Xu Dingming lu 續定命錄
Xu Ning 徐凝
Xu Xuanguai lu 續玄怪錄
Xu Yougong 徐有功
Xuanguai lu 玄怪錄
Xuānzong （唐）宣宗
Xuánzong （唐）玄宗
Xue Juncao 薛君曹

Xue Tiao 薛調
Xue Yongruo 薛用弱
Xun Shuang 荀爽

Yang Guifei 楊貴妃
Yang Guifei waizhuan 楊貴妃
    外傳
Yang Guozhong 楊國忠
Yang Juyuan 楊巨源
Yang Wanqing 楊萬頃
Yang Yan 楊炎
Yang Yu 楊豫
yanshi 豔詩
Yao Chong 姚崇
Ye Fashan 葉法善
Ye Jingneng 葉靜能/淨能
"Ye Jingneng shi" 葉淨能詩
Yi shi 逸史
Yi Yin 伊尹
Yijian zhi 夷堅志
yin 淫
yingxiong 英雄
"Yingying zhuan" 鶯鶯/鸎鸎傳
Yinhua lu 因話錄
yinshi 引詩
yinyang 陰陽
yinyi 隱逸
yipin baishan 一品白衫
yiyou 乙酉
Yizhi 宜之
Yong Tao 雍陶
youdi 友悌
youshi zhi shi 有識之士
youwu 尤物
"Youxia liezhuan" 遊俠列傳
youxian shi 遊仙詩
Youyang zazu 酉陽雜俎
yu 羽
Yu Dingguo 于定國
Yuan Can 袁參

Yuan Jiazuo 袁嘉祚
Yuan Mei 袁枚
Yuan Zhen 元稹
"Yuanhe shengde shi" 元和聖德詩
Yuchen yaolüe 御臣要略
Yue Shi 樂史
yuefu 樂府
Yuewei caotang biji 閱微草堂筆記
yuning 諛佞
Yunxi youyi 雲谿友議
yushi 餘食

zashi 雜史
Zeng Bu 曾布
Zhang (sheng) 張生
Zhang Baoyin 張保胤
Zhang Guo 張果
Zhang Hu 張祜
Zhang Huang 張瑝
Zhang Jiazhen 張嘉貞
Zhang Jiuling 張九齡
Zhang Shizhi 張釋之
Zhang Xiu 張琇
Zhang Yanshang 張延賞
Zhang Yichao 張義潮/議潮
Zhang Ying 張嬰
Zhang Yǐng 張穎
Zhang Yue 張說
Zhang Zhuo 張鷟
Zhao Gu 趙嘏
Zhao He 趙合
Zhao Lin 趙璘
Zhao Rui 趙蕤
Zhao Xiang 趙象
Zhao Xiu 趙修
Zhao yilou 趙倚樓
Zhao Ziqin 趙自勤
Zhao Zongru 趙宗儒
zhaoshu 兆庶
"Zhenzhong ji" 枕中記

Zheng Chuhui 鄭處誨
Zheng Huangu 鄭還古
Zheng Tao 鄭騊
Zheng Yu 鄭嵎
Zheng Yuqing 鄭餘慶
zhengneng 政能
Zhenguan zhengyao 貞觀政要
zhexian 謫仙
zhi 徵
Zhi yan （唐）摭言
zhi yu buzhi 知與不知
zhiguai 志怪
zhiji 知己
zhiju 制舉
zhiwei 知微
zhiyin 知音
zhong 眾
Zhong Lu 鍾籟/輅

Zhongchen men 忠臣門
zhonglie 忠烈
Zhongzong （唐）中宗
Zhou Ju 周矩
Zhu Ci 朱泚
Zhu Jun 朱均
Zhu Ze 朱澤
zhuan 傳
Zhuangzi 莊子
Zhuangzong （後唐）莊宗
Zhujia kemu ji 諸家科目記
Zhuo Wenjun 卓文君
Zi bu yu 子不語
Zuanyi ji 纂異記
Zuo Ci 左慈
Zuo zhuan 左傳
zuoyou 左右
zuozhu 座主

INTRODUCTION

1. Barbara Hardy, "Toward a Poetics of Fiction," 5.

2. Jerome Bruner, "Life as Narrative," 31.

3. W. S. Penn, *The Telling of the World*, 6.

4. Variant terms include *shi dafu, shiren, shizu, shi junzi, yiguan*, and *wenren*. Critics prefer different translations to underscore the characteristics of the *shi* in different periods, such as "aristocrats," "bureaucrats," "scholars," "men of letters," and "gentry." I adopt "literati" and "scholar-officials" throughout this book because they are widely accepted translations, especially in the scholarship on medieval China.

5. Ying-shih Yü, *Shi yu Zhongguo wenhua*, 3–74.

6. Naitō Konan (1866–1934) first proposed the idea of the Tang-Song Transition, arguing that the collapse of aristocracy with the demise of the Tang and the founding of the Song marked the end of the medieval period (*chūsei*). I use the term "late medieval" to refer specifically to the last two centuries in this process of dissolution. Although the term "medieval" has rich connotations in the studies of European history, I do not assume that China had exactly the same historical conditions and processes as its European counterparts. For Naitō's theory, see his "Gaikatsuteki Tō Sō jidai kan," 111–19. For Naitō's influences, see Miyakawa Hisayuki, "An Outline of the Naitō Hypothesis," 533–52; Zhang Guangda, "Naitō Konan de Tang Song biange shuo," 5–71.

7. Scholarship on this topic is extensive. For examples, see David Johnson, *The Medieval Chinese Oligarchy*; Patricia B. Ebrey, *The Aristocratic Families*; Robert P. Hymes, *Statesmen and Gentlemen*; Peter K. Bol, *"This Culture of Ours"*; Beverly J. Bossler, *Powerful Relations*; John W. Chaffee, *The Thorny Gates of Learning*; Hilde De Weerdt, *Competition over Content*.

8. Robert Hartwell, "Demographic, Political, and Social Transformations of China, 750–1550," 365–422; Qiu Tiansheng, *Tang Song biange qi de zhengjing yu shehui*; Satake Yasuhiko, *Tō Sō henkaku no chiikiteki kenkyū*; Wang Jianchuan and Pi Qingsheng, *Zhongguo jinshi minjian xinyang*, 1–30.

9. For the rise of military governors and the repercussions, see Mark Edward Lewis, *China's Cosmopolitan Empire*, 58–84; Huang Zhengjian et

al., *Zhong wan Tang shehui yu zhengzhi*; David McMullen, *State and Scholars in T'ang China*.

10. The Tang system included the annual degree examinations held by the Ministry of Rites and the irregular decree examinations by the emperor. Candidates for the Presented Scholar degree were chosen by prefectures mainly for their poetic talent and presented to the emperor along with other annual tribute goods. About twenty to thirty people who further passed the court-administered tests in poetic composition, policy discussion, and memorization of Confucian classics earned their eligibility for office. From the eighth century, they had to wait three years before they could be assessed and given appointments by the Ministry of Personnel.

11. See Benjamin A. Elman, *A Cultural History of Civil Examinations*. The short-lived conquest dynasty Yuan (1271–1368) was an exception because the Mongols refused to restore civil service examinations until 1313, and even then they severely restricted the quota for Chinese literati.

12. For histories of Tang poetry, see Xu Zong, *Tangshi shi*; Stephen Owen, *The Poetry of the Early T'ang*; Owen, *The Great Age of Chinese Poetry*; Owen, *The Late Tang*. For histories of Tang stories, see Cheng Yizhong, *Tangdai xiaoshuo shi*; Li Jianguo, *Tang Wudai zhiguai chuanqi xulu*.

13. Leo Tak-hung Chan, *The Discourse on Foxes and Ghosts*.

14. William H. Nienhauser Jr., "Creativity and Storytelling in the *Ch'uanch'i*," 31–70.

15. For examples, see Glen Dudbridge, *Religious Experience and Lay society*; Jia Erqiang, *Tang Song minjian xinyang*.

16. *TPGJ*, 452.3697.

17. Gao Yanxiu, *Que shi*, 1.1.

18. Although scholars have traditionally believed that the compilation and circulation of story collections could have helped examination candidates advance their careers, the theory has been refuted by Victor Mair. See Mair, "Scroll Presentation in the T'ang Dynasty," 35–60. For a summary of the traditional belief, see Cheng Qianfan, *Tangdai jinshi xingjuan yu wenxue*, 79–87.

19. The numbers are only approximate. I do not count the collections on objects, arts, theoretical treatises, and the like; collections believed to have variant titles are counted only once. See Ning Jiayu, *Zhongguo wenyan xiaoshuo zongmu tiyao*, 6–128. For an earlier bibliography, see Yuan Xingpei and Hou Zhongyi, *Zhongguo wenyan xiaoshuo shumu*, 8–93.

20. Lu Xun, *Zhongguo xiaoshuo shilüe*, 44–57. *Chuanqi* was first used as a generic term by Hu Yinglin (1551–1602) to refer to lengthy tales on romantic affairs and later by Lu Xun for the lengthy and artistic Tang tales. See Laura Hua Wu, "From *Xiaoshuo* to Fiction," 339–71.

21. For example, Y. W. Ma, "Fact and Fantasy in T'ang Tales," 167–81.

22. Luo Ning, *Han Tang xiaoshuo guannian lungao*; Han Yunbo, *Tangdai xiaoshuo guannian yu xiaoshuo xingqi yanjiu*.

23. Regardless of their differences, most scholars of Tang narrative literature have accepted the framework of "fiction" in their studies. For examples, see Mizobe Yoshie, "Denki botsukō izen no Tōdai shōsetsu," 90–104;

Nienhauser Jr., "Creativity and Storytelling in the *Ch'uan-ch'i*," 31–70;
Song Lunmei, *Tangren xiaoshuo* Xuanguai lu *yanjiu*; Li Pengfei, *Tangdai
fei xieshi xiaoshuo*; Cheng Yizhong, *Tangdai xiaoshuo shi*; Liu Yongqiang,
Zhongguo gudai xiaoshuo shi xulun, 106–34.

24. Dudbridge, *Religious Experience and Lay society*, 16. Parallel to this
study of religious beliefs, his most recent work treats collections of anecdotes
as memoirs. See Dudbridge, *A Portrait of Five Dynasties China*.

25. Sarah M. Allen, "Tales Retold," 105–43; Allen, "Tang Stories."

26. Inglis, *Hong Mai's* Record of the Listener; Leo Tak-hung Chan, *The
Discourse on Foxes and Ghosts*.

27. He also offers by far the most forceful theoretical refutation of the fiction argument. See Campany, *Making Transcendents*, esp. 1–38.

28. Gabrielle M. Spiegel, *The Past as Text*, xviii.

29. Rania Huntington, *Alien Kind*, 17.

30. Christopher M. B. Nugent, *Manifest in Words, Written on Paper*;
also, Xiaofei Tian, *Tao Yuanming and Manuscript Culture*.

31. Allen, "Tales Retold," 126–36.

32. Ann Swidler, *Talk of Love*, 158.

33. Ibid., 111–59.

34. Robert Darnton, *The Great Cat Massacre*, 9–72.

35. Bol, *"This Culture of Ours,"* 32–35.

36. Duan Chengshi, *Youyang zazu*, 12.95.

37. I am not concerned here with distinguishing the term "theme" from
other related ones, including "motif" and "topos." For discussions of "motif"
and "topos," see Stith Thompson, *The Folktale*, 413–27; Lynette Hunter,
Toward a Definition of Topos.

38. Charles Holcombe, *In the Shadow of the Han*, 13, 127.

39. See Owen, *The End of the Chinese "Middle Ages,"* 83–106; Xiaoshan
Yang, *Metamorphosis of the Private Sphere*. Moreover, Tang literati also
played an important role in iconizing the recluse-poet Tao Yuanming, although
their attitudes were often ambivalent because of their own commitment to official service. See Wendy Swartz, *Reading Tao Yuanming*, 48–73, 160–85.

40. Fan Shu, *Yunxi youyi*, 2.27–28.

41. Bol, *"This Culture of Ours,"* 41–48.

42. Charles Hartman, *Han Yü*, 115–18.

43. Owen, *The Late Tang*, 45–65.

44. Contradiction and ambivalence in late medieval stories are broader
and more complex than negation. The model of negation is embodied by the
clichéd statement that traditional Chinese scholar-officials were often torn
between an impulse to serve the court and the people (*rushi* or *jianji*) and
another to repudiate such social responsibilities and pursue personal happiness (*chushi* or *dushan*). See Zhang Zhongmou, *Jianji yu dushan*.

45. Denis C. Twitchett, *The Birth of the Chinese Meritocracy*, 15; Wu
Zongguo, *Tangdai keju zhidu yanjiu*, 21; Fu Xuancong, *Tangdai keju yu
wenxue*, 47–50.

46. Twitchett, *The Birth of the Chinese Meritocracy*, 8–17; Wu Zongguo,
Tangdai keju zhidu yanjiu, 21.

47. Dai Weihua, *Tang fangzhen wenzhi liaozuo kao.*
48. Chaffee, *The Thorny Gates of Learning,* 35.
49. Anthony DeBlasi, *Reform in the Balance.*
50. Bol, *"This Culture of Ours,"* 108–47; Hartman, *Han Yü*; Sun Changwu, *Tangdai guwen yundong tonglun.*
51. Johnson, "The Last Years of a Great Clan," 5–102; Ebrey, *The Aristocratic Families,* 119; Bol, *"This Culture of Ours,"* 45–47; Nicolas Tackett, "The Transformation of Medieval Chinese Elites."
52. For discussions of the Song centralization, see Miyazaki Ichisada, *Tōyōteki kinsei*; Deng Xiaonan, *Zuzong zhi fa.*
53. Bol, *"This Culture of Ours,"* 52.
54. I use this epithet throughout this book because his posthumous title, Xuánzong, is indistinguishable in romanization from that of a later Tang emperor Xuānzong (r. 846–859).
55. Darnton, *The Great Cat Massacre,* 23.

CHAPTER 1

1. For the emperor's annals, see *JTS,* 8.165–9.238; *XTS,* 5.121–54. Also see Twitchett and John K. Fairbank, *The Cambridge History of China,* vol. 3, pt. 1, 333–463.
2. Twitchett, "How to Be an Emperor," 1–102; DeBlasi, "Contemplating Rulership," 203–32.
3. Martin Kern, *The Stele Inscriptions of Ch'in Shih-huang*; Michael Loewe, *Divination, Mythology, and Monarchy,* 85–111, 121–41; Howard J. Wechsler, *Offerings of Jade and Silk*; Andrew Eisenberg, *Kingship in Early Medieval China.*
4. Robert E. Harrist Jr., *The Landscape of Words,* 219–70.
5. Jack W. Chen, *The Poetics of Sovereignty*; Paul W. Kroll, "Four Vignettes from the Court of Tang Xuanzong," 1–27.
6. Twitchett, *The Writing of Official History*; Mark Strange, "Representations of Liang Emperor Wu," 53–112.
7. Arthur F. Wright, "T'ang T'ai-tsung," 17–32; Wright, "Sui Yang-Ti," 47–76; Xiaofei Tian, "The Representation of Sovereignty," 211–31.
8. John Watkins, *Representing Elizabeth in Stuart England.*
9. David I. Kertzer, *Ritual, Politics, and Power,* 11.
10. For a discussion of the structure of the two texts, see Luo Liantian, "Changhen ge yu Changhen ge zhuan," 727–43.
11. For the Presented Scholar degree, see the introduction, note 10. In the Tang, new entrants into officialdom usually had to wait for a certain period before they could be appointed to offices; special examinations held by the Ministry of Personnel, the Pre-eminent in Legal Judgments (*shupan bacui*) and the Erudite Learning and Grand Composition (*boxue hongci*), allowed the most outstanding among them to bypass the mandatory wait period. The decree examination was presided over by the emperor in person to recruit special talents for the court; successful candidates could get appointments immediately.

12. For Bai's life, see *JTS*, 166.4340–60; *XTS*, 119.4300–5; Zhu Jincheng, *Bai Juyi nianpu*; Arthur Waley, *The Life and Times of Po Chü-I*.

13. For Chen Hong's life, see Li Jianguo, *Tang Wudai zhiguai chuanqi xulu*, 326–28.

14. *QTS*, 336.3760.

15. Ibid., 309.3496.

16. Ibid., 217.2276.

17. For a discussion of this belief, see Owen, "The Difficulty of Pleasure," 9–30.

18. See Fan-pen Li Chen, "Yang Kuei-fei," 1–48.

19. Bai Juyi, *Bai Juyi ji*, 12.239.

20. Ibid., 12.238. For a discussion of such debates, see Zhang Zhongyu, *Bai Juyi* Changhen ge *yanjiu*.

21. For a discussion of the term, see Dudbridge, *The Tale of Li Wa*, 67–72.

22. *WYYH*, 794.8b.

23. Y. W. Ma sees the second half as marking a shift from "factual description of the events" to "the mystic setting," or from "fact" to "fantasy." Ma, "Fact and Fantasy in T'ang Tales," 167–69.

24. *WYYH*, 794.10a.

25. Ibid., 794.7b.

26. Ibid., 794.8b–9a.

27. Owen, "What Did Liu Zhi Hear?" 81–118. For a detailed study, see Yue Hong, "A Discourse of Romantic Love."

28. For instance, while commenting on the story of a scholar-official who dies of grief after the passing of his beloved concubine, the ninth-century literati storyteller Gao Yanxiu points out that obsessions for female beauty "can [cause a man] to lose a state on a big scale of things and on a small one lead to his demise." Gao Yanxiu, *Que shi*, 2.30–31.

29. Anna M. Shields, "Defining Experience," 61–78.

30. *WYYH*, 794.10a–b.

31. This is a presumption that came true. Bai Juyi himself was surprised by how popular his ballad was among his contemporaries. See Bai Juyi, "Yu Yuan Jiu shu," *Bai Juyi ji*, 45.963–64. The ballad was even transmitted and influential beyond the borders of China. See Masako Nakagawa Graham, *The Yang Kuei-fei Legend*.

32. For examples, see Li Deyu, *Ci Liu shi jiuwen*, 1.4–5; Zheng Qi, *Kai Tian chuanxin ji*, 1.4–5, 1.9–10; Nan Zhuo, *Jiegu lu*, 1.3–6.

33. Fan Shu, *Yunxi youyi*, 3.76–77.

34. For a discussion of poems on the topic, see Jin Jicang, *Changhen ge jiqi tong ticai shi xiangjie*.

35. Wang Renyu, *Kaiyuan Tianbao yishi*, 1.21, 2.40.

36. Li Zhao, *Tang guoshi bu*, 1.19.

37. Kroll, "Nostalgia and History,'" 309.

38. Li Zhao, *Tang Guoshi bu*, 1.18–19.

39. Che Ruoshui, *Jiaoqi ji*, 3b. For another criticism, see Zhang Jie (fl. twelfth century), *Suihantang shihua*, 1.7.

40. See Bol, *"This Culture of Ours,"* 108–47; Sun Changwu, *Tangdai guwen yundong tonglun*; DeBlasi, *Reform in the Balance*.

41. A more detailed analysis of these collections has been published in Manling Luo, "Remembering Kaiyuan and Tianbao," 263–300.

42. *JTS*, 17.562–65. For a discussion of the incident, see Hu Kexian, *Tangdai zhongda lishi shijian*, 495–565.

43. Normally a male heir would strengthen the status of a crown prince. Because Princess Taiping sought to undermine the future Illustrious Emperor, the baby would have made her more desperate and hence more inclined to do harm. Princess Taiping was very influential during the reign of Emperor Ruizong as his favorite sister. She gradually developed an antagonistic relationship with her nephew, the crown prince and future Illustrious Emperor, who eventually took actions against her and her allies.

44. Li Deyu, *Ci Liu shi jiuwen*, 1.1–2.

45. Ibid., 1.2.

46. Ibid., 1.3.

47. Ibid., 1.4–5.

48. Li's effort was probably encouraged by his previous success. In 825, Li submitted a group of six poems entitled "Danyi zhen" to Emperor Jingzong (r. 824–827), the elder brother of Wenzong, to encourage him to devote himself to monarchic duties. Jingzong is said to have responded warmly to Li's presentation. *JTS*, 124.4514–15.

49. For a study of Li's role as Wuzong's chief minister, see Michael R. Drompp, *Tang China and the Collapse of the Uighur Empire*.

50. For biographies of Zheng Chuhui, see *JTS*, 158.4168–69; *XTS*, 165.5062.

51. *XTS*, 165.5062. Zheng might have accessed archival sources when he worked as a collator in the imperial library. See Kroll, "The Dancing Horses of T'ang," 244.

52. See Kroll, "Nostalgia and History," 298n22. Supporting evidence can be seen in the account of Li Deyu demoting an official Wei Wen to a provincial post for his association with Li's enemies. Wei is said to have enlisted Zheng Chuhui on his staff, a move that further displeased Li. See *JTS*, 168.4380.

53. Zheng Chuhui, *Minghuang zalu*, 1.12.

54. Ibid., 1.12–13.

55. Another drunken genius in Tang stories associated with the Illustrious Emperor's court is Li Bai, who acquired a much more prominent status than Su Ting in post-Tang representations.

56. Zheng Chuhui, *Minghuang zalu*, 2.25.

57. Ibid., 1.16.

58. In a version by Meng Qi, the poem Li Shizhi composed after his demotion plays a more active role in the story: described as Li's defiant gesture, it angers his enemy and leads to his death. Meng Qi, *Benshi shi*, 4.18. For a discussion, see Marc Nürnberger, *Das "Ben shi shi" des Meng Qi*, 211–12.

59. There was a third collection, *Kai Tian chuanxin ji* by Zheng Qi (fl. late ninth century). Zheng Qi only reiterates the emphases of Li Deyu and

Zheng Chuhui on political intimacy, with additional examples. See Luo, "Remembering Kaiyuan and Tianbao," 285–89.

60. One of the captives taken by the Later Tang army, Wang survived and became an official at the new court. For biographies of Wang Renyu, see *Jiu Wudai shi*, 128.1689–90; *Xin Wudai shi*, 57.661–62. For a detailed study of his life, see Dudbridge, *A Portrait of Five Dynasties China*, 1–38.

61. Wang Renyu, *Kaiyuan Tianbao yishi*, 9.

62. Ibid., 1.11.

63. The nickname was noted by Li Zhao in his "Hanlin zhi." See Fu Xuancong and Shi Chunde, *Hanxue sanshu*, 1–7. For discussions of the institution, see F. A. Bischoff, *La Forêt des Pinceaux*; Mao Lei, *Tangdai hanlin xueshi*; Li Fuchang, *Tangdai xueshi yu wenren zhengzhi*, 219–302.

64. In his two other collections, *Yutang xianhua* and *Wang shi jianwen lu*, Wang Renyu also shows his admiration of men with literary talent like himself. Dudbridge, *A Portrait of Five Dynasties China*, 15–16.

65. See Fu Xuancong, "Tang Xuan Su liangchao hanlin xueshi kaolun," 55–64. A seemingly anachronistic reference to Li Bai as Hanlin academician may, however, be an honorific tribute, as we can see in the tomb inscription composed by Fan Chuanzheng around 817. Fan Chuanzheng, "Tang zuo shiyi hanlin xueshi Li gong xin mubei bing xu," 31.1461–68.

66. For examples, see Zheng Qi, *Kai Tian chuanxin ji*, 6; Zheng Chuhui, *Minghuang zalu*, 2.25–26, 2.28–30; Wang Renyu, *Kaiyuan Tianbao yishi*, 2.46, 2.52, 2.54, 2.59.

67. Zheng Chuhui, *Minghuang zalu*, 2.25; Wang Renyu, *Kaiyuan Tianbao yishi*, 1.23; Liu Su, *Da Tang xinyu*, 1.12.

68. The old man in Zheng Yu's poem was at least 110 years old. See Kroll, "Nostalgia and History," 293.

69. For authorship, see Chen Yinke, *Chen Yinke xiansheng wenshi lunji*, 149–55; Wang Meng'ou, *Tangren xiaoshuo yanjiu*, vol. 4, 213–21.

70. *TPGJ*, 485.3992–95.

71. Cutter, "History and 'The Old Man of the Eastern Wall,'" 503–28. Cutter believes that the old man's change of identity has an ironic edge and that his name Jia Chang is a pun for "false glory."

72. Cutter, *The Brush and the Spur*, 9–107.

73. *JTS*, 8.166–67; *XTS*, 5.121.

74. Li Han, *Xian Qin liang Han zhi yinyang wuxing xueshuo*.

75. *TPGJ*, 485.3993.

76. Like the Presented Scholar degree, the Canonical Expert degree in Confucian classics was conferred through the annual recruitment examinations. It was easier and had a higher success rate than the Presented Scholar examination. Successful candidates also earned their eligibility for office but had to wait before getting appointments.

77. For Yuan Zhen's life, see *JTS*, 166.4327–39; *XTS*, 174.5223–29; Bian Xiaoxuan, *Yuan Zhen nianpu*.

78. Charles Hartman has argued that the movement emphasized "a new sense of didacticism." Hartman, *Han Yü*, 225–35.

79. Bai Juyi, "Yu Yuan Jiu shu," *Bai Juyi ji*, 45.962–63.

80. Yuan Zhen, *Yuan Zhen ji*, 24.313.

81. Ibid.

82. *JTS*, 116.4333–34.

83. For a detailed discussion and translation of the poem, see Kroll, "Nostalgia and History," 286–366.

84. Stanley Weinstein, *Buddhism under the T'ang*, 114–36.

85. *QTS*, 567.6565.

86. Weinstein, *Buddhism under the T'ang*, 137–44.

87. *QTS*, 567.6566.

88. *JTS*, 18.629–30; *XTS*, 216.6107–8.

89. Strange, "Representations of Liang Emperor Wu"; Tian, "The Representation of Sovereignty"; Thomas E. Smith, "Ritual and the Shaping of Narrative."

90. In 733, the emperor ordered that each family hold a copy of the *Laozi* and that policy questions on the text be added to annual recruitment examinations held by the Ministry of Rites. Eight years later, he set up Laozi temples across the country and created an examination degree for Daoist learning. In 755, he issued his personal commentaries on the *Laozi*. See *JTS*, 8.199, 9.213, 9.230; *XTS*, 44.1164.

91. Zheng Yu, "Jinyang men shi," *QTS*, 567.6563; Duan Chengshi, *Youyang zazu*, 3.32.

92. Li Deyu, *Ci Liu shi jiuwen*, 1.4; Duan Chengshi, *Youyang zazu*, 3.32.

93. Zheng Chuhui, *Minghuang zalu*, 2.30–32; *TPGJ*, 26.172.

94. Campany, *Making Transcendents*, 214, 129.

95. For discussions, see Wang Yongping, *Daojiao yu Tangdai shehui*; Sun Changwu, *Daojiao yu Tangdai wenxue*; Sun Changwu, *Tangdai wenxue yu fojiao*.

96. Campany, *Making Transcendents*, 208–13.

97. *Kaiyuan yishi*, cited in Chen Jingyi, *Quanfang beizu*, houji, 3.13a.

98. Zheng Qi, *Kai Tian chuanxin ji*, 1.6.

99. *Shi* usually means "poetry," but its meaning in the title here is unclear. I have translated it as "story" for the sake of convenience.

100. Zheng Zhenduo, *Zhongguo su wenxue shi*, vol. 1, 180–270; Victor H. Mair, *Tang Transformation Texts*; Mair, *Painting and Performance*.

101. Zhang Hongxun, *Dunhuang su wenxue yanjiu*, 260–86.

102. Ibid., 273–78.

103. *JTS*, 7.182, 51.2174–75.

104. Zhang Hongxun calls Ye an "archery target" type of character. Zhang, *Dunhuang su wenxue yanjiu*, 264.

105. Zhao Lin, *Yinhua lu*, 5.106.

106. God Indra (Di Shi) is a deity of Buddhist origin, and the All-Encompassing Heaven (Daluo tian) is the highest of the thirty-six Daoist heavens. This mixture of Buddhist and Daoist elements is not unusual in Dunhuang transformation texts, often taken as one of their characteristics as popular literature.

107. Wang Chongmin, *Dunhuang bianwen ji*, 2.216–28.

108. Ibid., 2.216.

109. Ibid., 2.225.

110. Jack Chen, *The Poetics of Sovereignty*, 18.

111. Wang Chongmin, *Dunhuang bianwen ji*, 2.228.

112. The unflattering image of the Illustrious Emperor here parallels that of Taizong in another transformation text, "Emperor Taizong of the Tang Enters the Underworld" (Tang Taizong ru ming ji). In this narrative, Taizong is summoned to hell and tries to bribe his way back to life by promising wealth and rank in the living world to the presiding administrative assistant. Wang Chongmin, *Dunhuang bianwen ji*, 209–15.

113. *Lunyu jishi*, 16.540. For a detailed discussion of recluses, see Alan Berkowitz, *Patterns of Disengagement*.

CHAPTER 2

1. See Cen Zhongmian, *Tangshi yushen*, passim.

2. Jack Chen, "Blank Spaces and Secret Histories," 1071–73.

3. See Luo, "Remembering Kaiyuan and Tianbao," 263–300. For examples of such clichéd statements, see Li Deyu, *Ci Liu shi jiuwen*, 1; Wang Renyu, *Kaiyuan Tianbao yishi*, 9.

4. It is sometimes assumed that the Presented Scholar examination was the typical career starting point for Tang literati. See Shang Yongliang, *Keju zhi lu yu huanhai fuchen*. But less than thirty a year passed this competitive examination, and most people entered through other avenues.

5. Twitchett, *The Writing of Official History*, 4.

6. *XTS*, 58.1467.

7. Nanxiu Qian, *Spirit and Self in Medieval China*, 211–32.

8. Paul F. Rouzer, *Articulated Ladies*, 94.

9. Liu Su, *Da Tang xinyu*, 10.160.

10. Ibid., 1.4.

11. Ibid., 4.57–58.

12. Ibid., 9.143.

13. Ibid., 12.182–83.

14. For a recent discussion of didacticism, see Anthony E. Clark, "Praise and Blame." For an overview of premodern official historiography, see Oncho Ng and Q. Edward Wang, *Mirroring the Past*.

15. In fact, Qing court historians considered Liu Su's inclusion of humorous entries as a major flaw, expunging the collection from the "history"(*shi*) division and relegating it to the "schools of minor discourses" (*xiaoshuo jia lei*) section. See Ji Yun et al., *Siku quanshu zongmu*, 140.1183.

16. Liu Su, *Da Tang xinyu*, 1.7–8, 9.144, 12.185–86.

17. Ibid., 11.171.

18. Ibid., 6.84.

19. Ibid., 7.101. For Zhang Shizhi's biography, see Ban Gu, *Han shu*, 50.2307–12.

20. For Yu Dingguo's biography, see Ban Gu, *Han shu*, 71.3041–46.

21. Liu Su, *Da Tang xinyu*, 5.81–82.

22. Ibid., 3.41.

23. Wu Jing, *Zhenguan zhengyao jijiao*, 7.390–92. For a discussion of Taizong's anxiety over his image in the historical record, see Jack Chen, *The Poetics of Sovereignty*, 14–32.

24. Zuo Qiuming, *Chunqiu Zuo zhuan zhu*, Xiang 25, 1099.

25. *JTS*, 8.187–88.

26. Liu Su, *Da Tang xinyu*, 3.50.

27. A major advisor to the founding king of the Shang dynasty (ca. 16–11th century BCE), Yi Yin exiled the tyrannical new king Taijia for three years, forcing him to reform before he brought him back and reinstalled him. See Sima Qian, *Shi ji*, 3.99. A high minister at the Han court, Huo Guang (d. 68 BCE) removed the new emperor after he soon turned out to be unqualified, enthroning another one in his place. See Ban Gu, *Han shu*, 68.2937–47.

28. Liu Su, *Da Tang xinyu*, 11.171.

29. Zhou Xunchu, *Tangren biji xiaoshuo kaosuo*, 146–64.

30. *Li ji Zheng zhu*, 10.7b.

31. Zhao Lin, *Yinhua lu*, 2.75.

32. Ibid., 4.92.

33. Ibid., 5.101.

34. Ibid., 4.94.

35. Ibid., 2.79.

36. Ibid., 1.71–72.

37. Ibid., 6.115.

38. Ibid., 5.110.

39. Zhao Zongru died at roughly the same time as Du and Song. Zhao Lin's statement here is inaccurate, perhaps due to his faulty personal memory or some flawed details in his source.

40. Zhao Lin, *Yinhua lu*, 2.76–77.

41. *JTS*, 167.4370–72; *XTS*, 152.4844–46.

42. Cited in *TPGJ*, 122.864–65.

43. Shields, "Alternate Views of Literary History," 22.

44. Zhao Lin, *Yinhua lu*, 2.75–76.

45. *JTS*, 18.602–3.

46. See Oliver Moore, *Rituals of Recruitment in Tang China*, 55–57.

47. Zhao Lin, *Yinhua lu*, 3.89–90.

48. For studies of the change, see Johnson, *The Medieval Chinese Oligarchy*; Ebrey, *The Aristocratic Families*.

49. Zhao Lin, *Yinhua lu*, 2.77–78.

50. Zhao Lin was not the only one who admired such success. For another collection preoccupied with examples of family success, see Li Ao, *Zhuoyi ji*.

51. Zhao Lin, *Yinhua lu*, 3.86.

52. Ibid., 2.79.

53. Ibid., 3.83.

54. Ibid., 3.86.

55. Ibid., 1.74.

56. Ibid., 1.68.

57. Ibid., 3.90. The italicized sentences in parenthesis are Zhao Lin's interlinear notes.

58. Moore, *Rituals of Recruitment in Tang China*, 75–76.
59. Zhao Lin, *Yinhua lu*, 2.78.
60. Ibid., 5.105–6.
61. *XTS*, 59.1542.
62. *QTS*, 646.7406.
63. Owen, *The End of the Chinese "Middle Ages,"* 1–129; Owen, *The Late Tang*, 1–40, 89–182, 226–54.
64. Graham M. Sanders, *Words Well Put*, 281.
65. Xu Youfu, *Tangdai funü shenghuo yu shi*.
66. Fan Shu, *Yunxi youyi*, 1.4–5.
67. Ibid.
68. For the abandoned woman persona, see Maija Bell Samei, *Gendered Persona and Poetic Voice*.
69. For discussions of historical women's poetic voices, see Maureen Robertson, "Voicing the Feminine," 63–110; Wilt L. Idema and Beata Grant, *The Red Brush*; Grace S. Fong, *Herself an Author*; Xiaorong Li, *Women's Poetry of Late Imperial China*.
70. Such gender assumptions still prompt modern scholars to read historical women's poetry as autobiographical. For a criticism, see Ronald Egan, "Why Didn't Zhao Mingcheng Send Letters to His Wife?," 57–77.
71. Fan Shu, *Yunxi youyi*, 1.12–13.
72. Ibid., 1.2–3.
73. See *Yue jue shu*, 12.1b–2a; Zhao Ye, *Wu Yue chunqiu*, 9.249–51.
74. Tian, *Tao Yuanming and Manuscript Culture*, 196–219.
75. For the tale of an ugly woman who tries to imitate Xi Shi, see *Zhuangzi jishi*, "Tian yun," 5.515. This ugly woman is later known as the Eastern Neighbor, an addition that plays with the literal meaning of the *xi* (west) in Xi Shi's name.
76. For a discussion of female ghosts and historical sites, see Judith Zeitlin, *The Phantom Heroine*, 87–97. For discussions of *huaigu* poetry, see Hans H. Frankel, "The Contemplation of the Past," 345–65; Owen, "Place," 417–57; Chi Xiao, "Lyric Archi-Occasion," 17–35.
77. The anthology *Gujin shiren xiuju* by Yuan Jing (late seventh century) indicates that outstanding lines became an important way of assessing literary history. The collection is not extant, but its preface has survived. See Kūkai, *Wenjing mifu lun jiaozhu*, 354–55. Bai Juyi praised two parallel couplets by his friend Liu Yuxi as the best of his works. Bai Juyi, "Liu Bai changhe ji jie," in *Bai Juyi ji*, 69.1452–53. Many other ninth-century poetic craftsmen were preoccupied with parallel couplets. See Owen, *The Late Tang*, 89–155.
78. Yu-kung Kao, "The Aesthetics of Regulated Verse," 332–85; Owen, *Traditional Chinese Poetry and Poetics*, 78–107.
79. Fan Shu, *Yunxi youyi*, 2.31–32.
80. Wang Dingbao, *Tang zhi yan*, 7.80.
81. Fan Shu, *Yunxi youyi*, 1.8.
82. Mair, "Scroll Presentation in the T'ang Dynasty," 35–60.
83. Wei Xuan, *Liu Binke jiahua lu*, 4.

84. Fan Shu, *Yunxi youyi*, 1.5–6.

85. For discussions of travel writing and landscape inscriptions, see Harrist Jr., *The Landscape of Words*; James Hargett, *Stairway to Heaven*. For a translated anthology, see Richard E. Strassberg, *Inscribed Landscapes*.

86. Fan Shu, *Yunxi youyi*, 2.42.

87. For anthologizing literature, see David R. Knechtges, "Culling the Weeds and Selecting Prime Blossoms," 200–41; Pauline Yu, "Poems in Their Place," 163–96; Yu, "Charting the Landscape of Chinese Poetry," 71–87.

88. Fan Shu, *Yunxi youyi*, 3.55.

89. Zeng Qinliang, *Zuo zhuan yinshi fushi zhi shijiao yanjiu*; David Schaberg, *A Patterned Past*, 72–80.

90. Fan Shu, *Yunxi youyi*, 3.61–63.

91. Zeng Qinliang, *Zuo zhuan yinshi fushi zhi shijiao yanjiu*; Schaberg, *A Patterned Past*, 234–43.

92. For a study of poetry production and circulation in the Tang, see Nugent, *Manifest in Words, Written on Paper*.

93. Moore, *Rituals of Recruitment in Tang China*, 26–44.

94. For discussions of the recruitment examinations, see Twitchett, *The Birth of the Chinese Meritocracy*; Wu Zongguo, *Tangdai keju zhidu yanjiu*; Fu Xuancong, *Tangdai keju yu wenxue*. The assessment and selection by the Ministry of Personnel was of a different nature because candidates presented evidence of their eligibility and were evaluated on account of their appearance, speech, calligraphy, and legal judgment. See Wang Xuncheng, *Tangdai quanxuan yu wenxue*, 138–228.

95. Wang Dingbao, *Tang zhi yan*, 1.2. Shi Jianwu, who passed the Presented Scholar examination in 820, complained to the chief examiner about his lack of social connections in a poem; the poem states that despite his talent, he was the only one with the surname of Shi among the 800 examinees. Shi Jianwu, "Shang libu shilang chenqing," *QTS*, 494.5587. For estimates of the candidate pool, see Fu Xuancong, *Tangdai keju yu wenxue*, 47–50; Twitchett, *The Birth of the Chinese Meritocracy*, 15; Wu Zongguo, *Tangdai keju zhidu yanjiu*, 21.

96. Wang Dingbao, *Tang zhi yan*, 8.90–91.

97. For discussions of this examination culture, see Moore, *Rituals of Recruitment in Tang China*, 67–280; Yang Bo, *Chang'an de chuntian*.

98. Rouzer, *Articulated Ladies*, 249–83.

99. Wang Dingbao, *Tang zhi yan*, 1.3, 15.159 (with slight variations).

100. Moore, *Rituals of Recruitment in Tang China*, 2.

101. Liu Shao, *Renwu zhi*, 2.6b. Some versions show a variation of *cao* 草 (grass) instead of *zhang* 章 (pattern).

102. Ibid., 2.6a–7b. Another well-known story, "The Story of the Curly Bearded Hero" (Qiuran ke zhuan), follows precisely the same rationale in casting the future Emperor Taizong as a true hero who is destined to outshine his competitors and become the new Son of Heaven. See *TPGJ*, 193.1445–48.

103. To late medieval scholar-officials, *wen* is superior to *wu* because it encompasses the latter. A Presented Scholar degree holder, chief minister Pei

Du, for instance, was admired because he also served as a military governor and led a campaign that pacified the rebellion of Wu Yuanji (783–817) in 817. Like many others, he demonstrated his qualifications to "be a general in the field and a minister at court" (*chu jiang ru xiang*). Although late medieval scholar-officials looked down upon uncultured military men, they had not yet associated literati only with civil administration and even physical fragility, as in later periods.

104. Wang Dingbao, *Tang zhi yan*, 1.5.

105. Ibid., 6.63–64, 7.75–76 (with slight variations). Huangfu Shi actually passed the Presented Scholar examination one year later than Niu Seng-ru and thus could not possibly be the latter's patron.

106. Ibid., 1.4. After the examinees acquired entry positions, they could forsake their uncolored hemp robes and change to the colored robes of officials in the "shedding the coarse robe" (*shihe*) ceremony.

107. Ibid., 3.43–44.

108. Ibid., 12.137–39, 12.141.

109. Ibid., 8.86.

110. Ibid., 10.106–19. Wang Dingbao's list is built upon that of Wei Zhuang (836–910), who tried to petition the throne to award posthumous Presented Scholar degree to candidates.

111. Ibid., 8.93.

112. Ibid., 2.20–23, 11.123–24.

113. Ibid., 8.87.

114. Ibid., 4.53.

115. Ibid., 8.89–90.

116. Moore, *Rituals of Recruitment in Tang China*, 181–229.

CHAPTER 3

1. These stories do not touch upon male homosexuality. For discussions of homosexuality, see Bret Hinsch, *Passions of the Cut Sleeve*; Shi Ye, *Zhongguo gudai wenxue zhong de tongxinglian*.

2. Daniel Hsieh, *Love and Women*. Although Zhang Zhuo's "Youxian ku" describes an official's temporary liaison with a widow, the story is set in an otherworldly locale, making her more like an immortal. For a discussion of this story, see Rouzer, *Articulated Ladies*, 202–16.

3. An early reference to Sima Xiangru's affair can be found in Sima Qian, *Shi ji*, 117.3000–1. For a later version, see Liu Xin (attributed), *Xijing zaji*, 1.10a–b. For the story's later evolutions, see W. L. Idema, "The Story of Ssu-ma Hsiang-ju and Cho Wen-chün," 60–109. For the story of Han Shou, see Liu Yiqing, *Shishuo xinyu jiaojian*, "Huoni," 3.491–92.

4. In addition to his principal wife, a man could also take concubines, often women of lesser backgrounds, such as commoners or former courtesans. See Xiang Shuyun, *Tangdai hunyin fa yu hunyin shitai*; Yao Ping, *Tangdai funü de shengming licheng*; Wong Yu-Hsuan, "Tōdai ni okeru kannin kaikyū no konyin keitai," 131–59.

5. For studies of the genre, see Li Zongwei, *Tangren chuanqi*; Wu Zhida, *Tangren chuanqi*; Liu Ying, *Tangdai chuanqi yanjiu*; Liu Kairong, *Tangdai xiaoshuo yanjiu*.

6. Owen, "What Did Liu Zhi Hear?" 81–118; Rouzer, *Articulated Ladies*, 249–83; Zheng Zhimin, *Xishuo Tangji*, 71–188.

7. Shields, *Crafting a Collection*, 17–65; Li Jianliang, *Tang Song ci yu Tang Song geji zhidu*; Kang-i Sun Chang, *The Evolution of Chinese Tz'u Poetry*.

8. Linda Rui Feng, "Unmasking *fengliu* in Urban Chang'an," 1–21.

9. Owen, *The End of the Chinese "Middle Ages,"* 130–48; Rouzer, *Articulated Ladies*, 201–83.

10. Meng Jian received his Presented Scholar degree only one year earlier than Ouyang Zhan and subsequently enjoyed a rather successful career. For Meng Jian's biography, see *JTS*, 163.4257–58; *XTS*, 160.4968–69. Upon Ouyang's death, his friend Han Yu composed a eulogy; in 852, a relative, Li Yisun (fl. 780–852), wrote a preface to his anthology. Neither mentioned his love affair. For a discussion of the commemorations of Ouyang, see Nienhauser Jr., "Literature as a Source for Traditional History," 1–14.

11. *TPGJ*, 274.2161–62. Meng Jian's version survived as part of an entry on Ouyang Zhan in the *Minchuan mingshi zhuan* compiled by Huang Pu (867–950).

12. The couple's relationship is not illicit in these two stories. In the "Huashan ji," the young man becomes lovesick for the daughter of an innkeeper; he dies from swallowing her apron, which she sends as a talisman to cure him. When his coffin passes by, the girl sings a song beckoning him to open it, and she jumps in. See Guo Maoqian, comp., *Yuefu shiji*, 46.546–47. In the "Lujiang xiaoli" (also known as "Kongque dongnan fei" or "Gushi wei Jiao Zhongqing qi zuo"), the heroine is expelled by her mother-in-law and forced by her natal family to remarry. She commits suicide to remain loyal to her ex-husband, who follows suit. Xu Ling, *Yutai xinyong jianzhu*, 1.42–54.

13. *TPGJ*, 274.2162.

14. Female and male commitments to their liaison are thus dictated by a "double standard." See Nienhauser Jr., "Female Sexuality and the Double Standard," 1–20.

15. Feng, "Youthful Displacement."

16. Owen, *The End of the Chinese "Middle Ages,"* 83–106.

17. Mikhail Bakhtin's concept of "carnival" has been particularly influential. See Bakhtin, *Rabelais and His World*. For an example of studies on specific rituals of carnival, see David D. Gilmore, *Carnival and Culture*.

18. A maid was a slave, while a household entertainer was usually purchased for her musical skills. Both were lower in status than a concubine. The Tang state and local government owned women who offered musical entertainments at the banquets of officials. See Bossler, "Vocabularies of Pleasure," 71–99; Zheng Zhimin, *Xishuo Tangji*, 26–46.

19. For a detailed study, see Rouzer, *Articulated Ladies*. For a discussion of male homosocial dynamic outside the Chinese tradition, see Eve Sedgwick, *Between Men*.

20. Li Bai, *Li Taibai quanji*, 15.708.

21. Examples include "Yu Han Jingzhou shu" and "Shang Anzhou Pei zhangshi shu." Ibid., 26.1239–50.

22. Waley, *The Life and Times of Po Chü-I*, 18–19.

23. For discussion of Meng Qi's collection, see Sanders, *Words Well Put*, 157–278.

24. There is no record of Wu Yansi in extant sources. Earlier versions of the story identify Empress Wu's nephew Wu Chengsi (d. 698) instead. See Liu Su, *Sui Tang jiahua*, 3.39; Zhang Zhuo, *Chaoye qianzai*, 2.31.

25. Meng Qi, *Benshi shi*, 5–6.

26. Sanders, *Words Well Put*, 265–68.

27. Meng Qi, *Benshi shi*, 11–12. This anonymous censor is identified as Liu Yuxi in another version. See *TPGJ*, 273.2153–54. Some believe that this identification is a misattribution. See Wang Meng'ou, *Tangren xiaoshuo yanjiu*, vol. 3, 47–48.

28. Sanders, *Words Well Put*, 274–77.

29. Meng Qi, *Benshi shi*, 7–8.

30. In these variants, the sexual triangle exists among Minister of Work Yu Di (d. 818), scholar Cui Jiao (n.d.), and a maid of Cui's aunt, or among Yu Di, Rong Yu, and the prefectural singing girl. See Fan Shu, *Yunxi youyi*, 1.7–8.

31. Sanders, *Words Well Put*, 271–74.

32. Yue Hong, "A Structural Study of Ninth Century Anecdotes,'" 65–83.

33. Meng Qi, *Benshi shi*, 11. For variant versions, see *TPGJ*, 177.1318; Fan Shu, *Yunxi youyi*, 2.49–50; Hu Zi, *Tiaoxi yuyin conghua*, houji, 9.64. These are all apocryphal. See Cen Zhongmian, *Tangshi yushen*, 3.173–75.

34. Li Jianguo, *Tang Wudai zhiguai chuanqi xulu*, 857–75.

35. Pei Xing, *Chuan qi*, 10–11.

36. For the term "Kunlun," see Edward H. Schafer, *The Golden Peaches of Samarkand*, 45–46.

37. For discussions, see Feng, "Negotiating Vertical Space," 27–44; James J. Y. Liu, *The Chinese Knight-errant*; Cao Yibing, *Xiayi gongan xiaoshuo shi*.

38. Pei Xing, *Chuan qi*, 11.

39. See Li Jianguo, *Tang Wudai zhiguai chuanqi xulu*, 574–75.

40. *TPGJ*, 486.4001–5.

41. Rouzer, *Articulated Ladies*, 232.

42. Ibid., 231.

43. Sun Qi, *Beili zhi*, 29.

44. Ibid., 32–35.

45. Li Jianguo, *Tang Wudai zhiguai chuanqi xulu*, 276–81.

46. *TPGJ*, 484.3985–91.

47. Ibid., 484.3985.

48. Dudbridge, *The Tale of Li Wa*, 38; Rouzer, *Articulated Ladies*, 252–54.

49. *TPGJ*, 484.3986.

50. Dudbridge, *The Tale of Li Wa*, 127n85.

51. Kevin Tsai, "Ritual and Gender," 104–11.

52. Kominami Ichirō, "Li A den no kōzō," 284–91; Dudbridge, *The Tale of Li Wa*, 52–57; Tsai emphasizes the role of gender in this rite of passage. Tsai, "Ritual and Gender," 99–127. Feng foregrounds the role of urban space and culture. Feng, "Youthful Displacement," 66–84, 98–118; Feng, "Chang'an and Narratives of Experience," 35–68.

53. Rouzer, *Articulated Ladies*, 244.

54. Senō Tatsuhiko, "Tōdai kōhanki no chōan," 488; Rouzer, *Articulated Ladies*, 244–45.

55. For the Tang sumptuary rules, see Zhou Xibao, *Zhongguo gudai fushi shi*, 174–93.

56. Rouzer, *Articulated Ladies*, 246; Tsai, "Ritual and Gender," 119–22.

57. Dudbridge, *The Tale of Li Wa*, 75; Rouzer, *Articulated Ladies*, 246–47.

58. Such a happy union was not realistic in the Tang. See Yu-hwa Lee, *Fantasy and Realism*, xi; Dudbridge, *The Tale of Li Wa*, 72–80.

59. *TPGJ*, 484.3991.

60. Hu Yinglin, *Shaoshi shanfang bicong*, 41.567.

61. Feng Menglong, *Qing shi*, 16.9a–b.

62. For the story's later adaptations, see Dudbridge, *The Tale of Li Wa*, 80–99.

63. *Mengzi zhengyi*, 8.124. For Confucian norms of sexuality and family, see Ebrey's discussion and translations in "Confucianism," 367–414.

64. *Li ji Zheng zhu*, 8.18a.

65. Tsai, "Ritual and Gender," 114.

66. Li Wa's spontaneous recognition of the young man's voice (*yin*) alludes to the well-known story of Zhong Ziqi, who understands Boya's music (*yin*) without Boya's saying a word of explanation about it (*zhiyin*). *Liezi*, 5.71. Rouzer argues that Li Wa's act of recognition turns her into the young man's patron (*zhiji*). Rouzer, *Articulated Ladies*, 245.

67. Li Jianguo, *Tang Wudai zhiguai chuanqi xulu*, 446–49.

68. Li Jianguo argues that because Xiaoyu is the daughter of Prince Huo, the reference to her family name as Huo was a misattribution. Ibid., 452. Bian Xiaoxuan believes that the story was meant to slander the historical Li Yi (748–827). Bian Xiaoxuan, *Tang chuanqi xintan*, 50–59. For the historical Li Yi, see Wang Meng'ou, *Tang shiren Li Yi shengping jiqi zuopin*.

69. *TPGJ*, 484.3985–91.

70. Owen, *The End of the Chinese "Middle Ages,"* 137–42; Feng, "Youthful Displacement," 185–94.

71. Owen, *The End of the Chinese "Middle Ages,"* 143–45.

72. Jack Chen, "Blank Spaces and Secret Histories," 1087.

73. Owen, *The End of the Chinese "Middle Ages,"* 142.

74. Mark Edward Lewis, *Sanctioned Violence in Early China*, 3. Because of her sacrifice, Xiaoyu was much applauded by later literati. See Feng Menglong, *Qing shi*, 16.31a–b.

75. *TPGJ*, 487.4011.

76. Owen, *The End of the Chinese "Middle Ages,"* 148.

77. Dai De, *Da Dai Li ji huijiao jijie*, 13.1305; *Kongzi jiayu shuzheng*, 6.170–71.

78. Zhangsun Wuji et al., *Tanglü shuyi jianjie*, 14.1055–56.

79. Ibid., 26.1836–48.

80. Jo-shui Ch'en, *Liu Tsung-yüan*.

81. Liu Zongyuan, *Liu Hedong ji*, 46.794–97.

82. Hu Yin, *Dushi guanjian*, 24.888. Bian Xiaoxuan further elaborates on the theory by explaining why Liu would attack Xianzong. Bian Xiaoxuan, *Tang chuanqi xintan*, 115–26. Other critics have emphasized the fictional nature of this story. See Richard Wang, "Liu Tsung-yüan's 'Tale of Ho-chien' and Fiction," 21–48.

83. This emphasis that untested virtue is not true virtue echoes Sima Xiangru's rhapsody "Meiren fu." For a discussion of this rhapsody, see Rouzer, *Articulated Ladies*, 49–52.

84. For Shen's life and his works, see Nienhauser Jr., "Creativity and Storytelling in the *Ch'uan-ch'i*," 31–70.

85. Shen Yazhi, *Shen Xiaxian ji jiaozhu*, 4.73–75.

86. Ibid., 4.74.

87. Ibid.

88. For a discussion of the retellings, see Huang Meiling, "'Feng Yan zhuan,' 'Feng Yan ge,' 'Shuidiao qibian,'" 171–90.

89. *QTS*, 634.7283.

90. Ibid.

91. The story is cited in Wen Yu, *Xu bu shier xiaoming lu*, 1.5a–6a.

92. Li Jianguo, *Tang Wudai zhiguai chuanqi xulu*, 960–62.

93. See Wang Pijiang, *Tangren xiaoshuo*, 292–95. Also, "Feiyan zhuan" (missing Huangfu Mei's comments), *TPGJ*, 491.4033–36.

94. For discussion of such rituals in an earlier story "You xianku," see Rouzer, *Articulated Ladies*, 202–16.

95. Wang Pijiang, *Tangren xiaoshuo*, 295.

96. Ibid.

97. Ibid.

98. Ibid.

99. Ibid.

100. A more detailed analysis of this story has appeared in Manling Luo, "The Seduction of Authenticity," 40–70.

101. The attribution can be seen as part of the story's seductive "effects of authenticity." See Luo, "The Seduction of Authenticity," 40–70. The conventional attribution underlies a long list of scholarship. For influential earlier examples, see Chen Yinke, "Du Yingying zhuan," in *Chen Yinke xiansheng wenshi lunji*, 397–406; Uchiyama Chinari, "Ōō den no kōzō to shudai ni tsuite," 156–68; James R. Hightower, "Yuan Chen and 'The Story of Yingying,'" 90–123.

102. *TPGJ*, 488.4012–17. For a discussion of the story's textual history, see Li Jianguo, *Tang Wudai zhiguai chuanqi xulu*, 310–14.

103. *Mengzi zhengyi*, 6.18.

104. Owen, *The End of the Chinese "Middle Ages,"* 165.

105. Wai-yee Li, "Mixture of Genres and Motives for Fiction," 190.
106. Owen, *The End of the Chinese "Middle Ages,"* 153.
107. *TPGJ*, 358.2831–32.
108. Ibid., 488.4015.
109. Owen, *The End of the Chinese "Middle Ages,"* 151–52.
110. *TPGJ*, 488.4016.
111. Ibid., 488.4017.
112. See Rouzer, *Articulated Ladies*, 1–72; Owen, "One Sight," 239–59.
113. Gao Shiyu, *Tangdai funü*; Duan Tali, *Tangdai funü diwei yanjiu*.
114. Song Geng, *The Fragile Scholar*, 19–67.

CHAPTER 4

1. Campany, *Strange Writing*, 273–394.
2. The 498 entries include 34 gathered from sources outside the received versions of the collection. See Gan Bao, *Soushen ji*.
3. Noting that Tang tales feature a higher number of literati protagonists encountering the supernatural than the pre-Tang counterparts, Linda Feng focuses her analysis on those about examination candidates. See Feng, "Youthful Displacement," 207–13.
4. The edition used here is a collated one. See Tang Lin, *Mingbao ji*.
5. The collated version of the *Xuanguai lu* includes 57 entries, while that of the *Xu Xuanguai lu* has 29 (the story "Ni Miaoji" is listed in the former collection but belongs in the latter). See Niu Sengru, *Xuanguai lu*; Li Fuyan, *Xu Xuanguai lu*.
6. David Schaberg, "Command and the Content of Tradition," 23–48; Michael Puett, "Following the Commands of Heaven," 49–69; Lisa Raphals, "Languages of Fate," 70–106; Chen Ning, *Zhongguo gudai mingyun guan*.
7. Mu-chou Poo, "How to Steer through Life," 107–25.
8. Campany, "Living off the Books," 129–50; Stephen R. Bokenkamp, "Simple Twists of Fate," 151–68.
9. Li Jianguo, *Tang Wudai zhiguai chuanqi xulu*, 236–37, 602–8, 628–33, 644–46, 1075–78.
10. Zhong Lu, *Qianding lu*, 1a–b.
11. Ibid., 11b–12b.
12. See stories from Lu Zhao, *Yi shi*, cited in *TPGJ*, 149.1072, 153.1096, 153.1097, 156.1125.
13. Zhong Lu, *Qianding lu*, 1a.
14. Ibid., 15a. For a variant with different protagonists, see Anon., *Huichang jieyi lu*, cited in *TPGJ*, 149.1070–71.
15. Wen She, *Xu Dingming lu*, cited in *TPGJ*, 154.1109–10, 156.1119–20.
16. Lü Daosheng, *Dingming lu*, cited in *TPGJ*, 147.1060.
17. Ibid., 221.1700.
18. Ibid., 146.1053.
19. Zhong Lu, *Qianding lu*, 3a–4b.
20. Lü Daosheng, *Dingming lu*, cited in *TPGJ*, 222.1702.
21. Huangfu shi, *Yuanhua ji*, cited in *TPGJ*, 77.488–89. Also Lu Zhao, *Yi shi*, cited in *TPGJ*, 153.1099–100.

22. Li Fuyan, *Xu Xuanguai lu*, 2.162–63.

23. Dai Fu, *Guangyi ji*, cited in *TPGJ*, 112.776–77, 334.2656–57; Li Mei, *Zuanyi ji*, cited in *TPGJ*, 350.2773–75.

24. Lü Daosheng, *Dingming lu*, cited in *TPGJ*, 221.1700–1.

25. Kang Pian, *Jutan lu*, 1.8b–10a. For variant versions, see Anon., *Yehou waizhuan*, cited in *TPGJ*, 38.244; Anon., *Ganding lu* (believed to be an abbreviated title of the *Gan dingming lu*), cited in *TPGJ*, 150.1079.

26. For examples, see Zhong Lu, *Qianding lu*, 1b–3a; Lü Daosheng, *Dingming lu*, cited in *TPGJ*, 221.1696.

27. Lü Daosheng, *Dingming lu*, cited in *TPGJ*, 146.1052.

28. Ibid., 147.1063.

29. Ibid., 147.1062–63.

30. Li Fuyan, *Xu Xuanguai lu*, 2.165.

31. Ibid., 4.186–88. For a variant version, see Wang Renyu, *Yutang xianhua*, cited in *TPGJ*, 160.1151–52.

32. Lü Daosheng, *Dingming lu*, cited in *TPGJ*, 159.1143–44.

33. Ying-shih Yü, "O Soul Come Back," 384–85.

34. See Richard von Glahn, *The Sinister Way*, 19–77; Stephen F. Teiser, *The Ghost Festival in Medieval China*; Bokenkamp, *Ancestors and Anxiety*.

35. Teiser, *The Scripture on the Ten Kings*; Teiser, "The Growth of Purgatory," 115–45; Teiser, "'Having Once Died and Returned to Life,'" 433–64.

36. Campany, "Ghosts Matter," 32.

37. Campany, "Return-From-Death Narratives," 91–125. These narratives have parallels in other cultures. See James McClenon, "Near-Death Folklore in Medieval China and Japan," 319–42.

38. Here I do not consider collections with Buddhist agendas, such as Tang Lin's *Mingbao ji* and Meng Xianzhong's *Jingang bore jing jiyan ji*. Return-from-death stories in such collections usually describe the efficacy of Buddhist devotion, especially the recitation of Buddhist scriptures, in winning one's release from the underworld.

39. Li Jianguo, *Tang Wudai zhiguai chuanqi xulu*, 463–89.

40. Dudbridge, *Religious Experience and Lay society*, 52–53, 57–58.

41. Dai Fu, *Guangyi ji*, cited in *TPGJ*, 379.3019–20.

42. Emily Martin Ahern, *Chinese Ritual and Politics*, 109.

43. Dudbridge, *Religious Experience and Lay Society*, 52–54.

44. Dai Fu, *Guangyi ji*, cited in *TPGJ*, 336.2665–67.

45. Xue Yongruo, *Jiyi ji*, 46–47.

46. Niu Sengru, *Xuanguai lu*, 10.110–11.

47. Ibid., buyi, 131–35; also cited in *TPGJ*, 385.3068–73.

48. Campany, "Return-From-Death Narratives," 114–20.

49. Campany, "Living off the Books," 129–31.

50. Dai Fu, *Guangyi ji*, cited in *TPGJ*, 381.3035–36.

51. Teiser, "The Growth of Purgatory," 133–35. For studies of paper money and other offerings, see Fred C. Blake, *Burning Money*; Janet L. Scott, *For Gods, Ghosts, and Ancestors*.

52. Dai Fu, *Guangyi ji*, cited in *TPGJ*, 381.3038–39.

53. Ibid., 302.2398, 303.2402–3, 301.2390–92.

54. Dudbridge, *Religious Experience and Lay Society*, 86–116.

55. Niu Sengru, *Xuanguai lu*, 7.71.

56. Dai Fu, *Guangyi ji*, cited in *TPGJ*, 381.3033–35.

57. Duan Chengshi, *Youyang zazu*, 2.10.

58. See Campany, *Making Transcendents*, 39–61; Ute Engelhardt, "Longevity Techniques and Chinese Medicine," 53–73; Benjamin Penny, "Immortality and Transcendence," 74–108.

59. Yan Jinxiong, *Tangdai youxian shi yanjiu*.

60. Timothy H. Barrett, *Taoism under the T'ang*; Wang Yongping, *Daojiao yu Tangdai shehui*.

61. Li Fengmao, *You yu you*, 6–12; Huo Mingkun, *Tangren de shenxian shijie*, 7–28.

62. For Lu's life, see *JTS*, 145.3937–38; *XTS*, 151.4822–23.

63. Lu Changyuan, *Bianyi zhi*, cited in *TPGJ*, 289.2297–98, 289.2298–99, 288.2296. The last story is cited in Tao Zongyi, *Shuo fu*, 34.20b.

64. See *XTS*, 196.5262–63.

65. Pei Xing, *Chuan qi*, 16–17.

66. One can earn such a name through moral powers (*de*), deeds (*gong*), or words (*yan*). See Zuo Qiuming, *Zuo zhuan*, Xiang 24, 1087–88.

67. Li Jianguo, *Tang Wudai zhiguai chuanqi xulu*, 609–26, 670–92, 1013–16, 1025–40.

68. Dai Fu, *Guangyi ji*, cited in *TPGJ*, 23.158; Niu Sengru, *Xuanguai lu*, 1.12–15.

69. Sing-chen Lydia Chiang, "Daoist Transcendence and Tang Literati Identities," 7–11.

70. Lu Zhao, *Yi shi*, cited in *TPGJ*, 17.118–19; Du Guangting, *Xianzhuan shiyi*, cited in *TPGJ*, 17.120–21.

71. Lu Zhao, *Yi shi*, cited in *TPGJ*, 35.222–23.

72. Ibid., 39.245–46.

73. Ibid., 19.129–31.

74. For stories that condemn Li Linfu, see Liu Su, *Da Tang xinyu*, 11.173, 8.122; Zheng Chuhui, *Minghuang zalu*, 1.13–14, 1.16–17, 2.25–26, 2.28–29; Hu Qu, *Tanbin lu*, 2a–b, 3a–4a; Fan Shu, *Yunxi youyi*, 2.34–35.

75. The story was included in the *Yiwen ji* (not extant) by Chen Han and later cited in *TPGJ*, 419.3410–17. For authorship and textual history of this story, see Li Jianguo, *Tang Wudai zhiguai chuanqi xulu*, 286–92.

76. Pei Xing, *Chuan qi*, 6–7.

77. Li Fang et al., *Taiping yulan*, 41.2b–3a.

78. Pei Xing, *Chuan qi*, 7.

79. Li Jianguo, *Tang Wudai zhiguai chuanqi xulu*, 657–69.

80. Gushenzi, *Boyi zhi*, 18–20.

81. See Li Fuyan, *Xu Xuanguai lu*, 1.149; buyi, 198–99. Also, Lu Zhao, *Yi shi*, cited in *TPGJ*, 45.279, 48.299; Meng Qi, *Benshi shi*, 15.

82. For authorship and textual history, see Li Jianguo, *Tang Wudai zhiguai chuanqi xulu*, 706–15.

83. Li Mei, *Zuanyi ji*, cited in *TPGJ*, 50.309–12.

84. Niu Sengru, *Xuanguai lu*, 7.62–64.

85. Ibid., 7.63.

86. Wai-yee Li, "On Becoming a Fish," 29–56.

87. Song Zhenhao, "Jiaguwen zhong de meng yu zhanmeng," 61–71.

88. John Brennan, "Dreams, Divination, and Statecraft," 73–102.

89. Wai-yee Li, "Dreams of Interpretation," 17–42.

90. Zheng Binglin and Yang Ping, *Dunhuang ben meng shu*; Liu Wenying, *Zhongguo gudai de meng shu*.

91. Wai-yee Li, "Dreams of Interpretation," 29–39; Lu Ying, *Zhongguo meng wenhua*, 66–69.

92. For a detailed explanation of the uses of the dream metaphor in Buddhist texts, see Xingyun dashi et al., *Foguang da cidian*, 5776–81.

93. Chen Dakang, *Zhongguo gudai huameng lu*; Wu Kang, *Zhongguo gudai menghuan*; Fu Zhenggu, *Zhongguo gudai meng wenxue shi*; Fu Zhenggu, *Zhongguo meng wenhua*; Wang Weidi, *Zhongguo meng wenhua*; Zhuo Songsheng, *Zhongguo meng wenhua*.

94. Li Hanbin, *Taiping guangji de meng yanjiu*.

95. The story was included in Chen Han's *Yiwen ji*, later cited in *TPGJ*, 82.526–28.

96. Huang Jingjin, "'Zhenzhong ji' de jiegou fenxi," 592–93; Takeda Akira, "Chinchūki," 209–12.

97. Li Jianguo, *Tang Wudai zhiguai chuanqi xulu*, 265–66, 269–73; Inui Kazuo, "Chinchūki no kōsō," 219–32.

98. Carrie Reed, "Parallel Worlds, Stretched Time, and Illusory Reality," 309–42.

99. *TPGJ*, 82.528.

100. This perspective has been seen as Daoist, while some critics also believe in a Buddhist influence on the story. See Matsuo Yoshihiro, "'Sō Shū no yume' de toku 'Chinchūki,'" 15–28; Mei Jialing, "Lun 'Du Zichun' yu 'Zhenzhong ji' de rensheng taidu," 123; Huo Shixiu, "Tangdai chuanqiwen yu Yindu gushi," 130–61, 404.

101. Liu Ying, *Tangdai chuanqi yanjiu*, 55.

102. In fact, a similar story, "The Maid Carrying Cherries" (Yingtao Qingyi), resorts precisely to this solution by having the young protagonist, also named Lu, leave the world in quest of immortality. See Xue Yusi, *Hedong ji*, cited in *TPGJ*, 281.2242–44. Later adaptations of "The World Inside a Pillow" also allow the young man to become a disciple of the Daoist priest. See Tang Xianzu, "Handan ji," in *Tang Xianzu ji*, vol. 4, 2277–432.

103. Li Jianguo, *Tang Wudai zhiguai chuanqi xulu*, 305–10.

104. The story is included in *Yiwen lu*, often taken to be a variant title of Chen Han's *Yiwen ji*. For the story, see *TPGJ*, 475.3910–15.

105. Wang Pijiang, *Tangren xiaoshuo*, 90; Li Jianguo, *Tang Wudai zhiguai chuanqi xulu*, 309.

106. For discussions of dreams as the adventures of the departed spirit somewhere away from where the body is, see Huo Shixiu, "Tangdai chuanqiwen yu Yindu gushi," 135–41; Liao Tengye, *Zhongguo mengxi yanjiu*, 20–24.

107. See *TPGJ*, 475.3915.

108. Ibid. This Li Zhao is usually taken to be the same person as the compiler of *Supplements to the State History* (Guoshi bu); in this collection, however, "The Story of the Governor of the Southern Branch" is actually disparaged as one of the "monsters of literature" (*wen zhi yao*). I have thus treated them as two different persons. See Li Zhao, *Tang guoshi bu*, 3.55.

109. Carrie Reed has discussed the interconnections between the realms of the ants and the dead. See Reed, "Message from the Dead," 121–30.

110. *TPGJ*, 475.3915.

111. Reed points out that this story presents death as "homecoming," without its stereotypical sting. See Reed, "Message from the Dead," 125–26.

112. Shen Yazhi, *Shen Xiaxian ji jiaozhu*, 2.35–37.

113. Nienhauser Jr., "Creativity and Storytelling in the *Ch'uan-ch'i*," 65–66.

114. Ibid.

CONCLUSION

1. For example, Wu Zongguo, *Tangdai keju zhidu yanjiu*; Fu Xuancong, *Tangdai keju yu wenxue*.

2. This is not to suggest that the examination communities in the Song and later were homogeneous. For in-depth discussions, see Chaffee, *The Thorny Gates of Learning*; De Weerdt, *Competition over Content*; Elman, *A Cultural History of Civil Examinations*.

3. See Bol, *"This Culture of Ours,"* 108–47; DeBlasi, *Reform in the Balance*.

4. Johnson, "The Last Years of a Great Clan," 5–102; Ebrey, *The Aristocratic Families*; Tackett, "The Transformation of Medieval Chinese Elites (850–1000 C.E.)."

5. Owen, *The End of the Chinese "Middle Ages,"* 107–29; Owen, *The Late Tang*, 89–182, 226–54.

6. See Shields, "Defining Experience," 61–78; Rouzer, *Articulated Ladies*, 285–309.

7. Owen, *The End of the Chinese "Middle Ages,"* 83–106; Xiaoshan Yang, *Metamorphosis of the Private Sphere*.

8. For a discussion of this circle, see Ma Minghao, *Tangdai shehui yu Yuan Bai wenxue jituan*.

9. For a few examples of discussion on poetic circles, see Ping Wang, *The Age of Courtly Writing*; Jia Jinhua, *Tangdai jihui zongji yu shiren qun yanjiu*. For poetic intertextuality, see Joseph R. Allen, *In the Voice of Others*; Owen, *The Late Tang*.

10. Cheng Guofu, *Tangdai xiaoshuo shanbian yanjiu*. Also see Kang Yunmei, *Tangdai xiaoshuo chengyan de xushi yanjiu*; Huang Dahong, *Tangdai xiaoshuo chongxie yanjiu*.

11. Wang Jisi, *Cong Yingying zhuan dao Xixiang ji*. For a discussion and translation of the drama, see Stephen H. West and Wilt L. Idema, *The Moon and the Zither*.

12. For a survey of these adaptations, see Lorraine Dong, "The Creation and Life of Cui Yingying."

13. For examples, see Maram Epstein, *Competing Discourses*; Martin W. Huang, *Desire and Fictional Narrative*; Haiyan Lee, *Revolution of the Heart*.

14. Ning Jiayu, *Zhongguo wenyan xiaoshuo zongmu tiyao*, 129–458.

15. Roughly half of the collection is extant. See Inglis, *Hong Mai's* Record of the Listener, 1–22.

16. Leo Tak-hung Chan, *Discourse on Foxes and Ghosts*, 1–37.

17. Works on these famous collections are too numerous to list here. For a few examples, see Zeitlin, *Historian of the Strange*; Liu Shaoxin, *Liaozhai zhiyi xushi yanjiu*; Chiang, *Collecting the Self*. In addition, there is a quarterly journal dedicated exclusively to scholarship on Pu Songling, entitled *Pu Songling yanjiu*.

18. See Ruth Finnegan, *Literacy and Orality*.

19. Liangyan Ge, *Out of the Margins*.

BIBLIOGRAPHY

ABBREVIATIONS

JTS	*Jiu Tang shu*
QTS	*Quan Tang shi*
TPGJ	*Taiping guangji*
WYYH	*Wenyuan yinghua*
XTS	*Xin Tang shu*

PRIMARY SOURCES

Bai Juyi 白居易. *Bai Juyi ji* 白居易集. Collated by Gu Xuejie 顧學頡. Beijing: Zhonghua shuju, 1979.

Ban Gu 班固, comp. *Han shu* 漢書. Beijing: Zhonghua shuju, 1962.

Che Ruoshui 車若水. *Jiaoqi ji* 腳氣集. Taipei: Shangwu yinshuguan, 1982.

Chen Jingyi 陳景沂. *Quanfang beizu* 全芳備祖. Taipei: Shangwu yinshuguan, 1974.

Dai De 戴德, ed. *Da Dai Li ji huijiao jijie* 大戴禮記滙校集解. Collated by Fang Xiangdong 方向東. Beijing: Zhonghua shuju, 2008.

Duan Chengshi 段成式. *Youyang zazu* 酉陽雜俎. *Congshu jicheng* 叢書集成 edition. Shanghai: Shangwu yinshuguan, 1937.

Fan Chuanzheng 范傳正. "Tang zuo shiyi hanlin xueshi Li gong xin mubei bing xu" 唐左拾遺翰林學士李公新墓碑并序. In *Li Taibai quanji* 李太白全集, 31.1461–68. Beijing: Zhonghua shuju, 1977.

Fan Shu 范攄. *Yunxi youyi* 雲谿友議. Shanghai: Zhonghua shuju, 1959.

Feng Menglong 馮夢龍, comp. *Qing shi* 情史. *Guben xiaoshuo jicheng* 古本小說集成 edition. Shanghai: Shanghai guji chubanshe, 1990.

Fu Xuancong 傅璇琮 and Shi Chunde 施純德, eds. *Hanxue sanshu* 翰學三書. Shenyang: Liaoning jiaoyu chubanshe, 2003.

Gan Bao 干寶. *Soushen ji* 搜神記. Beijing: Zhonghua shuju, 1979.

Gao Yanxiu 高彥休. *Que shi* 闕史. Beijing: Zhonghua shuju, 1985.

Guo Maoqian 郭茂倩, comp. *Yuefu shiji* 樂府詩集. Taipei: Taiwan Shangwu yinshuguan, 1968.

Gushenzi 谷神子. *Boyi zhi* 博異志. Beijing: Zhonghua shuju, 1980.

Hu Qu 胡璩. *Tanbin lu* 譚賓錄. *Xuxiu siku quanshu* 續修四庫全書 edition. Shanghai: Shanghai guji chubanshe, 1995.

Hu Yin 胡寅. *Dushi guanjian* 讀史管見. Changsha: Yuelu shushe, 2011.

Hu Yinglin 胡應麟. *Shaoshi shanfang bicong* 少室山房筆叢. Taipei: Shijie shuju, 1963.

Hu Zi 胡仔. *Tiaoxi yuyin conghua* 苕溪漁隱叢話. Taipei: Taiwan Shangwu yinshuguan, 1968.

Kang Pian 康駢. *Jutan lu* 劇談錄. *Xuejin taoyuan* 學津討源 edition. Taipei: Yiwen yinshuguan, 1965.

Kongzi jiayu shuzheng 孔子家語疏證. Annotated by Chen Shike 陳士珂. Taipei: Taiwan Shangwu yinshuguan, 1968.

Kūkai 空海. *Wenjing mifu lun jiaozhu* 文鏡秘府論校注. Collated and annotated by Wang Liqi 王利器. Beijing: Zhongguo shehui kexue chubanshe, 1983.

Li Ao 李翱. *Zhuoyi ji* 卓異記. *Baibu congshu jicheng* 百部叢書集成 edition. Taipei: Yiwen yinshuguan, 1965.

Li Bai 李白. *Li Taibai quanji* 李太白全集. Annotated by Wang Qi 王琦. Beijing: Zhonghua shuju, 1977.

Li Deyu 李德裕. *Ci Liu shi jiuwen* 次柳氏舊聞. *Congshu jicheng* 叢書集成 edition. Changsha: Shangwu yinshuguan, 1940.

Li Fang 李昉 et al., comps. *Taiping guangji* 太平廣記. Beijing: Zhonghua shuju, 1961.

———. *Taiping yulan* 太平御覽. Taipei: Xinxing shuju, 1959.

———. *Wenyuan yinghua* 文苑英華. Collated by Peng Shuxia 彭叔夏 et al. Taipei: Huawen shuju, 1965.

Li Fuyan 李復言. *Xu Xuanguai lu* 續玄怪錄. Beijing: Zhonghua shuju, 2006.

Li ji Zheng zhu 禮記鄭注. Annotated by Zheng Xuan 鄭玄. Taipei: Xinxing shuju, 1977.

Li Zhao 李肇. *Tang guoshi bu* 唐國史補. Shanghai: Gudian wenxue chubanshe, 1958.

Liezi 列子. *Guoxue jiben congshu* 國學基本叢書 edition. Taipei: Taiwan Shangwu yinshuguan, 1968.

Liu Shao 劉邵. *Renwu zhi* 人物志. *Sibu beiyao* 四部備要 edition. Shanghai: Zhonghua shuju, 1927.

Liu Su 劉肅. *Da Tang xinyu* 大唐新語. Beijing: Zhonghua shuju, 1984.

Liu Su 劉餗. *Sui Tang jiahua* 隋唐嘉話. Beijing: Zhonghua shuju, 1979.

Liu Xin 劉歆 (attributed). *Xijing zaji* 西京雜記. Edited by Ge Hong 葛洪. *Bao-jingtang congshu* 抱經堂叢書 edition. Taipei: Yiwen yinshuguan, 1968.

Liu Xu 劉昫 et al., comps. *Jiu Tang shu* 舊唐書. Beijing: Zhonghua shuju, 1975.

Liu Yiqing 劉義慶. *Shishuo xinyu jiaojian* 世說新語校箋. Collated and annotated by Xu Zhen'e 徐震堮. Hong Kong: Zhonghua shuju Xianggang fenju, 1987.

Liu Zongyuan 柳宗元. *Liu Hedong ji* 柳河東集. Hong Kong: Zhonghua shuju, 1972.

Lunyu jishi 論語集釋. Collated by Cheng Shude 程樹德. Beijing: Zhonghua shuju, 1990.

Meng Qi 孟棨. *Benshi shi* 本事詩. Shanghai: Gudian wenxue chubanshe, 1957.

Mengzi zhengyi 孟子正義. Annotated by Jiao Xun 焦循. Taipei: Taiwan Shangwu yinshuguan, 1968.

Nan Zhuo 南卓. *Jiegu lu* 羯鼓錄. Shanghai: Shanghai guji chubanshe, 1958.

Niu Sengru 牛僧孺. *Xuanguai lu* 玄怪錄. Beijing: Zhonghua shuju, 2006.

Ouyang Xiu 歐陽修 et al., comps. *Xin Tang shu* 新唐書. Beijing: Zhonghua shuju, 1975.

———. *Xin Wudai shi* 新五代史. Beijing: Zhonghua shuju, 1974.

Pei Xing 裴鉶. *Chuan qi* 傳奇. Taipei: Shijie shuju, 1962.

Peng Dingqiu 彭定求 et al., comps. *Quan Tang shi* 全唐詩. Beijing: Zhong-hua shuju, 1979.

Shen Yazhi 沈亞之. *Shen Xiaxian ji jiaozhu* 沈下賢集校注. Collated and annotated by Xiao Zhanpeng 肖占鵬 and Li Boyang 李勃洋. Tianjin: Nan-kai daxue chubanshe, 2003.

Sima Qian 司馬遷. *Shi ji* 史記. Beijing: Zhonghua shuju, 1964.

Sun Qi 孫棨. *Beili zhi* 北里誌. Shanghai: Gudian wenxue chubanshe, 1957.

Tang Lin 唐臨. *Mingbao ji* 冥報記. Beijing: Zhonghua shuju, 1992.

Tang Xianzu 湯顯祖. *Tang Xianzu ji* 湯顯祖集. Collated and Annotated by Xu Shuofang 徐朔方. Beijing: Zhonghua shuju, 1962.

Tao Zongyi 陶宗儀, comp. *Shuo fu* 說郛. Shanghai: Shangwu yinshuguan, 1927.

Wang Chongmin 王重民, comp. *Dunhuang bianwen ji* 敦煌變文集. Beijing: Renmin wenxue chubanshe, 1984.

Wang Dingbao 王定保. *Tang zhi yan* 唐摭言. Shanghai: Shanghai guji chubanshe, 1978.

Wang Pijiang 汪辟疆, ed. *Tangren xiaoshuo* 唐人小說. Shanghai: Shanghai guji chubanshe, 1978.

Wang Renyu 王仁裕. *Kaiyuan Tianbao yishi* 開元天寶遺事. Beijing: Zhonghua shuju, 2006.

Wei Xuan 韋絢. *Liu Binke jiahua lu* 劉賓客嘉話錄. Beijing: Zhonghua shuju,
1985.

Wen Yu 溫豫. *Xu bu shier xiaoming lu* 續補侍兒小名錄. In *Bai hai* 稗海,
vol. 3, *Baibu congshu jicheng* 百部叢書集成 edition. Taipei: Yiwen yinshuguan, 1965.

Wu Jing 吳兢. *Zhenguan zhengyao jijiao* 貞觀政要集校. Collated by Xie Bao-
cheng 謝保成. Beijing: Zhonghua shuju, 2003.

Xu Ling 徐陵, comp. *Yutai xinyong jianzhu* 玉臺新詠箋注. Annotated by Wu
Zhaoyi 吳兆宜. Edited by Cheng Yan 程琰. Collated by Mu Kehong 穆克
宏. Beijing: Zhonghua shuju, 1985.

Xue Juzheng 薛居正 et al., comps. *Jiu Wudai shi* 舊五代史. Beijing: Zhonghua shuju, 1976.

Xue Yongruo 薛用弱. *Jiyi ji* 集異記. Beijing: Zhonghua shuju, 1980.

Yuan Zhen 元稹. *Yuan Zhen ji* 元稹集. Collated by Ji Qin 冀勤. Beijing:
Zhonghua shuju, 1982.

Yue jue shu 越絕書. Authorship disputed. Collated by Zhang Zongxiang 張
宗祥. Shanghai: Shangwu yinshuguan, 1956.

Zhang Jie 張戒. *Suihantang shihua* 歲寒堂詩話. Changsha: Shangwu yinshuguan, 1939.

Zhang Zhuo 張鷟. *Chaoye qianzai* 朝野僉載. Beijing: Zhonghua shuju,
1979.

Zhangsun Wuji 長孫無忌 et al., comps. *Tanglü shuyi jianjie* 唐律疏議箋解.
Annotated by Liu Junwen 劉俊文. Beijing: Zhonghua shuju, 1996.

Zhao Lin 趙璘. *Yinhua lu* 因話錄. Shanghai: Gudian wenxue chubanshe,
1958.

Zhao Ye 趙曄. *Wu Yue chunqiu* 吳越春秋. Taipei: Shijie shuju, 1962.

Zheng Chuhui 鄭處誨. *Minghuang zalu* 明皇雜錄. Collated by Tian Tingzhu
田廷柱. Beijing: Zhonghua shuju, 1994.

Zheng Qi 鄭棨. *Kai Tian chuanxin ji* 開天傳信記. *Congshu jicheng* 叢書集成
edition. Changsha: Shangwu yinshuguan, 1940.

Zhong Lu 鍾籟. *Qianding lu* 前定錄. *Baichuan xuehai* 百川學海 edition. Taipei: Yiwen yinshuguan, 1965.

Zhuangzi jishi 莊子集釋. Collated and annotated by Guo Qingfan 郭慶藩.
Beijing: Zhonghua shuju, 1961.

Zuo Qiuming 左丘明. *Chunqiu Zuo zhuan zhu* 春秋左傳注. Annotated by
Yang Bojun 楊伯峻. Beijing: Zhonghua shuju, 1990.

WORKS CITED

Ahern, Emily Martin. *Chinese Ritual and Politics*. Cambridge: Cambridge University Press, 1981.

Allen, Joseph R. *In the Voice of Others: Chinese Music Bureau Poetry*. Ann Arbor: University of Michigan Press, 1992.

Allen, Sarah M. "Tales Retold: Narrative Variation in a Tang Story." *Harvard Journal of Asiatic Studies* 66, no. 1 (2006): 105–43.

———. "Tang Stories: Tales and Texts." PhD diss., Harvard University, 2003.

Bakhtin, Mikhail. *Rabelais and His World*. Translated by Helene Iswolsky. Bloomington: Indiana University Press, 1984.

Barrett, Timothy H. *Taoism under the T'ang: Religion and Empire during the Golden Age of Chinese History*. London: Wellsweep, 1996.

Berkowitz, Alan. *Patterns of Disengagement: The Practice and Portrayal of Reclusion in Early Medieval China*. Stanford: Stanford University Press, 2000.

Bian Xiaoxuan 卞孝萱. *Tang chuanqi xintan* 唐傳奇新探. Nanjing: Jiangsu jiaoyu chubanshe, 2001.

———. *Yuan Zhen nianpu* 元稹年譜. Jinan: Qilu shushe, 1980.

Bischoff, F. A. *La Forêt des Pinceaux: Étude sur l'Académie du Han-lin sous la dynastie des T'ang et traduction du Han lin tche*. Paris: Presses Universitaires de France, 1963.

Blake, Fred C. *Burning Money: The Material Spirit of the Chinese Lifeworld*. Honolulu: University of Hawai'i Press, 2011.

Bokenkamp, Stephen R. *Ancestors and Anxiety: Daoism and the Birth of Rebirth in China*. Berkeley: University of California Press, 2007.

———. "Simple Twists of Fate: The Daoist Body and Its *Ming*." In Lupke, *The Magnitude of* Ming, 151–68.

Bol, Peter K. *"This Culture of Ours": Intellectual Transitions in T'ang and Sung China*. Stanford: Stanford University Press, 1992.

Bossler, Beverly J. *Powerful Relations: Kinship, Status, and the State in Sung China (960–1279)*. Cambridge, MA: Harvard University Council on East Asian Studies, 1998.

———. "Vocabularies of Pleasure: Categorizing Female Entertainers in the Late Tang Dynasty." *Harvard Journal of Asiatic Studies* 72, no. 1 (2012): 71–99.

Brennan, John. "Dreams, Divination, and Statecraft: The Politics of Dreams in Early Chinese History and Literature." In *The Dream and the Text:*

Essays on Literature and Language, edited by Carol Shreier Rupprecht, 73–102. Albany: State University of New York Press, 1993.

Bruner, Jerome. "Life as Narrative." *Social Research* 54 (1987): 11–32.

Campany, Robert Ford. "Ghosts Matter: The Culture of Ghosts in Six Dynasties *Zhiguai.*" *Chinese Literature: Essays, Articles, Reviews* 13 (1991): 15–34.

———. "Living off the Books: Fifty Ways to Dodge *Ming* in Early Medieval China." In Lupke, *The Magnitude of* Ming, 129–50.

———. *Making Transcendents: Ascetics and Social Memory in Early Medieval China.* Honolulu: University of Hawai'i Press, 2009.

———. "Return-From-Death Narratives in Early Medieval China." *Journal of Chinese Religions* 18 (1990): 91–125.

———. *Strange Writing: Anomaly Accounts in Early Medieval China.* Albany: State University of New York Press, 1995.

Cao Yibing 曹亦冰. *Xiayi gongan xiaoshuo shi* 俠義公案小說史. Hangzhou: Zhejiang guji chubanshe, 1998.

Cen Zhongmian 岑仲勉. *Tangshi yushen* 唐史餘瀋. Shanghai: Shanghai guji chubanshe, 1979.

Chaffee, John W. *The Thorny Gates of Learning in Sung China.* Cambridge: Cambridge University Press, 1986.

Chan, Leo Tak-hung. *The Discourse on Foxes and Ghosts: Ji Yun and Eighteenth-Century Literati Storytelling.* Honolulu: University of Hawai'i Press, 1998.

Chang, Kang-i Sun. *The Evolution of Chinese Tz'u Poetry.* Princeton: Princeton University Press, 1980.

Chen, Fan-pen Li. "Yang Kuei-fei: Changing Images of a Historical Beauty in Chinese Literature." PhD diss., Columbia University, 1984.

Chen, Jack W. "Blank Spaces and Secret Histories: Questions of Historiographic Epistemology in Medieval China." *Journal of Asian Studies* 69, no. 4 (2010): 1071–91.

———. *The Poetics of Sovereignty: On Emperor Taizong of the Tang Dynasty.* Cambridge, MA: Harvard University Asia Center, 2010.

Ch'en, Jo-shui. *Liu Tsung-yüan and Intellectual Change in T'ang China, 773–819.* Cambridge: Cambridge University Press, 1992.

Chen Dakang 陳大康. *Zhongguo gudai huameng lu* 中國古代話夢錄. Taipei: Yeqiang shuju, 1994.

Chen Ning 陳寧. *Zhongguo gudai mingyun guan de xiandai quanshi* 中國古代命運觀的現代詮釋. Liaoyang: Liaoning jiaoyu chubanshe, 1999.

Chen Yinke 陳寅恪. *Chen Yinke xiansheng wenshi lunji* 陳寅恪先生文史論集. Vol. 2. Hong Kong: Wenwen chubanshe, 1973.

Cheng Guofu 程國賦. *Tangdai xiaoshuo shanbian yanjiu* 唐代小說嬗變研究. Guangzhou: Guangdong renmin chubanshe, 1997.

Cheng Qianfan 程千帆. *Tangdai jinshi xingjuan yu wenxue* 唐代進士行卷與文學. Shanghai: Shanghai guji chubanshe, 1980.

Cheng Yizhong 程毅中. *Tangdai xiaoshuo shi* 唐代小說史. Beijing: Renmin wenxue chubanshe, 2003.

Chiang, Sing-chen Lydia. *Collecting the Self: Body and Identity in Strange Tale Collections of Late Imperial China*. Leiden: Brill, 2005.

———. "Daoist Transcendence and Tang Literati Identities in *Records of Mysterious Anomalies*." *Chinese Literature: Essays, Articles, Reviews* 29 (2007): 1–21.

Clark, Anthony E. "Praise and Blame: Ruist Historiography in Ban Gu's *Hanshu*." *The Chinese Historical Review* 18, no. 1 (2011): 1–24.

Cutter, Robert Joe. *The Brush and the Spur: Chinese Culture and Cockfight*. Hong Kong: Chinese University Press, 1989.

———. "History and 'The Old Man of the Eastern Wall.'" *Journal of the American Oriental Society* 106, no. 3 (1986): 503–28.

Dai Weihua 戴偉華. *Tang fangzhen wenzhi liaozuo kao* 唐方鎮文職僚佐考. Guilin: Guangxi shifan daxue chubanshe, 2007.

Darnton, Robert. *The Great Cat Massacre and Other Episodes in French Cultural History*. New York: Basic Books, 1999.

De Weerdt, Hilde. *Competition over Content: Negotiating Standards for the Civil Service Examinations in Imperial China (1127–1279)*. Cambridge, MA: Harvard University Asia Center, 2007.

DeBlasi, Anthony. "Contemplating Rulership: The *Changduan Jing* and the Tang Political Thought." *T'ang Studies* 25 (2007): 203–32.

———. *Reform in the Balance: The Defense of Literary Culture in Mid-Tang China*. Albany: State University of New York Press, 2002.

Deng Xiaonan 鄧小南. *Zuzong zhi fa—Bei Song qianqi zhengzhi shulüe* 祖宗之法—北宋前期政治述略. Beijing: Sanlian shudian, 2006.

Dong, Lorraine. "The Creation and Life of Cui Yingying (c. 803–1969)." PhD diss., University of Washington, 1978.

Drompp, Michael R. *Tang China and the Collapse of the Uighur Empire: A Documentary History*. Leiden: Brill, 2005.

Duan Tali 段塔麗. *Tangdai funü diwei yanjiu* 唐代婦女地位研究. Beijing: Renmin chubanshe, 2000.

Dudbridge, Glen. *A Portrait of Five Dynasties China: From the Memoirs of Wang Renyu (880–956)*. Oxford: Oxford University Press, 2013.

———. *Religious Experience and Lay Society in T'ang China: A Reading of Tai Fu's* Kuang-i chi. Cambridge: Cambridge University Press, 1995.

————. *The Tale of Li Wa*. London: Ithica Press, 1983.

Ebrey, Patricia B. *The Aristocratic Families of Early Imperial China: A Case Study of the Po-ling Ts'ui Family*. Cambridge: Cambridge University Press, 1978.

————. "Confucianism." In *Sex, Marriage, and Family in World Religions*, edited by Don S. Browning, M. Christian Green, and John Witte Jr., 367–414. New York: Columbia University Press, 2006.

Egan, Ronald. "Why Didn't Zhao Mingcheng Send Letters to His Wife, Li Qingzhao, When He Was Away?" In *Hsiang Lectures on Chinese Poetry*, vol. 5, edited by Grace S. Fong, 57–77. Montreal: Center for East Asian Research, McGill University, 2010.

Eisenberg, Andrew. *Kingship in Early Medieval China*. Leiden: Brill, 2008.

Elman, Benjamin A. *A Cultural History of Civil Examinations in Late Imperial China*. Berkeley: University of California Press, 2000.

Engelhardt, Ute. "Longevity Techniques and Chinese Medicine." In Kohn, *Daoism Handbook*, 53–73.

Epstein, Maram. *Competing Discourses: Orthodoxy, Authenticity, and Engendered Meanings in Late Imperial Chinese Fiction*. Cambridge, MA: Harvard University Asia Center, 2001.

Feng, Linda Rui. "Chang'an and Narratives of Experience in Tang Tales." *Harvard Journal of Asiatic Studies* 71, no. 1 (2011): 35–68.

————. "Negotiating Vertical Space: Walls, Vistas, and the Topographical Imagination." *T'ang Studies* 29 (2011): 27–44.

————. "Unmasking *fengliu* 風流 in Urban Chang'an: Rereading *Beili zhi* 北里志 (Anecdotes from the Northern Ward)." *Chinese Literature: Essays, Articles, Reviews* 32 (2010): 1–21.

————. "Youthful Displacement: City, Travel and Narrative Formation in Tang Tales." PhD diss., Columbia University, 2008.

Finnegan, Ruth. *Literacy and Orality: Studies in the Technology of Communication*. New York: Blackwell, 1988.

Fong, Grace S. *Herself an Author: Gender, Agency, and Writing in Late Imperial China*. Honolulu: University of Hawai'i Press, 2008.

Frankel, Hans H. "The Contemplation of the Past in T'ang Poetry." In *Perspectives on the T'ang*, edited by Arthur F. Wright and Denis Twitchett, 345–65. New Haven, CT: Yale University Press, 1973.

Fu Xuancong 傅璇琮. "Tang Xuan Su liangchao hanlin xueshi kaolun" 唐玄蕭两朝翰林學士考論. *Wenxue yichan*, no. 4 (2000): 55–64.

————. *Tangdai keju yu wenxue* 唐代科舉與文學. Xi'an: Shanxi renmin chubanshe, 1986.

Fu Zhenggu 傅正谷. *Zhongguo gudai meng wenxue shi* 中國古代夢文學史. Beijing: Guangming ribao chubanshe, 1993.

——— . *Zhongguo meng wenhua* 中國夢文化. Beijing: Zhongguo shehui kexue chubanshe, 1993.

Gao Shiyu 高世瑜. *Tangdai funü* 唐代婦女. Xi'an: Sanqin chubanshe, 1988.

Ge, Liangyan. *Out of the Margins: The Rise of Chinese Vernacular Fiction.* Honolulu: University of Hawai'i Press, 2001.

Geng, Song. *The Fragile Scholar: Power and Masculinity in Chinese Culture.* Hong Kong: Hong Kong University Press, 2004.

Gilmore, David D. *Carnival and Culture: Sex, Symbol, and Status in Spain.* New Haven, CT: Yale University Press, 1998.

Graham, Masako Nakagawa. *The Yang Kuei-fei Legend in Japanese Literature.* Lewiston, NY: Edwin Mellen, 1998.

Han Yunbo 韓云波. *Tangdai xiaoshuo guannian yu xiaoshuo xingqi yanjiu* 唐代小說觀念與小說興起研究. Chengdu: Sichuan minzu chubanshe, 2002.

Hardy, Barbara. "Toward a Poetics of Fiction." *NOVEL: A Forum on Fiction* 2, no. 1 (1968): 5–14.

Hargett, James. *Stairway to Heaven: A Journey to the Summit of Mount Emei.* Albany: State University of New York Press, 2006.

Harrist, Jr., Robert E. *The Landscape of Words: Stone Inscriptions from Early and Medieval China.* Seattle: University of Washington Press, 2008.

Hartman, Charles. *Han Yü and the T'ang Search for Unity.* Princeton: Princeton University Press, 1986.

Hartwell, Robert. "Demographic, Political, and Social Transformations of China, 750–1550." *Harvard Journal of Asiatic Studies* 42, no. 2 (1982): 365–422.

Hightower, James R. "Yuan Chen and 'The Story of Ying-ying.'" *Harvard Journal of Asiatic Studies* 33 (1973): 90–123.

Hinsch, Bret. *Passions of the Cut Sleeve: The Male Homosexual Tradition in China.* Berkeley: University of California Press, 1990.

Holcombe, Charles. *In the Shadow of the Han: Literati Thought and Society at the Beginning of the Southern Dynasties.* Honolulu: University of Hawai'i Press, 1994.

Hong, Yue. "The Discourse of Romantic Love in Ninth Century Tang China." PhD diss., Harvard University, 2010.

——— . "A Structural Study of Ninth Century Anecdotes on 'Original Events.'" *T'ang Studies* 26 (2008): 65–83.

Hsieh, Daniel. *Love and Women in Early Chinese Fiction.* Hong Kong: Chinese University Press, 2008.

Hu Kexian 胡可先. *Tangdai zhongda lishi shijian yu wenxue yanjiu* 唐代重大歷史事件與文學研究. Hangzhou: Zhejiang daxue chubanshe, 2007.

Huang, Martin W. *Desire and Fictional Narrative in Late Imperial China.* Cambridge, MA: Harvard University Asia Center, 2001.

Huang Dahong 黃大宏. *Tangdai xiaoshuo chongxie yanjiu* 唐代小說重寫研究. Chongqing: Chongqing chubanshe, 2004.

Huang Jingjin 黃景進. "'Zhenzhong ji' de jiegou fenxi" 枕中記的結構分析. In *Tangdai yanjiu lunji* 唐代研究論集, vol. 4, 585–98. Taipei: Xinwenfeng, 1992.

Huang Meiling 黃美鈴. "'Feng Yan zhuan,' 'Feng Yan ge,' 'Shuidiao qibian' dui Feng Yan de ouge" <馮燕傳><馮燕歌><水調七遍>對馮燕的謳歌. *Hanxue yanjiu* 24, no. 2 (2006): 171–90.

Huang Zhengjian 黃正建 et al. *Zhong wan Tang shehui yu zhengzhi yanjiu* 中晚唐社會與政治研究. Beijing: Zhongguo shehui kexue chubanshe, 2006.

Hucker, Charles O. *A Dictionary of Official Titles in Imperial China* 中國古代官名辭典. Beijing: Beijing daxue chubanshe, 2008. Reprint.

Hunter, Lynette, ed. *Toward a Definition of Topos: Approaches to Analogical Reasoning.* Basingstoke, UK: MacMillan, 1991.

Huntington, Rania. *Alien Kind: Foxes and Late Imperial Chinese Narrative.* Cambridge, MA: Harvard University Asia Center, 2003.

Huo Mingkun 霍明琨. *Tangren de shenxian shijie:* Taiping guangji *Tang Wudai shenxian xiaoshuo de wenhua yanjiu* 唐人的神仙世界：《太平廣記》唐五代神仙小說的文化研究. Harbin: Heilongjiang daxue chubanshe, 2007.

Huo Shixiu 霍世休. "Tangdai chuanqiwen yu Yindu gushi" 唐代傳奇文與印度故事. In *Zhongguo bijiao wenxue* 中國比較文學, vol. 2, 130–61, 404. Hangzhou: Zhejiang wenyi chubanshe, 1985.

Hymes, Robert P. *Statesmen and Gentlemen: The Elite of Fu-chou, Chianghsi in Northern and Southern Sung.* Cambridge: Cambridge University Press, 1986.

Idema, W. L. "The Story of Ssu-ma Hsiang-ju and Cho Wen-chün in Vernacular Literature of the Yüan and Early Ming Dynasties." *T'oung Pao: International Journal of Chinese Studies* 70 (1984): 60–109.

Idema, Wilt L., and Beata Grant, trans. *The Red Brush: Writing Women of Imperial China.* Cambridge, MA: Harvard University Asia Center, 2004.

Inglis, Alister D. *Hong Mai's* Record of the Listener *and Its Song Dynasty Context.* Albany: State University of New York Press, 2006.

Inui Kazuo 乾一夫. "Chinchūki no kōsō—Tōdai denki shōsetsu no sekai"

枕中記の構想—唐代伝奇小説の世界. In *Bungaku to tetsugaku no aida: Chūgoku bungaku no sekai* 文学と哲学のあいだ: 中国文学の世界, vol. 3, 203–45. Tokyo: Kasama shoin, 1978.

Ji Yun 紀昀 et al., comps. *Siku quanshu zongmu* 四庫全書總目. Beijing: Zhonghua shuju, 1965.

Jia Erqiang 賈二強. *Tang Song minjian xinyang* 唐宋民間信仰. Fuzhou: Fujian renmin chubanshe, 2002.

Jia Jinhua 賈晉華. *Tangdai jihui zongji yu shiren qun yanjiu* 唐代集會總集與詩人羣研究. Beijing: Beijing daxue chubanshe, 2001.

Jin Jicang 靳极苍. *Changhen ge jiqi tong ticai shi xiangjie* 長恨歌及其同題材詩詳解. Taiyuan: Shanxi guji chubanshe, 2002.

Johnson, David. "The Last Years of a Great Clan: The Li Family of Chao Chün in the Late T'ang and Early Sung." *Harvard Journal of Asiatic Studies* 37, no. 1 (1977): 5–102.

———. *The Medieval Chinese Oligarchy*. Boulder, CO: Westview, 1977.

Kang Yunmei 康韻梅. *Tangdai xiaoshuo chengyan de xushi yanjiu* 唐代小說承衍的敘事研究. Taipei: Liren shuju, 2005.

Kao, Yu-kung. "The Aesthetics of Regulated Verse." In *The Vitality of the Lyric Voice*, edited by Shuen-fu Lin and Stephen Owen, 332–85. Princeton: Princeton University Press, 1986.

Kern, Martin. *The Stele Inscriptions of Ch'in Shih-huang: Text and Ritual in Early Chinese Imperial Representation*. New Haven, CT: American Oriental Society, 2000.

Kertzer, David I. *Ritual, Politics, and Power*. New Haven, CT: Yale University Press, 1988.

Knechtges, David R. "Culling the Weeds and Selecting Prime Blossoms: The Anthology in Early Medieval China." In *Culture and Power in the Reconstitution of the Chinese Realm, 200–600*, edited by Scott Pearce, Audrey Spiro, and Patricia Ebrey, 200–41. Cambridge, MA: Harvard University Asia Center, 2001.

Kohn, Livia, ed. *Daoism Handbook*. Leiden: Brill, 2000.

Kominami Ichirō 小南一郎. "Li A den no kōzō" 李娃伝の構造. *Tōhō gakuhō* 東方学報 62 (1990): 271–309.

Kroll, Paul W. "Basic Data on Reign-Dates and Local Government." *T'ang Studies* 5 (1987): 95–104.

———. "The Dancing Horses of T'ang." *T'oung Pao: International Journal of Chinese Studies* 67 (1981): 240–68.

———. "Four Vignettes from the Court of Tang Xuanzong." *T'ang Studies* 25 (2007): 1–27.

———. "Nostalgia and History in Mid-Ninth-Century Verse: Cheng Yü's

Poem on 'The Chin-yang Gate.'" *T'oung Pao: International Journal of Chinese Studies* 89 (2003): 286–366.

Lee, Haiyan. *Revolution of the Heart: A Genealogy of Love in China, 1900–1950*. Stanford: Stanford University Press, 2007.

Lee, Yu-hwa. *Fantasy and Realism in Chinese Fiction: T'ang Love Themes in Contrast*. San Francisco: Chinese Materials Center, 1984.

Lewis, Mark Edward. *China's Cosmopolitan Empire: The Tang Dynasty*. Cambridge, MA: Belknap Press of Harvard University Press, 2009.

———. *Sanctioned Violence in Early China*. Albany: State University of New York Press, 1990.

Li, Wai-yee. "On Becoming a Fish: Paradoxes of Immortality and Enlightenment in Chinese Literature." In *Self and Self-Transformation in the History of Religions*, edited by David Shulman and Guy G. Stroumsa, 29–56. Oxford: Oxford University Press, 2002.

———. "Dreams of Interpretation in Early Chinese Historical and Philosophical Writings." In *Dream Cultures: Explorations in the Comparative History of Dreaming*, edited by David Shulman and Guy G. Stroumsa, 17–42. Oxford: Oxford University Press, 1999.

———. "Mixture of Genres and Motives for Fiction in 'Yingying's Story.'" In *Ways with Words: Writing about Reading Texts from Early China*, edited by Pauline Yu et al., 185–92. Berkeley: University of California Press, 2000.

Li, Xiaorong. *Women's Poetry of Late Imperial China*. Seattle: University of Washington Press, 2012.

Li Fengmao 李丰楙. *You yu you: Liuchao Sui Tang xiandao wenxue* 憂與遊：六朝隋唐仙道文學. Beijing: Zhonghua shuju, 2010.

Li Fuchang 李福長. *Tangdai xueshi yu wenren zhengzhi* 唐代學士與文人政治. Jinan: Qilu shushe, 2005.

Li Han 李漢. *Xian Qin liang Han zhi yinyang wuxing xueshuo* 先秦兩漢之陰陽五行學説. Taipei: Zhongding wenhua gufen youxian gongsi, 1967.

Li Hanbin 李漢濱. *Taiping guangji de meng yanjiu* 《太平廣記》的夢研究. Taipei: Xuehai chubanshe, 2004.

Li Jianguo 李劍國. *Tang Wudai zhiguai chuanqi xulu* 唐五代志怪傳奇敍錄. Tianjin: Nankai daxue chubanshe, 1998.

Li Jianliang 李劍亮. *Tang Song ci yu Tang Song geji zhidu* 唐宋詞與唐宋歌妓制度. Hangzhou: Zhejiang daxue chubanshe, 1999.

Li Pengfei 李鵬飛. *Tangdai fei xieshi xiaoshuo zhi leixing yanjiu* 唐代非寫實小說之類型研究. Beijing: Beijing daxue chubanshe, 2004.

Li Zongwei 李宗爲. *Tangren chuanqi* 唐人傳奇. Beijing: Zhonghua shuju, 2003.

Liao Tengye 廖藤葉. *Zhongguo mengxi yanjiu* 中國夢戲研究. Taipei: Xuesi chubanshe, 2000.

Liu, James J. Y. *The Chinese Knight-errant*. Chicago: University of Chicago Press, 1967.

Liu Kairong 劉開榮. *Tangdai xiaoshuo yanjiu* 唐代小說研究. Shanghai: Shangwu yinshuguan, 1955.

Liu Shaoxin 劉紹信. *Liaozhai zhiyi xushi yanjiu* 聊齋誌異敘事研究. Beijing: Zhongguo shehui kexue chubanshe, 2012.

Liu Wenying 劉文英. *Zhongguo gudai de meng shu* 中國古代的夢書. Beijing: Zhonghua shuju, 1992.

Liu Ying 劉瑛. *Tangdai chuanqi yanjiu* 唐代傳奇研究. Taipei: Zhengzhong shuju, 1982.

Liu Yongqiang 劉勇強. *Zhongguo gudai xiaoshuo shi xulun* 中國古代小說史敘論. Beijing: Beijing daxue chubanshe, 2007.

Loewe, Michael. *Divination, Mythology, and Monarchy in Han China*. Cambridge: Cambridge University Press, 1994.

Lu Xun 魯迅. *Zhongguo xiaoshuo shilüe* 中國小說史略. Shanghai: Shanghai guji chubanshe, 1998. Reprint.

Lu Ying 路英. *Zhongguo meng wenhua* 中國夢文化. Beijing: Zhongguo sanxia chubanshe, 2005.

Luo, Manling. "Remembering Kaiyuan and Tianbao: The Construction of Mosaic Memory in Medieval Historical Miscellanies." *T'oung Pao: International Journal of Chinese Studies* 97 (2011): 263–300.

———. "The Seduction of Authenticity: 'The Story of Yingying.'" *Nannü: Men, Women, and Gender in China* 7, no. 1 (2005): 40–70.

———. "Tangdai xiaoshuo zhong yishi xingtai yiyi de 'yao'" 唐代小說中意識形態意義的"妖." *Beijing daxue xuebao* 50, no. 6 (2013): 93–101.

———. "What One has Heard and Seen: Intellectual Discourse in a Late Eighth-Century Miscellany." *Tang Studies* 30 (2012): 23–44.

Luo Liantian 羅聯添. "Changhen ge yu Changhen ge zhuan yiti jiegou wenti jiqi zhuti tantao" 長恨歌與長恨歌傳一體結構問題及其主題探討. In *Tangdai yanjiu lunji* 唐代研究論集, vol. 1, 727–43. Taipei: Xinwenfeng, 1992.

Luo Ning 羅寧. *Han Tang xiaoshuo guannian lungao* 漢唐小說觀念論稿. Chengdu: Bashu shushe, 2009.

Lupke, Christopher, ed. *The Magnitude of Ming: Command, Allotment, and Fate in Chinese Culture*. Honolulu: University of Hawai'i Press, 2005.

Ma, Y. W. "Fact and Fantasy in T'ang Tales." *Chinese Literature: Essays, Articles, Reviews* 2, no. 2 (1980): 167–81.

Ma Minghao 馬銘浩. *Tangdai shehui yu Yuan Bai wenxue jituan guanxi zhi yanjiu* 唐代社會與元白文學集團關係之研究. Taipei: Xuesheng shuju, 1991.

Mair, Victor H. *Painting and Performance: Chinese Picture Recitation and Its Indian Genesis*. Honolulu: University of Hawai'i Press, 1988.

———. "Scroll Presentation in the T'ang Dynasty." *Harvard Journal of Asiatic Studies* 38, no. 1 (1978): 35–60.

———. *T'ang Transformation Texts: A Study of the Buddhist Contribution to the Rise of Vernacular Fiction and Drama in China.* Cambridge, MA: Harvard Council on East Asian Studies, 1989.

Mao Lei 毛蕾. *Tangdai hanlin xueshi* 唐代翰林學士. Beijing: Shehui kexue wenxian chubanshe, 2000.

Matsuo Yoshihiro 松尾善弘. "'Sō Shū no yume' de toku 'Chinchūki'" 「莊週の夢」で解く「枕中記」. *Chūgoku bunka ronsō* 中國文化論叢 10 (2001): 15–28.

McClenon, James. "Near-Death Folklore in Medieval China and Japan: A Comparative Analysis." *Asian Folklore Studies* 50, no. 2 (1991): 319–42.

McMullen, David. *State and Scholars in T'ang China.* Cambridge: Cambridge University Press, 1988.

Mei Jialing 梅家玲. "Lun 'Du Zichun' yu 'Zhenzhong ji' de rensheng taidu" 論「杜子春」與「枕中記」的人生態度. *Zhongwai wenxue* 15, no. 12 (1987): 122–33.

Miyakawa Hisayuki 宮川尚志. "An Outline of the Naitō Hypothesis and Its Effects on Japanese Studies of China." *The Far Eastern Quarterly* 14, no. 4 (1955): 533–52.

Miyazaki Ichisada 宮崎市定. *Tōyōteki kinsei* 東洋的近世. Osaka: Kyōiku taimusu sha, 1950.

Mizobe Yoshie 溝部良恵. "Denki botsukō izen no Tōdai shōsetsu ni okeru kyokō ni tsuite: 'Enan ryōsha' (*Kibun*) to 'Annamu ryōsha' (*Kōiki*) no hikaku bunseki o chūshin to shite" 伝奇勃興以前の唐代小説における虚構について―「淮南猟者」(『紀聞』) と「安南猟者」(『広異記』) の比較分析を中心として―. *Nihon Chūgoku gakkaihō* 日本中國學會報 52 (2000): 90–104.

Moore, Oliver. *Rituals of Recruitment in Tang China: Reading an Annual Programme in the* Collected Statements *by Wang Dingbao (870–940).* Leiden: Brill, 2004.

Naitō Konan 内藤湖南. "Gaikatsuteki Tō Sō jidai kan" 概括的唐宋時代觀. In *Naitō Konan zenshū* 内藤湖南全集, vol. 8, 111–19. Tokyo: Chikuma shobo, 1969.

Ng, On-cho, and Wang, Q. Edward. *Mirroring the Past: The Writing and Use of History in Imperial China.* Honolulu: University of Hawai'i Press, 2005.

Nienhauser, Jr., William H. "Creativity and Storytelling in the *Ch'uan-ch'i*: Shen Ya-chih's T'ang Tales." *Chinese Literature: Essays, Articles, Reviews* 20 (1998): 31–70.

———. "Female Sexuality and the Double Standard in Tang Narratives: A

Preliminary Survey." In *Paradoxes of Traditional Chinese Literature*, edited by Eva Hung, 1–20. Hong Kong: Chinese University Press, 1994.

———. "Literature as a Source for Traditional History: The Case of Ou-yang Chan." *Chinese Literature: Essays, Articles, Reviews* 12 (1990): 1–14.

Ning Jiayu 寧稼雨. *Zhongguo wenyan xiaoshuo zongmu tiyao* 中國文言小說總目提要. Jinan: Qilu shushe, 1996.

Nugent, Christopher M. B. *Manifest in Words, Written on Paper: Producing and Circulating Poetry in Tang Dynasty China*. Cambridge, MA: Harvard University Asia Center, 2010.

Nürnberger, Marc. *Das "Ben shi shi" des Meng Qi*. Wiesbaden: Harrossowitz Verlag, 2010.

Owen, Stephen. "The Difficulty of Pleasure." *Extrême-Orient, Extrême-Occident* 20 (1998): 9–30.

———. *The End of the Chinese 'Middle Ages.'* Stanford: Stanford University Press, 1996.

———. *The Great Age of Chinese Poetry: The High T'ang*. New Haven, CT: Yale University Press, 1981.

———. *The Late Tang: Chinese Poetry of the Mid-Ninth Century (827–860)*. Cambridge, MA: Harvard University Asia Center, 2006.

———. "One Sight: The *Han shu* Biography of Lady Li." In *Rhetoric and the Discourses of Power in Court Culture*, edited by David R. Knechtges and Eugene Vance, 239–59. Seattle: University of Washington Press, 2005.

———. "Place: Meditation on the Past at Chin-ling." *Harvard Journal of Asiatic Studies* 50, no. 2 (1990): 417–57.

———. *The Poetry of the Early T'ang*. New Haven, CT: Yale University Press, 1977.

———. *Traditional Chinese Poetry and Poetics*. Madison: University of Wisconsin Press, 1985.

———. "What Did Liu Zhi Hear? The 'Yan Terrace Poems' and the Culture of Romance." *T'ang Studies* 13 (1995): 81–118.

Penn, W. S. *The Telling of the World: Native American Stories and Art*. New York: Stewart, Tabori & Chang, 1996.

Penny, Benjamin. "Immortality and Transcendence." In Kohn, *Daoism Handbook*, 74–108.

Poo, Mu-chou. "How to Steer through Life: Negotiating Fate in the *Daybook*." In Lupke, *The Magnitude of* Ming, 107–25.

Puett, Michael. "Following the Commands of Heaven: The Notion of *Ming* in Early China." In Lupke, *The Magnitude of* Ming, 49–69.

Qian, Nanxiu. *Spirit and Self in Medieval China: The* Shih-shuo hsin-yü *and Its Legacy*. Honolulu: University of Hawai'i Press, 2001.

Qiu Tiansheng 邱添生. *Tang Song bianke qi de zhengjing yu shehui* 唐宋變革期的政經與社會. Taipei: Wenjin chubanshe, 1999.

Raphals, Lisa. "Languages of Fate: Semantic Fields in Chinese and Greek." In Lupke, *The Magnitude of* Ming, 70–106.

Reed, Carrie. "Message from the Dead in 'Nanke Taishou zhuan.'" *Chinese Literature: Essays, Articles, Reviews* 31 (2009): 121–30.

———. "Parallel Worlds, Stretched Time, and Illusory Reality: The Tang Tale 'Du Zichun.'" *Harvard Journal of Asiatic Studies* 69, no. 2 (2009): 309–42.

Robertson, Maureen. "Voicing the Feminine: Constructions of the Gendered Subject in Lyric Poetry by Women of Medieval and Late Imperial China." *Late Imperial China* 13, no. 1 (1992): 63–110.

Rouzer, Paul F. *Articulated Ladies: Gender and the Male Community in Early Chinese Texts.* Cambridge, MA: Harvard University Asia Center, 2001.

Samei, Maija Bell. *Gendered Persona and Poetic Voice: The Abandoned Woman in Early Chinese Song Lyrics.* Lanham: Lexington, 2004.

Sanders, Graham M. *Words Well Put: Visions of Poetic Competence in the Chinese Tradition.* Cambridge, MA: Harvard University Asia Center, 2006.

Satake Yasuhiko 佐竹靖彦. *Tō Sō henkaku no chiikiteki kenkyū* 唐宋変革の地域的研究. Kyoto: Dōhōsha shuppan, 1990.

Schaberg, David. "Command and the Content of Tradition." In Lupke, *The Magnitude of* Ming, 23–48.

———. *A Patterned Past: Form and Thought in Early Chinese Historiography.* Cambridge, MA: Harvard University Asia Center, 2001.

Schafer, Edward H. *The Golden Peaches of Samarkand: A Study of T'ang Exotics.* Berkeley: University of California Press, 1963.

Scott, Janet L. *For Gods, Ghosts, and Ancestors: The Chinese Tradition of Paper Offerings.* Seattle: University of Washington Press, 2007.

Sedgwich, Eve. *Between Men: English Literature and Male Homosocial Desire.* New York: Columbia University Press, 1985.

Senō Tatsuhiko 妹尾達彦. "Tōdai kōhanki no chōan to denki shōsetsu—'Li A den' no bunseki o chūshin to shite" 唐代後半期の長安と傳奇小説——「李娃傳」の分析を中心として. In *Ronshū Chūgoku shakai seido bunkashi no shomondai: Hino Kaizaburō hakushi shōju kinen* 論集中國社會‧制度‧文化史の諸問題: 日野開三郎博士頌壽記念, 476–505. Fukuoka: Chūgoku shoten, 1987.

Shang Yongliang 尚永亮. *Keju zhi lu yu huanhai fuchen: Tangdai wenren de shihuan shengya* 科舉之路與宦海浮沉: 唐代文人的仕宦生涯. Taipei: Wenjin chubanshe, 2000.

Shi Ye 施曄. *Zhongguo gudai wenxue zhong de tongxinglian shuxie yanjiu* 中國古代文學中的同性戀書寫研究. Shanghai: Shanghai renmin chubanshe, 2008.

Shields, Anna M. "Alternate Views of Literary History: The Yuanhe Reign Period in Tang and Five Dynasties Anecdotal Texts." *Chūgoku shigaku* 中國史學 20 (2010): 1–31.

———. *Crafting a Collection: The Cultural Contexts and Poetic Practice of the* Huajian ji *(Collection from Among the Flowers)*. Cambridge, MA: Harvard University Asia Center, 2006.

———. "Defining Experience: The 'Poems of Seductive Allure' (*Yanshi*) of the Mid-Tang Poet Yuan Zhen (779–831)." *Journal of the American Oriental Society* 122, no. 1 (2002): 61–78.

Smith, Thomas E. "Ritual and the Shaping of Narrative: The Legend of the Han Emperor Wu." PhD diss., University of Michigan, 1992.

Song Lunmei 宋倫美. *Tangren xiaoshuo* Xuanguai lu *yanjiu* 唐人小說《玄怪錄》研究. Beijing: Beijing daxue chubanshe, 2005.

Song Zhenhao 宋鎮豪. "Jiaguwen zhong de meng yu zhanmeng" 甲骨文中的夢與占夢. *Wenwu*, no. 6 (2006): 61–71.

Spiegel, Gabrielle M. *The Past as Text: The Theory and Practice of Medieval Historiography*. Baltimore: Johns Hopkins University Press, 1997.

Strange, Mark. "Representations of Liang Emperor Wu as a Buddhist Ruler in Sixth- and Seventh-century Texts." *Asia Major* 24, no. 2 (2011): 53–112.

Strassberg, Richard E., tran. *Inscribed Landscapes: Travel Writings from Imperial China*. Berkeley: University of California Press, 1994.

Sun Changwu 孫昌武. *Daojiao yu Tangdai wenxue* 道教與唐代文學. Beijing: Renmin wenxue chubanshe, 2001.

———. *Tangdai guwen yundong tonglun* 唐代古文運動通論. Tianjin: Baihua wenyi chubanshe, 1984.

———. *Tangdai wenxue yu fojiao* 唐代文學與佛教. Xi'an: Shanxi renmin chubanshe, 1985.

Swartz, Wendy. *Reading Tao Yuanming: Shifting Paradigms of Historical Reception (427–1900)*. Cambridge, MA: Harvard University Asia Center, 2008.

Swidler, Ann. *Talk of Love: How Culture Matters*. Chicago: University of Chicago Press, 2001.

Tackett, Nicolas. "The Transformation of Medieval Chinese Elites (850–1000 C.E.)." PhD diss., Columbia University, 2006.

Takeda Akira 竹田晃. "Chinchūki: Shin to ka no aida" 枕中記: 真と仮の間. In *Chūgoku no koten bungaku* 中国の古典文学, 203–13. Tokyo: Tokyo daigaku, 1981.

Teiser, Stephen F. *The Ghost Festival in Medieval China*. Princeton: Princeton University Press, 1988.

———. "The Growth of Purgatory." In *Religion and Society in T'ang and Sung China*, edited by Patricia B. Ebrey and Peter N. Gregory, 115–45. Honolulu: University of Hawai'i Press, 1993.

———. "'Having Once Died and Returned to Life': Representations of Hell in Medieval China." *Harvard Journal of Asiatic Studies* 48, no. 2 (1988): 433–64.

———. *The Scripture on the Ten Kings and the Making of Purgatory in Medieval Chinese Buddhism*. Honolulu: University of Hawai'i Press, 1994.

Thompson, Stith. *The Folktale*. Berkeley: University of California Press, 1977. Reprint.

Tian, Xiaofei. "The Representation of Sovereignty in Chinese Vernacular Fiction." In *Text, Performance, and Gender in Chinese Literature and Music*, edited by Maghiel van Crevel, Tian Yuan Tan, and Michel Hockx, 211–31. Leiden: Brill, 2009.

———. *Tao Yuanming and Manuscript Culture: The Record of a Dusty Table*. Seattle: University of Washington Press, 2005.

Tsai, S-C Kevin. "Ritual and Gender in 'The Tale of Li Wa.'" *Chinese Literature: Essays, Articles, Reviews* 26 (2004): 99–127.

Twitchett, Denis C. *The Birth of the Chinese Meritocracy: Bureaucrats and Examinations in T'ang China*. London: China Society, 1976.

———. "How to Be an Emperor: T'ang Tai-tsung's Vision of His Role." *Asia Major* 9, nos.1–2 (1996): 1–102.

———. *The Writing of Official History under the T'ang*. Cambridge: Cambridge University Press, 1992.

Twitchett, Denis C., and John K. Fairbank, eds. *The Cambridge History of China*. Vol. 3, Part 1, *Sui and T'ang China, 589–906*. Cambridge: Cambridge University Press, 1979.

Twitchett, Denis C., and Paul Jakov Smith, eds. *The Cambridge History of China*. Vol. 5, Part 1, *The Sung Dynasty and Its Precursors, 907–1279*. Cambridge: Cambridge University Press, 2009.

Uchiyama Chinari 内山知也. "Ōō den no kōzō to shudai ni tsuite" 鶯鶯傳の構造と主題について. *Nihon Chūgoku gakkaihō* 日本中國學會報 42 (1990): 156–68.

von Glahn, Richard. *The Sinister Way: The Divine and the Demonic in Chinese Religious Culture*. Berkeley: University of California Press, 2004.

Waley, Arthur. *The Life and Times of Po Chü-I*. New York: MacMillan, 1949.

Wang, Ping. *The Age of Courtly Writing:* Wen Xuan *Compiler Xiao Tong (501–531) and His Circle*. Leiden: Brill, 2012.

Wang, Richard. "Liu Tsung-yüan's 'Tale of Ho-chien' and Fiction." *T'ang Studies* 14 (1996): 21–48.

Wang Jianchuan 王見川 and Pi Qingsheng 皮慶生. *Zhongguo jinshi minjian xinyang* 中國近世民間信仰. Shanghai: Shanghai renmin chubanshe, 2010.

Wang Jisi 王季思. *Cong Yingying zhuan dao Xixiang ji* 從鶯鶯傳到西廂記. Shanghai: Shanghai gudian wenxue chubanshe, 1955.

Wang Meng'ou 王夢鷗. *Tang shiren Li Yi shengping jiqi zuopin* 唐詩人李益生平及其作品. Taipei: Yiwen yinshuguan, 1973.

———. *Tangren xiaoshuo yanjiu* 唐人小説研究. Vols. 1–4. Taipei: Yiwen yinshubuan, 1971–78.

Wang Weidi 王維堤. *Zhongguo meng wenhua* 中國夢文化. Shanghai: Shanghai guji chubanshe, 1993.

Wang Xuncheng 王勛成. *Tangdai quanxuan yu wenxue* 唐代銓選與文學. Beijing: Zhonghua shuju, 2001.

Wang Yongping 王永平. *Daojiao yu Tangdai shehui* 道教與唐代社會. Beijing: Shoudu shifan daxue chubanshe, 2002.

Watkins, John. *Representing Elizabeth in Stuart England: Literature, History, Sovereignty*. Cambridge: Cambridge University Press, 2002.

Wechsler, Howard J. *Offerings of Jade and Silk: Ritual and Symbol in the Legitimation of the T'ang Dynasty*. New Haven, CT: Yale University Press, 1985.

Weinstein, Stanley. *Buddhism under the T'ang*. Cambridge: Cambridge University Press, 1987.

West, Stephen H., and Wilt L. Idema, trans. *The Moon and the Zither:* The Story of the Western Wing. Berkeley: University of California Press, 1991.

Wong Yu-Hsuan 翁育瑄. "Tōdai ni okeru kannin kaikyū no konyin keitai—Boshimei o chūshin ni" 唐代における官人階級の婚姻形態—墓誌銘を中心に. *Tōyō gakuhō* 東洋學報 83, no. 2 (2001): 131–59.

Wright, Arthur F. "Sui Yang-Ti: Personality and Stereotype." In *The Confucian Persuasion*, edited by John Curtis Perry and Bardwell L. Smith, 47–76. Stanford: Stanford University Press, 1960.

———. "T'ang T'ai-tsung: The Man and the Persona." In *Essays on T'ang Society*, edited by John Curtis Perry and Bardwell L. Smith, 17–32. Leiden: Brill, 1976.

Wu, Laura Hua. "From *Xiaoshuo* to Fiction: Hu Yinglin's Genre Study of *Xiaoshuo*." *Harvard Journal of Asiatic Studies* 55, no. 2 (1995): 339–71.

Wu Kang 吳康. *Zhongguo gudai menghuan* 中國古代夢幻. Changsha: Hunan wenyi chubanshe, 1992.

Wu Zhida 吳志達. *Tangren chuanqi* 唐人傳奇. Shanghai: Shanghai guji chubanshe, 1983.

Wu Zongguo 吳宗國. *Tangdai keju zhidu yanjiu* 唐代科舉制度研究. Beijing:
Beijing daxue chubanshe, 2010.

Xiang Shuyun 向淑雲. *Tangdai hunyin fa yu hunyin shitai* 唐代婚姻法與婚姻
實態. Taipei: Taiwan Shangwu yinshuguan, 1991.

Xiao, Chi. "Lyric Archi-Occasion: Coexistence of 'Now' and Then." *Chinese Literature: Essays, Articles, Reviews* 15 (1993): 17–35.

Xingyun dashi 星雲大師 et al., comps. *Foguang da cidian* 佛光大辭典. Beijing: Shumu wenxian chubanshe, 1989–93.

Xu Youfu 徐有富. *Tangdai funü shenghuo yu shi* 唐代婦女生活與詩. Beijing:
Zhonghua shuju, 2005.

Xu Zong 許總. *Tangshi shi* 唐詩史. Nanjing: Jiangsu jiaoyu chubanshe, 1994.

Yan Jinxiong 顏進雄. *Tangdai youxian shi yanjiu* 唐代遊仙詩研究. Taipei:
Wenjin chubanshe, 1996.

Yang, Xiaoshan. *Metamorphosis of the Private Sphere: Gardens and Objects
in Tang-Song Poetry*. Cambridge, MA: Harvard University Asia Center,
2003.

Yang Bo 楊波. *Chang'an de chuntian: Tangdai keju yu jinshi shenghuo* 長安
的春天: 唐代科舉與進士生活. Beijing: Zhonghua shuju, 2007.

Yao, Ping 姚平. *Tangdai funü de shengming licheng* 唐代婦女的生命歷程.
Shanghai: Shanghai guji chubanshe, 2004.

Yu, Pauline. "Charting the Landscape of Chinese Poetry." *Chinese Literature: Essays, Articles, Reviews* 20 (1998): 71–87.

———. "Poems in Their Place: Collections and Canons in Early Chinese
Literature." *Harvard Journal of Asiatic Studies* 50, no. 1 (1990): 163–96.

Yü, Ying-shih 余英時. "O Soul Come Back! A Study in the Changing Conceptions of the Soul and Afterlife in Pre-Buddhist China." *Harvard Journal of Asiatic Studies* 47, no. 2 (1987): 363–95.

———. *Shi yu Zhongguo wenhua* 士與中國文化. Shanghai: Shanghai renmin
chubanshe, 2003.

Yuan Xingpei 袁行霈 and Hou Zhongyi 侯忠義. *Zhongguo wenyan xiaoshuo
shumu* 中國文言小說書目. Beijing: Beijing daxue chubanshe, 1981.

Zeitlin, Judith T. *Historian of the Strange: Pu Songling and the Chinese
Classical Tale*. Stanford: Stanford University Press, 1993.

———. *The Phantom Heroine*. Honolulu: University of Hawai'i Press, 2007.

Zeng Qinliang 曾勤良. *Zuo zhuan yinshi fushi zhi shijiao yanjiu* 左傳引詩賦
詩之詩教研究. Taipei: Wenjin chubanshe, 1993.

Zhang Guangda 張廣達. "Naitō Konan de Tang Song biange shuo jiqi ying-
xiang" 內藤湖南的唐宋變革說及其影響. *Tang yanjiu* 11 (2005): 5–71.

Zhang Hongxun 張鴻勳. *Dunhuang su wenxue yanjiu* 敦煌俗文學研究. Lanzhou: Gansu jiaoyu chubanshe, 2002.

Zhang Weizhi 张撝之, Shen Qiwei 沈起煒, and Liu Dezhong 劉德重, eds. *Zhongguo lidai renming da cidian* 中國歷代人名大辭典. Shanghai: Shanghai guji chubanshe, 1999.

Zhang Zhongmou 張仲謀. *Jianji yu dushan—Gudai shidafu chushi xinli pouxi* 兼濟與獨善—古代士大夫處世心理剖析. Beijing: Dongfang chubanshe, 1998.

Zhang Zhongyu 張中宇. *Bai Juyi* Changhen ge *yanjiu* 白居易《長恨歌》研究. Beijing: Zhonghua shuju, 2005.

Zheng Binglin 鄭炳林 and Yang Ping 羊萍, eds. *Dunhuang ben meng shu* 敦煌本夢書. Lanzhou: Gansu wenhua chubanshe, 1995.

Zheng Zhenduo 鄭振鐸. *Zhongguo su wenxue shi* 中國俗文學史. Changsha: Shangwu yinshuguan, 1938.

Zheng Zhimin 鄭志敏. *Xishuo Tangji* 細說唐妓. Taipei: Wenjin chubanshe, 1997.

Zhou Xibao 周錫保. *Zhongguo gudai fushi shi* 中國古代服飾史. Beijing: Zhongguo xiju chubanshe, 1984.

Zhou Xunchu 周勳初. *Tangren biji xiaoshuo kaosuo* 唐人筆記小說考索. Nanjing: Jiangsu guji chubanshe, 1996.

Zhu Jincheng 朱金城. *Bai Juyi nianpu* 白居易年譜. Shanghai: Shanghai guji chubanshe, 1982.

Zhuo Songsheng 卓松盛. *Zhongguo meng wenhua* 中國夢文化. Haikou: Sanhuan chubanshe, 1991.

INDEX

Liu Ji, 68
Liu Mian, 35
Liu Miaozhi, 142–43
Liu Qichu, 73, 76
Liu Shao, *Treatise on People* (Renwu
zhi), 91
Liu Su (fl. 728–742), *Fine Anecdotes
from the Sui and Tang* (Sui Tang
jiahua), 61, 80
Liu Su (fl. 806–820), *New Tales of
the Great Tang* (Da Tang xinyu),
63–71, 199n15
Liu Taizhen, 95
Liu Xiyi, 85, 87
Liu Xuanzuo, 77, 79
Liu Yan, 159
Liu Yi, 160
Liu Yiqing, *A New Account of the Tales
of the World* (Shishuo xinyu), 61,
63, 80
Liu Yuxi, 85, 86, 104–5, 201n77
Liu Zongyuan, "Story of Hejian"
(Hejian zhuan), 118–19, 121–22
Lu Changyuan, *Records of Exposing
the Dubious* (Bianyi zhi), 155–56
Lü Daosheng, *Records of Predetermined
Fate* (Dingming lu), 139, 142, 144
Lu Hong, 64
Lu Hongzhi, "Meng Sixian," 123
Lu Kang, 142–43
Lu Lun, 82
Lu Qi, 158
Lu Yu, 76, 78
Lu Zhao, *The Lost History* (Yi shi), 74,
156–60
Luo Gongyuan, 52

Ma Youqin, 141
Ma Zong, 149, 154
marriages: arranged, 100, 109, 113–14,
125, 145–46; fate in, 145–46;
gender hierarchy, 119, 146; wives
(and divorces), 81, 109, 112, 117.
See also adultery; concubines
Mencius, 112, 126
Meng Jian, 101, 116, 204n10
Meng Qi, *Original Occasions of Poems*
(Benshi shi), 80–81, 103–5, 196n58
Meng Sixian, 123
minor discourses in classical language
(wenyan xiaoshuo), 7–9
morality, 130, 132–33

Niu Sengru, 157; *Collection of the
Mysterious and the Strange*
(Xuanguai lu), 137, 156–57, 162–
63; story about, 92–93, 96

nonmarital bonds. *See* adultery;
courtesans; romance; sexuality

officialdom: avenues of entry, 17, 62, 88;
constraints and power of, 14, 102,
136, 137–38, 138–44, 146–47, 152–
54, 170–71; literati life centered
on, 5, 13–18, 25, 63–64, 98, 136,
172–75; meritocracy, 4, 18, 63, 73,
79, 95, 97. *See also* bureaucracy;
cosmic mobility; examinations;
hierarchies; literati
Ouyang Zhan, 101, 116, 204n10

Pan Haoli, 67
patriarchy: in families, 100–101, 110–
11, 112; in marriage, 119, 146;
romantic challenges to, 99, 100–
102, 109–10, 115–16, 125, 128–29,
133; subversion and submission in
stories, 101–2, 110–11, 125–34. *See
also* hierarchies
Pei Du, 79, 202–3n103
Pei Guangting, 141, 143
Pei Hang, 160
Pei Wu, 78
Pei Xing, *Transmission of the
Marvelous* (Chuan qi), 105–7, 156,
160
Pei Yan, 70–71
poetry: aficionados, 86–88; arbiters,
86; didacticism, 28, 45–47; literati
storytelling and, 80–81, 176–77;
meritocracy, 83–84; Music Bureau
(yuefu), 28, 45; new Music Bureau
(xin yuefu), 45, 46; outstanding
lines and poems, 84–85, 86–87,
201n77; romantic, 30, 100;
sentimentalism, 28, 30, 131; Tang,
5, 8, 11, 80, 176; women and, 81,
83
popular storytelling, 10, 57–58, 177–
78, 181
Precious Consort Yang (Yang Guifei):
Illustrious Emperor and, 24, 27,
28, 29, 30; poetry on, 27–28, 46;
stories about, 26, 27–31, 33, 41,
178, 179

Qi Ying, 157–58, 159
Qiao Zhizhi, 103

*Records of Reflections on
Predetermined Fate* (Gan dingming
lu), 139
return-from-death narratives, 147–53,
209n38